SNAPSHOT

Norway

WITHDRAWN

CONTENTS

INTRODUCTION

This Snapshot guide, excerpted from my guidebook *Rick Steves Scandinavia*, introduces you to a land with immigrant roots, modern European values, and the great outdoors like nowhere else—Norway.

Start in Oslo, Norway's sharp capital city, with its historic and walkable core, mural-slathered City Hall, and inspiring Nobel Peace Center. Oslo's excellent museums are dedicated to Norwegian art, the paintings of Edvard Munch, Viking ships, traditional folk life, Norway's WWII resistance, and more. Ogle the celebration-of-humanity statues at Vigeland Park, and relive Olympic memories at Holmenkollen Ski Jump.

Then head for Norway's countryside for a dose of natural wonder. The famous "Norway in a Nutshell" ride—by train, ferry, and bus—showcases the scenic splendor of the country, from snowcapped mountains to the striking Sognefjord. Choose a cozy fjordside hamlet (such as Balestrand, Solvorn, or Aurland) as your home base for touring mighty glaciers and evocative stave churches. Explore the Gudbrandsdal Valley, Lillehammer's excellent open-air folk museum, and the impressive Jotunheimen Mountains.

Dip into Bergen, Norway's salty port town, with its lively fish market, colorful Hanseatic quarter, and a funicular to the top of Mount Fløyen. You can round out your Norwegian experience in the lively city of Stavanger, the time-passed Setesdal Valley, and resorty Kristiansand.

To help you have the best trip possible, I've included the following topics in this book:

• **Planning Your Time,** with advice on how to make the most of your limited time

• **Orientation,** including tourist information (abbreviated as TI), tips on public transportation, local tour options, and helpful hints

• **Sights** with ratings:

▲▲▲—Don't miss

▲▲—Try hard to see

▲—Worthwhile if you can make it

No rating—Worth knowing about

• **Sleeping and Eating**, with good-value recommendations in every price range

• **Connections**, with tips on trains, buses, boats, and driving

Practicalities, near the end of this book, has information on money, phoning, hotel reservations, transportation, and more.

To travel smartly, read this little book in its entirety before you go. It's my hope that this guide will make your trip more meaningful and rewarding. Traveling like a temporary local, you'll get the absolute most out of every mile, minute, and dollar.

Ha en god tur!

Rick Steves

NORWAY

NORWAY

Norge

Norway is stacked with superlatives—it's the most mountainous, most scenic, and most prosperous of all the Scandinavian countries. Perhaps above all, Norway is a land of intense natural beauty, its famously steep mountains and deep fjords carved out and shaped by an ancient ice age.

Norway is also a land of rich harvests—timber, oil, and fish. In fact, its wealth of resources is a major reason why Norwegians have voted *"nei"* to membership in the European Union. They don't want to be forced to share fishing rights with EU countries.

The country's relatively recent independence (in 1905, from Sweden) makes Norwegians notably patriotic and proud of their traditions and history. They have a reputation for insularity, and controversially tightened immigration laws in 2014.

Norway's Viking past (c. A.D. 800-1050) can still be seen today in the country's 28 remaining stave churches—with their decorative nods to Viking ship prows—and the artifacts housed in Oslo's Viking Ship Museum.

The Vikings, who also lived in present-day Denmark and Sweden, were great traders, shipbuilders, and explorers. However, they are probably best known for their infamous invasions, which terrorized much of Europe. The sight of their dragon-prowed ships on the horizon struck fear into the hearts of people from Ireland to the Black Sea.

Named for the Norse word *vik,* which means "fjord" or "inlet," the Vikings sailed their sleek, seaworthy ships on extensive voyages, laden with amber and furs for trading—and weapons for fighting. They traveled up the Seine and deep into Russia, through the Mediterranean east to Constantinople, and across the Atlantic to Greenland and even "Vinland" (Canada). In fact, they touched the soil of the Americas centuries before Columbus, causing proud "ya sure ya betcha" Scandinavian immigrants in the US to display bumper stickers that boast, "Columbus used a Viking map!"

Both history and Hollywood have painted a picture of the Vikings as fierce barbarians, an image reinforced by the colorful names of leaders like Sven Forkbeard, Erik Bloodaxe, and Harald

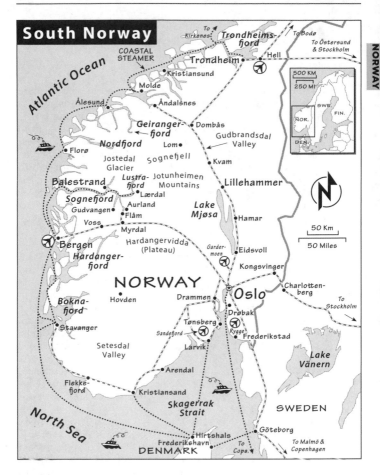

South Norway

To Kirkenes
To Bodø
To Östersund & Stockholm

Trondheims-fjord

COASTAL STEAMER

Trondheim
Hell

Atlantic Ocean

Kristiansund
Molde

Ålesund
Åndalsnes

500 KM
250 MI
SWE.
NOR.
FIN.
DEN.

Geiranger-fjord
Dombås

Gudbrandsdal Valley

Nordfjord
Lom

Florø
Jostedal Glacier
Sognefjell
Kvam

Lustra-fjord
Jotunheimen Mountains
Lillehammer

Balestrand
Lærdal

Sognefjord
Aurland
Lake Mjøsa

Gudvangen
Flåm
Hamar

Voss
Myrdal

Bergen
Hardangervidda (Plateau)
Garder-moen
Eidsvoll
50 Km
50 Miles

Hardanger-fjord
Kongsvinger

NORWAY
Charlotten-berg

Bokna-fjord
Hovden
Drammen
Oslo
To Stockholm

Stavanger
Tønsberg
Drøbak
Rygge
Frederikstad

Sandefjord
Larvik
Lake Vänern

Setesdal Valley

Arendal

Flekke-fjord
Kristiansand
Skagerrak Strait
SWEDEN

North Sea
Göteborg

Hirtshals
To Malmö & Copenhagen

Frederikshavn
To Cop.

DENMARK

Bluetooth. Unless you're handy with an axe, these don't sound like the kind of men you want to hoist a tankard of mead with. They kept slaves and were all-around cruel (though there is no evidence that they forced their subjects to eat lutefisk). But the Vikings also had a gentle side. Many were farmers, fishermen, and craftsmen who created delicate works with wood and metal. Faced with a growing population constrained by a lack of arable land, they traveled south not just to rape, pillage, and plunder, but in search of greener pastures. Sometimes they stayed and colonized, as in northeast England,

NORWAY

Norway Almanac

Official Name: Kongeriket Norge—"The Kingdom of Norway"—or simply Norge (Norway).

Population: Norway's 5.1 million people (about 35 per square mile) are mainly of Nordic and Germanic heritage, with a small population of indigenous Sami people in the north. The rapidly growing immigrant population is primarily from Pakistan, Sweden, Poland, Lithuania, and Somalia. Most Norwegians speak one of two official forms of Norwegian (Bokmål and Nynorsk), and the majority speak English as a second language. While church attendance is way down, the vast majority of Norwegian Christians consider themselves Lutheran.

Latitude and Longitude: 62°N and 10°E, similar latitude to Canada's Northwest Territories.

Area: 148,700 square miles, slightly larger than Montana.

Geography: Sharing the Scandinavian Peninsula with Sweden, Norway also has short northern borders with Finland and Russia. Its 51,575-mile coastline extends from the Barents Sea in the Arctic Ocean to the Norwegian Sea and North Sea in the North Atlantic. Shaped by glaciers, Norway has a rugged landscape of mountains, plateaus, and deep fjords. In the part of Norway that extends north of the Arctic Circle, the sun never sets at the height of summer, and never comes up in the deep of winter.

Biggest Cities: Norway's capital city, Oslo, has a population of 634,000; almost a million live in its metropolitan area. Bergen, Norway's second-largest city, has a population of about 240,000.

Economy: The Norwegian economy grows around 2 percent each year, contributing to a healthy $282 billion Gross Domestic Product and a per capita GDP of $55,400. Its primary export is oil—Norway ranks behind only Saudi Arabia and Russia in the amount of oil exported, making it one of the world's

which was called the "Danelaw," or in northwest France, which became known as Normandy ("Land of the North-men").

The Vikings worshipped many gods and had a rich tradition of mythology. Epic sagas were verbally passed down through generations or written in angular runic writing. The sagas told the heroic tales of the gods, who lived in Valhalla, the Viking heaven, presided over by Odin, the god of both wisdom and war. Like the Egyptians, the Vikings believed in life after death, and chieftains were often buried in their ships within burial mounds, along with prized possessions such as jewelry, cooking pots, food, and Hagar the Horrible cartoons.

Like the Greeks and Etruscans before them, the Vikings never richest countries. Thanks to this oil wealth, and the country's generally prudent approach to debt, the recent economic crisis has been relatively easy on Norway.

Currency: 6 Norwegian kroner (kr, officially NOK) = about $1.

Government: As the leader of Norway's constitutional monarchy, King Harald V has largely ceremonial powers. In September of 2013, Norwegian voters elected a right-wing government, which appointed Conservative Party leader Erna Solberg as prime minister. She is Norway's second woman prime minister (after the Labor Party's Gro Harlem Brundtland) and the country's first Conservative leader since 1990. Though Solberg's party formed a coalition with the far-right anti-immigration Progress Party, the government still does not have enough votes in Parliament to enact far-reaching changes to the Norwegian welfare state. Norway's legislative body is the Stortinget (Parliament), with 169 members elected for four-year terms. The Conservative-Progress Party coalition currently holds 77 seats, followed by the Labor Party at 55 seats, and the Christian Democratic and Center parties with 10 seats each. The remaining seats are divided among smaller political parties.

Flag: The Norwegian flag is red with a blue Scandinavian cross outlined in white.

The Average Norwegian...is 39 years old, has 1.86 children, and will live to be 82. Three in four Norwegians are employed in the service sector, one in five in industry, and only 2 percent in agriculture.

organized on a large national scale and eventually faded away due to bigger, better-organized enemies and the powerful influence of Christianity. By 1150, the Vikings had become Christianized and assimilated into European society. But their memory lives on in Norway.

Beginning in the 14th century, Norway came under Danish rule for more than 400 years, until the Danes took the wrong side in the Napoleonic Wars. The Treaty of Kiel forced Denmark to cede Norway to Sweden in 1814. Sweden's rule of Norway lasted until 1905, when Norway voted to dissolve the union. Like many European countries, Norway was taken over by Germany during World War II. April 9, 1940, marked the start of five years of Nazi occupation, during which a strong resistance movement developed, hindering some of the Nazi war efforts.

Each year on May 17, Norwegians celebrate their idealistic 1814 constitution with fervor and plenty of flag-waving. Men and women wear folk costumes *(bunads)*, each specific to a region of Norway. Parades are held throughout the country. The parade in Oslo marches past the Royal Palace, where the royal family waves to the populace from their balcony. While the king holds almost zero political power (Norway has a parliament chaired by a prime minister), the royal family is still highly revered and respected.

Several holidays in spring and early summer disrupt transportation schedules: the aforementioned Constitution Day (May 17), Ascension Day (May 14 in 2015, May 6 in 2016), and Whitsunday and Whitmonday (a.k.a. Pentecost and the following day, May 24-25 in 2015, May 15-16 in 2016).

High taxes contribute to Norway's high standard of living. Norwegians receive cradle-to-grave social care: university education, health care, nearly yearlong paternity leave, and an annual six weeks of vacation. Norwegians feel there is no better place than home. Norway regularly shows up in first place on the annual UN Human Development Index.

Visitors enjoy the agreeable demeanor of the Norwegian people—friendly but not overbearing, organized but not uptight, and with a lust for adventure befitting their gorgeous landscape. Known for their ability to suffer any misfortune with an accepting (if a bit pessimistic) attitude, Norwegians are easy to get along with.

Despite being looked down upon as less sophisticated by their Scandinavian neighbors, Norwegians are proud of their rich folk

traditions—from handmade sweaters and folk costumes to the small farms that produce a sweet cheese called *geitost*. Less than 7 percent of the country's land is arable, resulting in numerous small farms. The government recognizes the value of farming, especially in the remote reaches of the country, and provides rich subsidies to keep this tradition alive. These subsidies would not be allowed if Norway joined the European Union—yet another reason the country remains an EU holdout.

Appropriate for a land with countless fjords and waterfalls, Norway is known for its pristine water. Norwegian-bottled artisanal water has an international reputation for its crisp, clean taste. Although the designer Voss water—the H2O of choice for Hollywood celebrities—comes with a high price tag, the blue-collar Olden is just as good. (The tap water is actually wonderful, too—and much cheaper.)

While the Norwegian people speak a collection of mutually understandable dialects, the Norwegian language has two official forms: *bokmål* (book language) and *nynorsk* (New Norse). During the centuries of Danish rule, people in Norway's cities and upper classes adopted a Danish-influenced style of speech and writing (called Dano-Norwegian), while rural language remained closer to Old Norse. After independence, Dano-Norwegian was renamed *bokmål,* and the rural dialects were formalized as *nynorsk,* as part of a nationalistic drive for a more purely Norwegian language. Despite later efforts to combine the two forms, *bokmål* remains the most commonly used, especially in urban areas, books, newspapers, and government agencies. Students learn both.

The majority of the population under 70 years of age also speaks English, but a few words in Norwegian will serve you well. If you visit a Norwegian home, be sure to leave your shoes at the door; indoors is usually meant for stocking-feet only. At the end of a meal, it's polite to say "Thanks for the food"—*"Takk for maten"* (tahk for MAH-ten). Norwegians rarely feel their guests have eaten enough food, so be prepared to say *"Nei, takk"* (nay tahk; "No, thanks"). You can always try *"Jeg er mett"* (yay ehr met; "I am full"), but be careful not to say *"Jeg er full"*—"I am drunk."

STAVE CHURCHES

Norway's most distinctive architecture is the stave church. These medieval houses of worship—tall, skinny, wooden pagodas with dragon's-head gargoyles—are distinctly Norwegian and palpably historic, transporting you right back to the Viking days. On your visit, make it a point to visit at least one stave church.

Stave churches are the finest architecture to come out of medieval Norway. Wood was plentiful and cheap, and locals had an expertise with woodworking (from all that boat-building). In 1300, there were as many as 1,000 stave churches in Norway.

After a 14th-century plague, Norway's population dropped, and many churches fell into disuse or burned down. By the 19th century, only a few dozen stave churches survived. Fortunately, they became recognized as part of the national heritage and were protected. Virtually all of Norway's surviving stave churches have been rebuilt or renovated, with painstaking attention to the original details.

A distinguishing feature of the "stave" design is its frame of tall, stout vertical staves (Norwegian *stav*, or "staff"). The churches typically sit on stone foundations, to keep the wooden structure away from the damp ground (otherwise it would rot). Most stave churches were made of specially grown pine, carefully prepared before being felled for construction. As the trees grew, the tips and most of the branches were cut off, leaving the trunks just barely alive to stand in the woods for about a decade. This allowed the sap to penetrate the wood and lock in the resin, strengthening the wood while keeping it elastic. Once built, a stave church was slathered with black tar to protect it from the elements.

Stave churches are notable for their resilience and flexibility. Just as old houses creak and settle over the years, wooden stave churches can flex to withstand fierce winds and the march of time. When the wind shifts with the seasons, stave churches groan and moan for a couple of weeks...until they've adjusted to the new influences, and settle in.

Even after the Vikings stopped raiding, they ornamented the exteriors of their churches with warlike, evil spirit-fighting drag-

ons reminiscent of their ships. Inside, a stave church's structure makes you feel like you're huddled under an overturned ship. The churches are dark, with almost no windows (aside from a few small "portholes" high up). Typical decorations include carved, X-shaped crossbeams; these symbolize the cross of St. Andrew (who was crucified on such a cross). Round, Romanesque arches near the tops of the staves were made from the "knees" of a tree, where the roots bend to meet the trunk (typically the hardest wood in a tree). Overall, these churches are extremely vertical: the beams inside and the roofline outside both lead the eye up, up, up to the heavens.

Most surviving stave churches were renovated during the Reformation (16th and 17th centuries), when they acquired more horizontal elements such as pews, balconies, pulpits, altars, and other decorations to draw attention to the front of the church. In some (such as the churches in Lom and Urnes), the additions make the church feel almost cluttered. But the most authentic (including Hopperstad near Vik) feel truly medieval. These time-machine churches take visitors back to early Christian days: no pews (worshippers stood through the service), no pulpit, and a barrier between the congregation and the priest, to symbolically separate the physical world from the spiritual one. Incense filled the church, and the priest and congregation chanted the service back and forth to each other, creating an otherworldly atmosphere that likely made worshippers feel close to God. (If you've traveled in Greece, Russia, or the Balkans, Norway's stave churches might remind you of Orthodox churches, which reflect the way all Christians once worshipped.)

When traveling through Norway, you'll be encouraged to see stave church after stave church. Sure, they're interesting, but there's no point in spending time seeing more than a few of them. Of Norway's 28 remaining stave churches, seven are described in this book. The easiest to see are the ones that have been moved to open-air museums in Oslo and Lillehammer. But I prefer to appreciate a stave church in its original fjords-and-rolling-hills setting. My two favorites are both near Sogne-

fjord: Borgund and Hopperstad. They are each delightfully situated, uncluttered by more recent additions, and evocative as can be. Borgund is in a pristine wooded valley, while Hopperstad is situated on a fjord. Borgund comes with the only good adjacent stave church museum. (Most stave churches on the Sognefjord are operated by the same preservation society; for more details, see www.stavechurch.com.)

Other noteworthy stave churches include the one in Lom, near the Jotunheimen Mountains, which is one of Norway's biggest, and is indeed quite impressive. The Urnes church, across from Solvorn, is technically the oldest of them all—but it's been thoroughly renovated in later ages (it is still worth considering, however, if only for its exquisite carvings and the fun excursion to get to it). The Fantoft church, just outside Bergen, burned down in 1992, and the replica built to replace it has none of the original's magic. The stave church in Undredal advertises itself as the smallest. I think it's also the dullest.

Norwegian Survival Phrases

Norwegian can be pronounced quite differently from region to region. These phrases and phonetics match the mainstream Oslo dialect, but you'll notice variations. Vowels can be tricky: *å* sounds like "oh," *æ* sounds like a bright "ah" (as in "apple"), and *u* sounds like the German *ü* (purse your lips and say u). Certain vowels at the ends of words (such as *d* and *t*) are sometimes barely pronounced (or not at all). In some dialects, the letters *sk* are pronounced "sh." In the phonetics, ī sounds like the long i in "light," and bolded syllables are stressed.

English	Norwegian	Pronunciation
Hello. (formal)	*God dag.*	goo dahg
Hi. / Bye. (informal)	*Hei. / Ha det.*	hī / hah deh
Do you speak English?	*Snakker du engelsk?*	**snahk**-kehr dew **eng**-ehlsk
Yes. / No.	*Ja. / Nei.*	yah / nī
Please.	*Vær så snill.*	vayr soh sneel
Thank you (very much).	*(Tusen) takk.*	**(tew**-sehn) tahk
You're welcome.	*Vær så god.*	vayr soh goo
Can I help you?	*Kan jeg hjelpe deg?*	kahn yī **yehl**-peh dī
Excuse me.	*Unnskyld.*	**ewn**-shuld
(Very) good.	*(Veldig) fint.*	**(vehl**-dee) feent
Goodbye.	*Farvel.*	fahr-**vehl**
one / two	*en / to*	ayn / toh
three / four	*tre / fire*	treh / **fee**-reh
five / six	*fem / seks*	fehm / sehks
seven / eight	*syv / åtte*	seev / **oh**-teh
nine / ten	*ni / ti*	nee / tee
hundred	*hundre*	**hewn**-dreh
thousand	*tusen*	**tew**-sehn
How much?	*Hvor mye?*	voor **mee**-yeh
local currency: (Norwegian) crown	*(Norske) kroner*	**(norsh**-keh) **kroh**-nehr
Where is...?	*Hvor er...?*	voor ehr
...the toilet	*...toalettet*	toh-ah-**leh**-teh
men	*menn / herrer*	mehn / **hehr**-rehr
women	*damer*	**dah**-mehr
water / coffee	*vann / kaffe*	vahn / **kah**-feh
beer / wine	*øl / vin*	uhl / veen
Cheers!	*Skål!*	skohl
The bill, please.	*Regningen, takk.*	**rī**-ning-ehn tahk

OSLO

While Oslo is the smallest of the Scandinavian capitals, this brisk little city offers more sightseeing thrills than you might expect. As an added bonus, you'll be inspired by a city that simply has its act together.

Sights of the Viking spirit—past and present—tell an exciting story. Prowl through the remains of ancient Viking ships, and marvel at more peaceful but equally gutsy modern boats (the *Kon-Tiki, Ra, Fram,* and *Gjøa*). Dive into the traditional folk culture at the Norwegian open-air folk museum, and get stirred up by the country's heroic spirit at the Norwegian Resistance Museum.

For a look at modern Oslo, tour the striking City Hall, take a peek at sculptor Gustav Vigeland's people-pillars, climb the exhilarating Holmenkollen Ski Jump, walk all over the Opera House, and then celebrate the world's greatest peacemakers at the Nobel Peace Center.

Situated at the head of a 60-mile-long fjord, surrounded by forests, and populated by more than a half-million people, Oslo is Norway's cultural hub. For 300 years (1624-1924), the city was called Christiania, after Danish King Christian IV. With independence, it reverted to the Old Norse name of Oslo. As an important port facing the Continent, Oslo has been one of Norway's main cities for a thousand years and the de facto capital since around 1300. Still, Oslo has always been small by European standards; in 1800, Oslo had 10,000 people, while cities such as Paris and London had 50 times as many.

But Oslo experienced a growth spurt with the Industrial Age, and in 50 years (from 1850 to 1900) its population exploded from about 10,000 to about 250,000. Logically, most of "old Oslo" dates from this period when the city's many churches and grand buildings were made of stone in the Historicism styles (neo-Gothic and neo-Romanesque) of the late 19th century.

And Oslo's old industrial quarter, with its evocative brick factories and warehouses, is a trendy bohemian-chic zone that comes with as much of an edge as you'll find in otherwise wholesome Norway. The entire city—full of rich Norwegians—is expensive.

Today the city sprawls out from its historic core to encompass nearly a million people in its metropolitan area, about one in five Norwegians. Oslo's port hums with international shipping and a sizeable cruise industry. Its waterfront, once traffic-congested and slummy, has already undergone a huge change, and the extreme urban makeover is just starting. The vision: a five-mile people-friendly and traffic-free promenade stretching from east to west the entire length of its

waterfront. Cars and trucks now travel in underground tunnels, upscale condos and restaurants are taking over, and the neighborhood has a splashy Opera House. Oslo seems to be constantly improving its infrastructure and redeveloping slummy old quarters along the waterfront into cutting-edge residential zones. The metropolis feels as if it's rushing to prepare for an Olympics-like deadline. But it isn't—it just wants to be the best city it can be.

You'll see a mix of grand Neoclassical facades, plain 1960s-style modernism, and a sprouting Nordic Manhattan-type skyline of skyscrapers nicknamed "the bar code buildings" for their sleek yet distinct boxiness.

But overall, the feel of this major capital is green and pastoral—spread out, dotted with parks and lakes, and surrounded by hills and forests. For the visitor, Oslo is an all-you-can-see *smörgåsbord* of historic sights, trees, art, and Nordic fun.

PLANNING YOUR TIME

Oslo offers an exciting slate of sightseeing thrills. Ideally, spend two days, and leave on the night boat to Copenhagen or on the scenic "Norway in a Nutshell" train to Bergen the third morning. Spend the two days like this:

Day 1: Take my self-guided "Welcome to Oslo" walk. Tour the Akershus Fortress and the Norwegian Resistance Museum. Catch the City Hall tour. Spend the afternoon at the National Gallery and at the Holmenkollen Ski Jump and museum.

Day 2: Ferry across the harbor to Bygdøy and tour the *Fram*, *Kon-Tiki*, and Viking Ship museums. Spend the afternoon at the

Norwegian Folk Museum. Finish the day at Vigeland Park, enjoying Gustav Vigeland's statues.

Keep in mind that the National Gallery and the Vigeland Museum (at Vigeland Park) are closed on Monday.

Orientation to Oslo

Oslo is easy to manage. Its sights cluster around the main boulevard, Karl Johans Gate (with the Royal Palace at one end and the
train station at the other), and in the Bygdøy (big-doy) district, a
10-minute ferry ride across the harbor. The city's other main sight,
Vigeland Park (with Gustav Vigeland's statues), is about a mile behind the palace.

The monumental, homogenous city center contains most of
the sights, but head out of the core to see the more colorful neighborhoods. Choose from Majorstuen and Frogner (chic boutiques,
trendy restaurants), Grünerløkka (bohemian cafés, hipsters), and
Grønland (multiethnic immigrants' zone).

TOURIST INFORMATION

The city's shiny new **Oslo Visitor Center** is in the Østbanehallen,
the traditional-looking building right next to the central train station. Standing in the square (Jernbanetorget) by the tiger statue
and facing the train station, you'll find the TI's entrance in the
red-painted section between the station and Østbanehallen. You
can also enter the TI from inside the train station (May-Sept daily
9:00-18:00, Oct-April daily 9:00-16:00, tel. 81 53 05 55, www.
visitoslo.com).

At the TI, pick up these freebies: an Oslo map, the helpful
public-transit map, the annual *Oslo Guide* (with plenty of details
on sightseeing, shopping, and eating), and the *You Are Here Oslo*
map and visitors guide (a young people's guide that's full of fun
and offbeat ideas). For entertainment ideas and more, the free
What's On in Oslo monthly has the most accurate record of museum hours and an extensive listing of happenings every day, such
as special events, tours, and concerts. If you like to bike, ask about
the public bike-rental system (100 kr/24 hours; you can rent a
card from TI to release simple one-speed bikes from racks around
town).

If you're traveling on, pick up the *Bergen Guide* and information for the rest of Norway, including the useful, annual *Fjord Norway Travel Guide*. Consider buying the Oslo Pass (described next).
It's valid for 24, 48, or 72 hours; and there is a special rate for
children ages 4-15 and for seniors who are 67 and older.

Use It, a hardworking information center, is officially geared
for those under age 26 but is generally happy to offer anyone its

OSLO

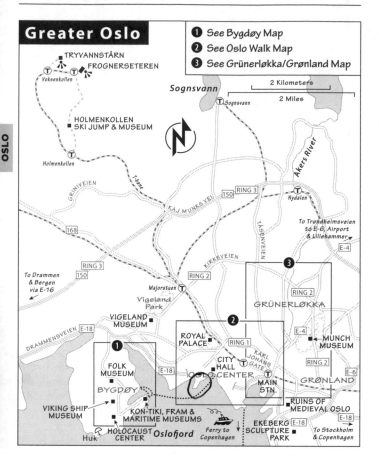

Greater Oslo

❶ See Bygdøy Map
❷ See Oslo Walk Map
❸ See Grünerløkka/Grønland Map

TRYVANNSTÅRN
FROGNERSETEREN
Voksenkollen

Sognsvann

Sognsvann

2 Kilometers
2 Miles

HOLMENKOLLEN
SKI JUMP & MUSEUM

Akers River

Holmenkollen

GRINIVEIEN

KAJ MUNKS VEI   RING 3   150   Nydalen

TÅSENVEIEN

To Trondheimsveien
to E-6, Airport
& Lillehammer   E-4

168

RING 3   150   KIRKEVEIEN

To Drammen
& Bergen
via E-16   RING 2

Majorstuen   ❸

RING 2

Vigeland
Park   GRÜNERLØKKA

VIGELAND
MUSEUM   ❷

DRAMMENSVEIEN   E-18   ROYAL
PALACE   RING 1   E-4   MUNCH
MUSEUM

❶   CITY
HALL   KARL
JOHANS
GATE   RING 2   E-6

FOLK
MUSEUM   E-18   OSLO CENTER   GRØNLAND

BYGDØY   MAIN
STN.

VIKING SHIP
MUSEUM   KON-TIKI, FRAM &
MARITIME MUSEUMS   RUINS OF
MEDIEVAL OSLO

Huk   HOLOCAUST
CENTER   Oslofjord   Ferry to
Copenhagen   EKEBERG
SCULPTURE
PARK   E-18   E-18   To Stockholm
& Copenhagen

solid, money-saving, experience-enhancing advice (Mon-Fri 11:00-17:00, Sat 12:00-17:00, longer hours July-early Aug, closed Sun; Møllergata 3, look for *Ungdomsinformasjonen* sign, tel. 24 14 98 20, www.use-it.no). They can help find you the cheapest beds in town (no booking fee) and they offer these free services: Wi-Fi and Internet access, phone use, and luggage storage. Their free *You Are Here Oslo* guide—with practical info, maps, ideas on eating cheap, good nightspots, tips on picking up a Norwegian, the best beaches, and so on—is a must for young travelers and worthwhile for anyone curious about probing the Oslo scene.

Oslo Pass: This pass covers the city's public transit, ferry boats, and entry to nearly every major sight—all described in a useful handbook (320 kr/24 hours, 470 kr/48 hours, 590 kr/72 hours; big discounts for kids ages 4-15 and seniors age 67 and over, www. visitoslo.com). Do the math before buying; add up the individual costs of the sights you want to see to determine whether an Oslo

Pass will save you money. (Here are some sample charges: one 24-hour transit pass-90 kr, Nobel Peace Center-90 kr, three boat museums at Bygdøy-270 kr, National Gallery-50 kr. These costs, which total 500 kr, justify buying a 48-hour pass.) Students with an ISIC card may be better off without the Oslo Pass. If you have a smartphone, you can download the Oslo Pass app; after activating the pass, you don't have to be online to use it.

ARRIVAL IN OSLO
By Train

The central train station (Oslo Sentralstasjon, or "Oslo S" for short) is slick and helpful. You'll find free Wi-Fi, an Internet café, ATMs, and two Forex exchange desks. The station is plugged into a lively modern shopping mall called Byporten (Mon-Fri 10:00-21:00, Sat 10:00-20:00, closed Sun). You'll also find a cheap Bit sandwich shop with seating, a Joker supermarket (Mon-Fri 6:00-23:00, Sat 8:00-23:00, Sun 9:00-23:00), and a Vinmonopolet liquor store (Oslo's most central place to buy wine or liquor—which is sold only at Vinmonopolet stores, Mon-Thu 10:00-18:00, Fri 9:00-18:00, Sat 9:00-15:00, closed Sun). The new TI is in the Østbanehallen, right next to the train station.

For tickets and train info, you can go to the station's ticket office located between tracks 8 and 9 (Mon-Fri 6:30-23:00, Sat-Sun 10:00-18:00—opens at 7:45 on summer weekends) or to the helpful train office at the National Theater railway and T-bane station, which can have shorter lines (Mon-Fri 7:30-17:00, closed Sat-Sun; Ruseløkkveien, southwest of National Theater). At either ticket office, you can buy domestic and Norway in a Nutshell tickets, and pick up leaflets on the Flåm and Bergen Railway, but only the station office sells international tickets. The TI also sells domestic train tickets (same price, likely friendlier and faster).

By Plane
Oslo Airport

Oslo Lufthavn, also called Gardermoen, is about 30 miles north of the city center and has a helpful 24-hour information center (airport code: OSL, tel. 91 50 64 00, www.osl.no).

Flytoget is the speedy train that zips travelers between the airport and the central train station in 20-25 minutes (170 kr, less for students and seniors, 4/hour, runs roughly 5:00-24:00, not covered by rail passes, simply swipe your credit card through card reader at gate before boarding, then swipe it again when you get off—or buy ticket from machine or at ticket counter, where you'll pay a 30-kr surcharge; tel. 81 50 07 77, www.flytoget.no). Note that Flytoget trains alternate between those that go only to the central train sta-

OSLO

tion, and others that also continue on through Oslo, stopping at the National Theater station (which is closer to some recommended hotels and uses the same ticket).

Local trains are nearly half the cost of Flytoget trains and nearly as fast (90 kr, roughly 2/hour, 25 minutes, covered by rail passes, some also serve National Theater station). You'll save about 30 kr on this trip with an Oslo Pass because the pass covers transportation within Oslo; you only need to pay the fare for the stretch between the airport and the edge of town.

To reach the Flytoget and local train counters at the airport: After you leave customs, exit right and walk all the way to the far corner; you'll see two separate ticket counters (one for Flytoget, NSB for the cheaper local trains) and separate TV screens showing the timetables for Flytoget and the "lokal-InterCity-fjerntog" trains.

Flybus airport buses stop directly outside the arrival hall and make several downtown stops, including the central train station (150 kr one-way, 3/hour, 40 minutes, tel. 67 98 04 80).

Taxis run to and from the airport (895-kr fixed rate until 17:00, 1,095-kr rate after 17:00, confirm price before you commit). **Oslo Taxi** is the most reliable (tel. 02323). I prefer the slick and faster Flytoget train, but the taxi can be a good value for families and those with lots of luggage.

Other Airports near Oslo

If you arrive at the Rygge or Sandefjord airports, catch a Flybus airport bus to downtown Oslo. If you're going from Oslo *to* either airport, note that buses depart Oslo's central bus terminal (next to the train station) about three hours before all flight departures.

Rygge Airport: Ryanair and Norwegian use this airport near the city of Moss, 40 miles south of Oslo (160 kr for Flybus ticket—buy from driver, www.rygge-ekspressen.no; airport code: RYG, tel. 69 23 00 00, www.en.ryg.no).

Sandefjord Airport Torp: Ryanair, WizzAir, and other discount airlines use this airport, 70 miles south of Oslo (250 kr for Flybus ticket from driver, www.torpekspressen.no; airport code: TRF, tel. 33 42 70 00, www.torp.no).

HELPFUL HINTS

Pickpocket Alert: They're a problem in Oslo, particularly in crowds on the street and in subways and buses. To call the police, dial 112.

Street People and Drug Addicts: Oslo's street population loiters around the train station. While a bit unnerving to some travelers, locals consider this rough-looking bunch harmless. The police have pretty much corralled them to the square called Christian Frederiks Plass, south of the station.

Money: Banks in Norway don't change money. Use ATMs or Forex exchange offices (outlets near City Hall at Fridtjof Nansens Plass 6, at train station, and at Egertorget at the crest of Karl Johans Gate; hours vary by location but generally Mon-Fri 9:00-18:00, Sat 9:00-17:00, closed Sun).

Internet Access: @rctic Internet Café is pricey but central, located in the train station's main hall and above track 13 (60 kr/hour, daily 8:00-23:00).

Post Office: It's in the train station.

Pharmacy: Jernbanetorgets Vitus Apotek is open 24 hours daily (across from train station on Jernbanetorget, tel. 23 35 81 00).

Laundry: Selva Laundry is on the corner of Wessels Gate and Ullevålsveien at Ullevålsveien 15, a half-mile north of the train station (daily self-serve 8:00-21:00, full-serve 10:00-19:00, walk or catch bus #37 from station, tel. 41 64 08 33).

Bike Rental: Viking Biking, run by Americans Curtis and Ben, rents bikes (125 kr/8 hours, 200 kr/24 hours, includes helmet, map, rain poncho, and lock, daily 9:30-18:00, Nedre Slottsgate 4, tel. 41 26 64 96, www. vikingbikingoslo.com; see

"Tours in Oslo," later, for their guided bike tours).

Or use the public bike-rental system to grab basic **city bikes** out of locked racks at various points throughout town (100 kr/24 hours; get card at TI).

Movies: The domed **Colosseum Kino** in Majorstuen, one of northern Europe's largest movie houses with 1,500 seats, is a fun place to catch a big-time spectacle. Built in 1928, this high-tech, four-screen theater shows first-run films in their original language (Fridtjof Nansens Vei 6, a short walk west from Marjorstuen T-bane station, www.oslokino.no).

Updates to This Book: For updates to this book, check www. ricksteves.com/update.

GETTING AROUND OSLO

By Public Transit: Commit yourself to taking advantage of Oslo's excellent transit system, made up of buses, trams, ferries, and a subway (*Tunnelbane,* or T-bane for short; see "Sightseeing by Public Transit" sidebar). Use the TI's free public transit map to navigate. The system runs like clockwork, with schedules clearly posted and followed. Many stops have handy electronic reader boards showing the time remaining before the next tram arrives (usually less than 10 minutes). **Ruter,** the public-transit information center, faces the train station under the glass tower; Mon-Fri 7:00-20:00, Sat-Sun 8:00-18:00, tel. 177 or 81 50 01 76, www. ruter.no).

Individual **tickets** work on buses, trams, ferries, and the T-bane for one hour (30 kr if bought at machines, transit office, Narvesen kiosks, convenience stores such as 7-Eleven or Deli de Luca, or via smartphone app—or 50 kr if bought on board). Other options include the **24-hour ticket** (90 kr; buy at machines, transit office, or via smartphone app; good for unlimited rides in 24-hour period) and the **Oslo Pass** (gives free run of entire system; described earlier). Validate your ticket or smartcard by holding it next to the card reader when you board.

By Taxi: Taxis come with a 150-kr drop charge that covers you for three or four kilometers—about two miles (more on evenings and weekends). Taxis can be a good value if you're with a group. If you use a minibus taxi, you are welcome to negotiate an hourly rate. To get a taxi, wave one down, find a taxi stand, or call 02323.

Tours in Oslo

Oslo Fjord Tours

A fascinating world of idyllic islands sprinkled with charming vacation cabins is minutes away from the Oslo harborfront. For locals, the fjord is a handy vacation getaway. Tourists can get a glimpse of this island world by public ferry or tour boat. Cheap ferries regularly connect the nearby islands with downtown (free with Oslo Pass).

Several tour boats leave regularly from pier 3 in front of City Hall. Båtservice has a relaxing and scenic 1.5-hour hop-on, hop-off service, with recorded multilanguage commentary. It departs from the City Hall dock (185 kr, daily at 9:45, 11:15, 12:45, and 14:15; departs 30 minutes later from Opera House and one hour later from Bygdøy; tel. 23 35 68 90, www.boatsightseeing.com). They won't scream if you bring something to munch. They also offer two-hour fjord tours with lame live commentary (269 kr, 3-4/ day late March-Sept) and a "Summer Evening on the Fjord" dinner cruise on a sailing ship (395 kr; joyride without narration that includes a "shrimp buffet"—just shrimp, bread, and butter; daily mid-June-Aug 19:00-22:00).

Bus Tours

Båtservice, which runs the harbor cruises, also offers four-hour **bus tours** of Oslo, with stops at the ski jump, Bygdøy museums,

Sightseeing by Public Transit

With a transit pass or an Oslo Pass, take full advantage of the T-bane and the trams. Just spend five minutes to get a grip on the system, and you'll become amazingly empowered. Here are the only T-bane stations you're likely to use:

Jernbanetorget (central station, bus and tram hub, express train to airport)

Stortinget (top of Karl Johans Gate, near Akershus Fortress)

Nationaltheatret (National Theater, also a train station, express train to airport, near City Hall, Aker Brygge, Royal Palace)

Majorstuen (walk to Vigeland Sculpture Park, trendy shops on Bogstadveien, Colosseum cinema)

Grønland (colorful immigrant neighborhood, cheap and fun restaurant zone, bottom of Grünerløkka district; the underground mall in the station is a virtual trip to Istanbul)

Nydalen (start of my Nydalen to Grünerløkka Walk)

Holmenkollen (famous ski jump, city view)

Frognerseteren (highest point in town, jumping-off point for forest walks and bike rides)

Sognsvann (idyllic lake in forest outside of town)

Trams and buses that matter:

Trams #11 and #12 ring the city (stops at central station, fortress, harborfront, City Hall, Aker Brygge, Vigeland Park, Bogstadveien, National Gallery, and Stortorvet)

Trams #11, #12, and #13 to Olaf Ryes Plass (center of Grünerløkka district)

Trams #13 and #19, and bus #31 (south and parallel to Karl Johans Gate to central station)

Bus #30 (Nydalen, Olaf Ryes Plass in Grünerløkka, train station, near Karl Johans Gate, National Theater, and Bygdøy, with stops at each Bygdøy museum)

and Vigeland Park (390 kr, 2/day mid-May-mid-Sept, departs next to City Hall, longer tours also available, tel. 23 35 68 90, www. boatsightseeing.com). HMK also does daily city bus tours (220 kr/2 hours, 350 kr/4 hours, departs next to City Hall, tel. 22 78 94 00, www.hmk.no).

Open Top Sightseeing runs **hop-on, hop-off bus tours** (260 kr/all day, 19 stops, www.opentopsightseeing.no; every 30 minutes, leaves from City Hall, English headphone commentary, buy ticket from driver). While the tours help you get your bearings, most of Oslo's sightseeing is concentrated in a few discrete zones that are well-connected by the excellent public-transportation network—

making pricey bus tours a lesser value. And if you hit the timing wrong, you may wait up to an hour at popular stops (such as Vigeland Park) for a chance to hop back on.

Biking Tours

Viking Biking gives several different guided tours in English, including a three-hour Oslo Highlights Tour (250 kr, May-Sept daily at 13:00, Nedre Slottsgate 4, tel. 41 26 64 96, www. vikingbikingoslo.com). They also rent bikes; see "Helpful Hints," earlier.

Guided Walking Tour

Oslo Guideservice offers 1.5-hour historic "Oslo Promenade" walks from June through August (150 kr, free with Oslo Pass; Mon, Wed, and Fri at 17:30; leaves from sea side of City Hall, confirm departures at TI, tel. 22 42 70 20, www.guideservice.no).

Local Guides

You can hire a private guide through **Oslo Guideservice** (2,000 kr/2 hours, tel. 22 42 70 20, www.guideservice.no); my guide Aksel had a passion for both history and his hometown of Oslo. Or try **Oslo Guidebureau** (prices start at 1,950 kr/3 hours, tel. 22 42 28 18, www.osloguide.no, mail@guideservice.no).

Oslo Tram Tour

Tram #12, which becomes tram #11 halfway through its loop (at Majorstuen), circles the city from the train station, lacing together many of Oslo's main sights. Apart from the practical value of being able to hop on and off as you sightsee your way around town (trams come by at least every 10 minutes), this 40-minute trip gives you a fine look at parts of the city you wouldn't otherwise see.

The route starts at the main train station, at the traffic-island tram stop located immediately in front of the transit office tower. The route makes almost a complete circle and finishes at Stortorvet (the cathedral square), dropping you off a three-minute walk from where you began the tour.

Starting out, you want tram #12 as it leaves from the second set of tracks, going toward Majorstuen. Confirm with your driver that the particular tram #12 you're boarding becomes tram #11 and finishes at Stortorvet; some of these may turn into tram #19 instead, which takes a different route. If yours becomes #19, simply hop out at Majorstuen and wait for the next #11. If #11 is canceled because of construction, leave #12 at Majorstuen and catch #19 through the center back to the train station, or hop on the T-bane (which zips every few minutes from Majorstuen to the National

Theater—closest to the harbor and City Hall—and then to the station). Here's what you'll see and ideas on where you might want to hop out:

From the **station,** you'll go through the old grid streets of 16th-century Christiania, King Christian IV's planned Renaissance town. After the city's 17th fire, in 1624, the king finally got fed up. He decreed that only brick and stone buildings would be permitted in the city center, with wide streets to serve as fire breaks.

You'll turn a corner at the **fortress** (Christiana Torv stop; get off here for the fortress and Norwegian Resistance Museum), then head for **City Hall** (Rådhus stop). Next comes the harbor and upscale **Aker Brygge** waterfront neighborhood (jump off at the Aker Brygge stop for the harbor and restaurant row). Passing the harbor, you'll see on the left a few old shipyard buildings that still survive. Then the tram goes uphill, past the **House of Oslo** (a mall of 20 shops highlighting Scandinavian interior design; Vikatorvet stop) and into a district of ugly 1960s buildings (when elegance was replaced by "functionality"). The tram then heads onto the street Norwegians renamed **Henrik Ibsens Gate** in 2006 to commemorate the centenary of Ibsen's death, honoring the man they claim is the greatest playwright since Shakespeare.

After Henrik Ibsens Gate, the tram follows Frognerveien through the chic **Frogner neighborhood.** Behind the fine old facades are fancy shops and spendy condos. Here and there you'll see 19th-century mansions built by aristocratic families who wanted to live near the Royal Palace; today, many of these house foreign embassies. Turning the corner, you roll along the edge of **Frogner Park** (which includes **Vigeland Park,** featuring Gustav Vigeland's sculptures), stopping at its grand gate (hop out at the Vigelandsparken stop).

Ahead on the left, a statue of 1930s ice queen Sonja Henie marks the arena where she learned to skate. Turning onto Bogstadveien, the tram usually becomes #11 at the Majorstuen stop. **Bogstadveien** is lined with trendy shops, restaurants, and cafés—it's a fun place to stroll and window-shop. (You could get out here and walk along this street all the way to the Royal Palace park and the top of Karl Johans Gate.) The tram veers left before the palace, passing the **National Historical Museum** and stopping at the **National Gallery** (Tullinløkka stop). As you trundle along, you may notice that lots of roads are ripped up for construction. It's too cold to fix the streets in winter, so, when possible, the work is done in summer. Jump out at **Stortorvet** (a big square filled with flower stalls and fronted by the cathedral and the big GlasMagasinet department store). From here, you're a three-minute walk from the station, where this tour began.

Welcome to Oslo Walk

This self-guided stroll, worth ▲▲, covers the heart of Oslo—the zone where most tourists find themselves walking—from the train station, up the main drag, and past City Hall to the harborfront. It takes a brisk 30 minutes if done nonstop.

Train Station: Start at the plaza just outside the main entrance of Oslo's central train station (Oslo Sentralstasjon). The statue of the tiger prowling around out front alludes to the town's nickname of Tigerstaden ("Tiger Town") and commemorates the 1,000th birthday of Oslo's founding, celebrated in the year 2000. In the 1800s, Oslo was considered an urban tiger, leaving its mark on the soul of simple country folk who ventured into the wild and crazy New York City of Norway.

(These days, the presence of so many beggars, or *tigger,* has prompted the nickname "Tiggerstaden.")

With your back to the train station, look for the glass Ruter tower that marks the **public transit office;** from here, trams zip to City Hall (harbor, boat to Bygdøy), and the underground subway (T-bane, or *Tunnelbane*—look for the *T* sign to your right) goes to Vigeland Park (statues) and Holmenkollen. Tram #12—featured in the self-guided tram tour described earlier—leaves from directly across the street.

The green building behind the Ruter tower is a shopping mall called **Byporten** (literally, "City Gate," see big sign on rooftop), built to greet those arriving from the airport on the shuttle train. Oslo's 37-floor pointed-glass **skyscraper,** the Radisson Blu Plaza Hotel, looms behind that. Its 34th-floor SkyBar welcomes the public with air-conditioned views and pricey drinks (Mon-Sat 17:00-24:00, closed Sun). The tower was built with reflective glass so that, from a distance, it almost disappears. The area behind the Radisson—the lively and colorful "Little Karachi," centered along a street called Grønland—is where most of Oslo's immigrant population settled. It's become a vibrant nightspot, offering a fun contrast to the predictable homogeneity of Norwegian cuisine and culture.

Oslo allows hard-drug addicts and prostitutes to mix and mingle in the station area. (While it's illegal to buy sex in Norway, those who sell it are not breaking the law.) Troubled young people come here from small towns in the countryside for anonymity and community. The two cameras near the top of the Ruter tower monitor drug deals. Signs warn that this is a "monitored area," but victimless crimes proceed while violence is minimized. (Watch your purse and wallet here.)

• *Note that you are near the Opera House if you'd like to side-trip there now. Otherwise, turn your attention to Norway's main drag, called...*

Karl Johans Gate: This grand boulevard leads directly from the train station to the Royal Palace. The street is named for the French general Jean Baptiste Bernadotte, who was given a Swedish name, established the current Swedish dynasty, and ruled as a popular king (1818-1844) during the period after Sweden took Norway from Denmark.

Walk three blocks up Karl Johans Gate. This stretch is referred to as **"Desolation Row"** by locals because it has no soul, just shops greedily looking to devour tourists' money. If you visit in the snowy winter, you'll walk on bare concrete: Most of downtown Oslo's pedestrian streets are heated.

• *Hook right around the curved old brick structure of an old market and walk to the...*

Oslo Cathedral (Domkirke): This Lutheran church (daily 10:00-16:00) is the third cathedral Oslo has had, built in 1697 after the second one burned down. It's where

Norway commemorates its royal marriages and deaths. Seventy-seven deaths were mourned here following the tragic shootings and bombing of July 2011. In the grass in front of the cathedral, you may see a semipermanent memorial to the victims, consisting of a row of stones shaped like a heart.

Look for the cathedral's cornerstone (right of entrance), a thousand-year-old carving from Oslo's first and long-gone cathedral showing how the forces of good and evil tug at each of us. Look high up on the tower. The tiny square windows midway up the copper cupola were once the lookout quarters of the fire watchman.

Step inside beneath the red, blue, and gold seal of Oslo and under an equally colorful ceiling (late Art Deco from the 1930s). The box above on the right is for the royal family. The fine Baroque pulpit and altarpiece date from 1700. The chandeliers are from the previous cathedral (which burned in the 17th century). The colorful windows in the choir (leading up to the altar) were made in 1910 by Emanuel Vigeland (Gustav's less famous brother).

Leaving the church, stroll around to the right, behind the church. The **courtyard** is lined by a circa-1850 circular row of stalls from an old market. Rusty meat hooks now decorate the lamps of

OSLO

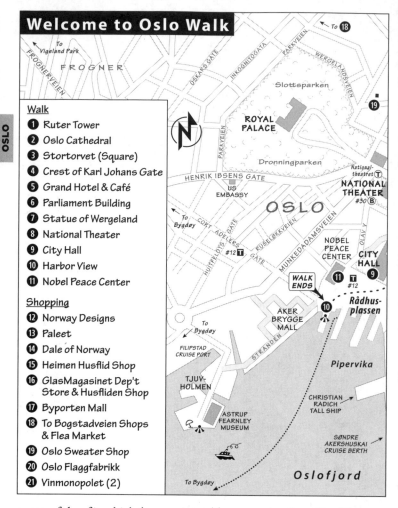

Welcome to Oslo Walk

To 18

To Vigeland Park

FROGNER

Slottsparken

ROYAL PALACE

Dronningparken

OSLO

Walk

❶ Ruter Tower
❷ Oslo Cathedral
❸ Stortorvet (Square)
❹ Crest of Karl Johans Gate
❺ Grand Hotel & Café
❻ Parliament Building
❼ Statue of Wergeland
❽ National Theater
❾ City Hall
❿ Harbor View
⓫ Nobel Peace Center

Shopping

⓬ Norway Designs
⓭ Paleet
⓮ Dale of Norway
⓯ Heimen Husflid Shop
⓰ GlasMagasinet Dep't Store & Husfliden Shop
⓱ Byporten Mall
⓲ To Bogstadveien Shops & Flea Market
⓳ Oslo Sweater Shop
⓴ Oslo Flaggfabrikk
㉑ Vinmonopolet (2)

HENRIK IBSENS GATE

US EMBASSY

NATIONAL THEATER

NØBEL PEACE CENTER

CITY HALL

WALK ENDS

Rådhus-plassen

AKER BRYGGE MALL

FILIPSTAD CRUISE PORT

TJUV-HOLMEN

ASTRUP FEARNLEY MUSEUM

Pipervika

CHRISTIAN RADICH TALL SHIP

SØNDRE AKERSHUSKAI CRUISE BERTH

To Bygdøy

Oslofjord

a peaceful café, which has quaint tables around a fountain. The atmospheric **Café Bacchus,** at the far left end of the arcade, serves food outside and in a classy café downstairs (light 150-200-kr meals, Mon-Fri 11:00-22:00, Sat 12:00-22:00, closed Sun, hamburgers, salads, good cakes, coffee, tel. 22 33 34 30).

• *The big square that faces the cathedral is called...*

Stortorvet: In the 17th century, when Oslo's wall was located about here, this was the point where farmers were allowed to enter and sell their goods. Today it's still lively as a flower and produce market (Mon-Fri). The statue shows Christian IV, the Danish king who ruled Norway around 1600, dramatically gesturing that-a-way. He named the city, rather immodestly, Chris-

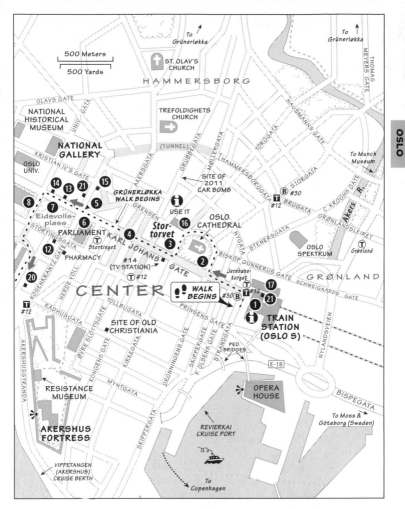

OSLO

tiania. (Oslo took back its old Norse name only in 1925.) Christian was serious about Norway. During his 60-year reign, he visited it 30 times (more than all other royal visits combined during 300 years of Danish rule). The big GlasMagasinet department store is a landmark on this square.

• *Return to Karl Johans Gate, and continue up the boulevard past street musicians, cafés, shops, and hordes of people. If you're here early in the morning (Mon-Fri) you may see a commotion at #14 (in the first block, on the*

left, look for the big 2 sign). This is the studio of a TV station (channel 2) where the Norwegian version of the Today *show is shot, and as on Rockefeller Plaza, locals gather here, clamoring to get their mugs on TV.*

At the next corner, Kongens Gate leads left, past the 17th-century grid-plan town to the fortress. But we'll continue hiking straight up to the crest of the hill, enjoying some of the street musicians along the way. Pause at the wide spot in the street just before Akersgata to appreciate the...

Crest of Karl Johans Gate: Look back at the train station. A thousand years ago, the original (pre-1624) Oslo was located at the foot of the wooded hill behind the station (described later). Now look ahead to the Royal Palace in the distance, which was built in the 1830s "with nature and God behind it and the people at its feet." If the flag flies atop the palace, the king is in the country. Karl Johans Gate, a parade ground laid out in about 1850 from here to the palace, is now the axis of modern Oslo. Each May 17, Norway's Constitution Day, an annual children's parade turns this street into a sea of marching student bands and costumed young flag-wavers, while the royal family watches from the palace balcony. Since 1814, Norway has preferred peace. Rather than celebrating its military on the national holiday, it celebrates its children.

King Harald V and Queen Sonja moved back into the palace in 2001, after extensive (and costly) renovations. To quell the controversy caused by this expense, the public is now allowed inside to visit each summer with a pricey one-hour guided tour (95 kr, 3 English tours/day late June-mid-Aug, fills fast—buy tickets in advance online or at many convenience stores, such as the Narvesen kiosk near the palace, or by calling 81 53 31 33, www.kongehuset. no).

In the middle of the small square, the *T* sign marks a stop of the T-bane (Oslo's subway). W. B. Samson's bakery is a good place for a quick, affordable lunch, with a handy cafeteria line (WC in back); duck inside if just to be tempted by the pastries. Two traditional favorites are *kanelboller* (cinnamon rolls) and *skolebrød* ("school bread," with an egg-and-cream filling). From here, the street called Akersgata kicks off a worthwhile stroll past the site of the July 2011 bombing, the national cemetery, and through a park-like river gorge to the trendy Grünerløkka quarter (an hour-long walk).

People-watching is great along Karl Johans Gate, but remember that if it's summer, half of the city's regular population is gone—vacationing in their cabins or farther away—and the city center is filled mostly with visitors.

Hike two blocks down Karl Johans Gate, past the big brick

Parliament building (on the left). On your right, seated in the square, is a statue of the 19th-century painter Christian Krohg. Continue down Karl Johans Gate. If you'd like to get a city view (and perhaps some refreshment), enter the glass doors at #27 and take the elevator to the eighth-floor roof-top bar, Etoile.

A few doors farther down Karl Johans Gate, just past the Freia shop (Norway's oldest and best chocolate), the venerable **Grand Hotel** (Oslo's celebrity hotel—Nobel Peace Prize winners sleep here) overlooks the boulevard.

• *Ask the waiter at the Grand Café—part of the Grand Hotel—if you can pop inside for a little sightseeing (he'll generally let you).*

Grand Café: This historic café was for many years the meeting place of Oslo's intellectual and creative elite (the playwright Henrik Ibsen was a regular here). Notice the photos and knickknacks on the wall. At the back of the café, a mural shows Norway's literary and artistic clientele—from a century ago—enjoying this fine hangout. On the far left, find Ibsen, coming in as he did every day at 13:00. Edvard Munch is on the right, leaning against the window, looking pretty drugged. Names are on the sill beneath the mural.

• *For a cheap bite with prime boulevard seating, continue past the corner to Deli de Luca, a convenience store with a super selection of takeaway food and a great people-watching perch. Across the street, a little park faces Norway's...*

Parliament Building (Stortinget): Norway's Parliament meets here (along with anyone participating in a peaceful protest outside). Built in 1866, the building seems to counter the Royal Palace at the other end of Karl Johans Gate. If the flag's flying, Parliament's in session. Today the king is a figurehead, and Norway is run by a unicameral parliament and a prime minister. Guided tours of the Stortinget are offered for those interested in Norwegian government (free, 45 minutes; mid-June-Aug Mon-Fri at 10:00 and 13:00 in English, at 11:30 in Norwegian; line up at gate in front of the main entrance off Karl Johans Gate, tel. 23 31 35 96, www.stortinget.no).

• *Cross over into the park and stroll toward the palace, past the fountain. Pause at the...*

Statue of Wergeland: The poet Henrik Wergeland helped inspire the national resurgence of Norway during the 19th century. Norway won its independence from Denmark in 1814, but within a year it lost its freedom to Sweden. For nearly a century, until Norway won independence in 1905, Norwegian culture and national spirit was stoked by artistic and literary patriots like Wergeland. In the winter, the pool here is frozen and covered with children happily ice-skating. Across the street behind Wergeland

Browsing

Oslo's pulse is best felt by strolling. Three good areas are along and near the central Karl Johans Gate, which runs from the train station to the palace (follow my self-guided "Welcome to Oslo" walk); in the trendy harborside Aker Brygge mall, a glass-and-chrome collection of sharp cafés, fine condos, and polished produce stalls (really lively at night, tram #12 from train station); and along Bogstadveien, a bustling shopping street with no-nonsense modern commerce, lots of locals, and no tourists (T-bane to Majorstuen and follow this street back toward the palace and tourist zone). While most tourists never get out of the harbor/Karl Johans Gate district, the real, down-to-earth Oslo is better seen elsewhere, in places such as Bogstadveien. The bohemian, artsy Grünerløkka district, described on page 56, is good for a daytime wander.

stands the **National Theater** and statues of Norway's favorite playwrights: Ibsen and Bjørnstjerne Bjørnson. Across Karl Johans Gate, the pale yellow building is the first university building in Norway, dating from 1854. A block behind that is the National Gallery, with Norway's best collection of paintings.

Take a moment here to do a 360-degree spin to notice how quiet and orderly everything is. Many communities suffer from a "free rider" problem—which occurs when someone does something that would mess things up for all if everyone did it. (The transgressor believes his actions are OK because most people toe the line.) Norwegian society, with its heightened sense of social responsibility, doesn't experience this phenomenon.

• *Facing the theater, follow Roald Amundsens Gate left, to the towering brick...*

City Hall (Rådhuset): Built mostly in the 1930s with contributions from Norway's leading artists, City Hall is full of great art and is worth touring. The mayor has his office here (at the base of one of the two 200-foot towers), and every December 10, this building is where the Nobel Peace Prize is presented. For the best exterior art, circle the courtyard clockwise, studying the colorful woodcuts in the arcade. Each shows a scene from Norwegian mythology, well-explained in English: Thor with his billy-goat chariot, Ask and Embla (a kind of Norse Adam and Eve), Odin on his eight-legged horse guided by ravens, the swan maidens shedding their swan disguises, and so on. Circle to the right around City Hall, until you reach the front. The statues (especially the six laborers on the other side of the building, facing the harbor, who seem to guard the facade) celebrate the nobility of the working class. Norway, a social democracy, believes in giving respect to the workers who built their society and made it what it is, and these laborers are viewed as heroes.

• *Walk to the...*

Harbor: A decade ago, you would have dodged several lanes of busy traffic to get to Oslo's harborfront. But today, most cars cross underneath the city in tunnels. In addition, the city has made its town center relatively quiet and pedestrian-friendly by levying a traffic-discouraging 35-kr toll for every car entering town. (This system, like a similar one in London, subsidizes public transit and the city's infrastructure.)

At the water's edge, find the shiny metal plaque (just left of center) listing the contents of a sealed time capsule planted in 2000 out in the harbor in the little Kavringen lighthouse straight ahead (to be opened in 1,000 years). Go to the end of the stubby pier (on the right). This is the ceremonial "enter the city" point for momentous occasions. One such instance was in 1905, when Norway gained its independence from Sweden and a Danish prince sailed in from Copenhagen to become the first modern king of Norway. Another milestone event occurred at the end of World War II, when the king returned to Norway after the country was liberated from the Nazis.

• *Stand at the harbor and give it a sweeping counterclockwise look.*

Harborfront Spin-Tour: Oslofjord is a huge playground, with 40 city-owned, park-like islands. Big white cruise ships—a large part of the local tourist economy—dock just under the Akershus Fortress on the left. Just past the fort's impressive 13th-century ramparts, a statue of FDR grabs the shade. He's here in gratitude for the safe refuge the US gave to members of the royal family (including the young prince who is now Norway's king) during World War II—while the king and his government-in-exile waged Norway's fight against the Nazis from London.

Enjoy the grand view of City Hall. The yellow building farther to the left was the old West Train Station; today it houses the **Nobel Peace Center,** which celebrates the work of Nobel Peace Prize winners. The next pier is the launchpad for harbor boat tours and the shuttle boat to the Bygdøy museums. A fisherman often moors his boat here, selling shrimp from the back.

Oslo at a Glance

▲▲▲**City Hall** Oslo's artsy 20th-century government building, lined with huge, vibrant, municipal-themed murals, best visited with included tour. **Hours:** Daily 9:00-18:00; 3 tours/day, tours run Wed only in winter. See page 32.

▲▲▲**National Gallery** Norway's cultural and natural essence, captured on canvas. **Hours:** Tue-Fri 10:00-18:00, Thu until 19:00, Sat-Sun 11:00-17:00, closed Mon. See page 38.

▲▲▲**Vigeland Park** Set in sprawling Frogner Park, with tons of statuary by Norway's greatest sculptor, Gustav Vigeland, and the studio where he worked (now a museum). **Hours:** Park—always open; Vigeland Museum—May-Aug Tue-Sun 10:00-17:00, Sept-April Tue-Sun 12:00-16:00, closed Mon year-round. See page 46.

▲▲▲**Norwegian Folk Museum** Norway condensed into 150 historic buildings in a large open-air park. **Hours:** Daily mid-May-mid-Sept 10:00-18:00, off-season park open Mon-Fri 11:00-15:00, Sat-Sun 11:00-16:00, but most historical buildings closed. See page 51.

▲▲**Norwegian Resistance Museum** Gripping look at Norway's tumultuous WWII experience. **Hours:** June-Aug Mon-Sat 10:00-17:00, Sun 11:00-17:00; Sept-May Mon-Fri 10:00-16:00, Sat-Sun 11:00-16:00. See page 37.

▲▲**Viking Ship Museum** An impressive trio of ninth-century Viking ships, with exhibits on the people who built them. **Hours:** Daily May-Sept 9:00-18:00, Oct-April 10:00-16:00. See page 52.

▲▲*Fram* **Museum** Captivating exhibit on the Arctic exploration ships *Fram* and *Gjøa*. **Hours:** June-Aug daily 9:00-18:00; May and Sept daily 10:00-17:00; Oct and March-April daily 10:00-16:00; Nov-Feb Mon-Fri 10:00-15:00, Sat-Sun 10:00-16:00. See page 54.

▲▲*Kon-Tiki* **Museum** Adventures of primitive *Kon-Tiki* and *Ra II* ships built by Thor Heyerdahl. **Hours:** Daily June-Aug 9:30-18:00, March-May and Sept-Oct 10:00-17:00, Nov-Feb 10:00-16:00. See page 54.

▲▲**Holmenkollen Ski Jump and Ski Museum** Dizzying vista and a schuss through skiing history. **Hours:** Daily June-Aug 9:00-20:00, May and Sept 10:00-17:00, Oct-April 10:00-16:00. See page 62.

▲**Nobel Peace Center** Exhibit celebrating the ideals of the Nobel Peace Prize and the lives of those who have won it. **Hours:** Mid-May-Aug daily 10:00-18:00; Sept-mid-May Tue-Sun 10:00-18:00, closed Mon. See page 34.

▲**Opera House** Stunning performance center that's helping re-vitalize the harborfront. **Hours:** Foyer and café/restaurant open Mon-Fri 10:00-23:00, Sat 11:00-23:00, Sun 12:00-22:00; usually 3 tours/day of Opera House in summer. See page 34.

▲**Akershus Fortress Complex and Tours** Historic military base and fortified old center, with guided tours, a ho-hum castle inte-rior, and a couple of museums (including the excellent Norwegian Resistance Museum, listed earlier). **Hours:** Park generally open daily 6:00-21:00; generally 3 one-hour tours/day, fewer off-sea-son. See page 36.

▲**Norwegian Maritime Museum** Dusty cruise through Norway's rich seafaring heritage. **Hours:** Mid-May-Aug daily 10:00-17:00; Sept-mid-May Tue-Fri 10:00-15:00, Sat-Sun 10:00-16:00, closed Mon. See page 55.

▲**Norwegian Holocaust Center** High-tech walk through rise of anti-Semitism, the Holocaust in Norway, and racism today. **Hours:** June-Aug daily 10:00-18:00, Sept-May Mon-Fri 10:00-16:00, Sat-Sun 11:00-16:00. See page 55.

▲**Ekeberg Sculpture Park** Hilly, hikeable 63-acre forest park dotted with striking contemporary art. **Hours:** Always open. See page 63.

▲**Edvard Munch Museum** Works of Norway's famous Expres-sionistic painter. **Hours:** Mid-June-Sept daily 10:00-17:00; Oct-mid-June Wed-Mon 11:00-17:00, closed Tue. See page 64.

▲**Grünerløkka** Oslo's bohemian district, with bustling cafés and pubs. **Hours:** Always open. See page 56.

▲**Aker Brygge and Tjuvholmen** Oslo's harborfront promenade, and nearby trendy Tjuvholmen neighborhood with Astrup Fearn-ley Museum, upscale galleries, shops, and cafés. **Hours:** Always strollable. See page 35.

At the other end of the harbor, shipyard buildings (this was the former heart of Norway's once-important shipbuilding industry) have been transformed into **Aker Brygge**—Oslo's thriving restaurant/shopping/nightclub zone (see "Eating in Oslo").

Just past the end of Aker Brygge is a new housing development—dubbed Norway's most expensive real estate—called **Tjuvholmen.** It's anchored by the Astrup Fearnley Museum, an international modern art museum complex designed by renowned architect Renzo Piano (most famous for Paris' Pompidou Center; www.afmuseet.no). This zone is just one more reminder of Oslo's bold march toward becoming a city that is at once futuristic and people-friendly.

An ambitious urban renewal project called Fjord City (Fjordbyen)—which kicked off years ago with Aker Brygge, and led to the construction of Oslo's dramatic Opera House—is making remarkable progress in turning the formerly industrial waterfront into a flourishing people zone.

• *From here, you can stroll out Aker Brygge and through Tjuvholmen to a tiny public beach at the far end, tour City Hall, visit the Nobel Peace Center, hike up to Akershus Fortress, take a harbor cruise (see "Tours in Oslo," earlier), or catch a boat across the harbor to the museums at Bygdøy (from pier 3). The sights just mentioned are described in detail in the following section.*

Sights in Oslo

NEAR THE HARBORFRONT
▲▲▲City Hall (Rådhuset)

In 1931, Oslo tore down a slum and began constructing its richly decorated City Hall. It was finally finished—after a WWII delay—in 1950 to celebrate the city's 900th birthday. Norway's leading artists all contributed to the building, which was an avant-garde thrill in its day. City halls, rather than churches, are the dominant buildings in Scandinavian capitals. The prominence of this building on the harborfront makes sense in this most humanistic, yet least churchgoing, northern end of the Continent. Up here, people pay high taxes, have high expectations, and are generally satisfied with what their governments do with their money.

Cost and Hours: Free, daily 9:00-18:00, free 50-minute guided tours daily at 10:00, 12:00, and 14:00 in summer, tours run Wed only in winter, free and fine WC, enter on Karl Johans Gate side, tel. 23 46 12 00.

Visiting City Hall: At Oslo's City Hall, the six statues facing the waterfront—dating from a period of Labor Party rule in Norway—celebrate the nobility of the working class. The art implies a classless society, showing everyone working together. The theme continues inside, with 20,000 square feet of bold and colorful Socialist Realist murals showing town folk, country folk, and people from all walks of life working harmoniously for a better society. The huge murals take you on a voyage through the collective psyche of Norway, from its simple rural beginnings through the scar tissue of the Nazi occupation and beyond. Filled with significance and symbolism—and well-described in English—the murals become even more meaningful with the excellent guided tours.

The main hall feels like a temple to good government, with its altar-like mural celebrating "work, play, and civic administration." The mural emphasizes Oslo's youth participating in community life—and rebuilding the country after Nazi occupation. Across the bottom, the slum that once cluttered up Oslo's harborfront is being cleared out to make way for this building. Above that, scenes show Norway's pride in its innovative health care and education systems. Left of center, near the top, Mother Norway rests on a church—reminding viewers that the Lutheran Church of Norway (the official state religion) provides a foundation for this society. On the right, four forms represent the arts; they il-

lustrate how creativity springs from children. And in the center, the figure of Charity is surrounded by Culture, Philosophy, and Family.

The "Mural of the Occupation" lines the left side of the hall. It tells the story of Norway's WWII experience. Looking left to right, you'll see the following: The German blitzkrieg overwhelms the country. Men head for the mountains to organize a resistance movement. Women huddle around the water well, traditionally where news is passed, while Quislings (traitors named after the Norwegian fascist who ruled the country as a Nazi puppet) listen in. While Germans bomb and occupy Norway, a family gathers in their living room. As a boy clenches his fist (showing determination) and a child holds the beloved Norwegian flag, the Gestapo steps in. Columns lie on the ground, symbolizing how Germans shut down the culture by closing newspapers and the university. Two resistance soldiers are executed. A cell of resistance fighters (wearing masks and using nicknames, so if tortured they can't reveal their compatriots' identities) plan a sabotage mission. Finally, prisoners are freed, the war is over, and Norway celebrates its happiest day: May 17, 1945—the first Constitution Day after five years under Nazi control.

While gazing at these murals, keep in mind that the Nobel Peace Prize is awarded in this central hall each December (though the general Nobel Prize ceremony occurs in Stockholm's City Hall). You can see videos of the ceremony and acceptance speeches in the adjacent Nobel Peace Center (see next).

Eating: Fans of the explorer Fridtjof Nansen might enjoy a coffee or beer across the street at Fridtjof, an atmospheric bar filled with memorabilia from Nansen's Arctic explorations. A model of his ship, the *Fram*, hangs from the ceiling, and 1894 photos and his own drawings are upstairs (Mon-Sat 12:00 until late, Sun 14:00-22:00, Nansens Plass 7, near Forex, tel. 93 25 22 30).

▲Nobel Peace Center (Nobels Fredssenter)

This thoughtful and thought-provoking museum, housed in the former West Train Station (Vestbanen), poses the question, "What is the opposite of conflict?" It celebrates the 800-some past and present Nobel Peace Prize winners with engaging audio and video exhibits and high-tech gadgetry (all with good English explanations). Allow time for reading about past prizewinners and listening to acceptance speeches by recipients from President Carter to Mother Theresa. Check out the astonishing interactive book detailing the life and work of Alfred Nobel, the Swedish inventor of dynamite, who initiated the prizes—perhaps to assuage his conscience.

Cost and Hours: 90 kr; mid-May-Aug daily 10:00-18:00; Sept-mid-May Tue-Sun 10:00-18:00, closed Mon; included English guided tours at 12:00 and 15:00, fewer in winter; Brynjulfs Bulls Plass 1, tel. 48 30 10 00, www.nobelpeacecenter.org.

▲Opera House

Opened in 2008, Oslo's striking Opera House is still the talk of the town and a huge hit. The building rises from the water on the city's eastern harbor, across the highway from the train station (use the sky-bridge). Its boxy, low-slung, glass center holds a state-of-the-art 1,400-seat main theater with a 99-piece orchestra "in

the pit," which can rise to put the orchestra "on the pedestal." The season is split between opera and ballet.

Information-packed, 50-minute tours explain what makes this one of the greenest buildings in Europe and why Norwegian taxpayers helped foot the half-billion dollar cost for this project—to make high culture (ballet and opera) accessible to the younger generation and a strata of society who normally wouldn't care. You'll see a workshop employing 50 people who hand-make costumes, and learn how the foundation of 700 pylons set 40 or 50 meters deep support the jigsaw puzzle of wood, glass, and 36,000 individual pieces of marble. The construction masterfully integrates land and water, inside and outside, nature and culture.

The jutting white marble planes of the Opera House's roof double as a public plaza. When visiting, you feel a need to walk all over it. The Opera House is part of a larger harbor-redevelopment plan that includes rerouting traffic into tunnels and turning a once-derelict industrial zone into an urban park.

Cost and Hours: Foyer and café/restaurant open Mon-Fri 10:00-23:00, Sat 11:00-23:00, Sun 12:00-22:00.

Tours: In summer, the Opera House offers sporadic foyer concerts (50 kr, generally at 13:00) and fascinating 50-minute guided tours of the stage, backstage area, and architecture (100 kr, usually 3 tours/day in English—generally at 11:00, 12:00, and 14:00, reserve by email at omvisninger@operaen.no or online at www.operaen.no, tel. 21 42 21 00).

Getting There: The easiest way to get to the Opera House is from the train station. Just follow signs for *Exit South/Utgang Syd* (standing in the main hall with the tracks to your back, it's to the left). Exiting the station, proceed straight ahead onto the pedestrian bridge (marked *Velkommen til Operaen*), which takes you effortlessly above traffic congestion to your goal.

▲Aker Brygge and Tjuvholmen

Oslo's harborfront was dominated by the Aker Brygge shipyard until it closed in 1986. Today this is the first finished part of a project (called Fjordbyen, or Fjord City) that will turn the central stretch of Oslo's harborfront into a people-friendly park and culture zone. Aker Brygge is a stretch of trendy yacht-club style restaurants facing a fine promenade—just the place to join in on a Nordic paseo on a balmy summer's eve.

The far end of Aker Brygge is marked by a big black anchor (from the German warship *Blücher,* sunk by Norwegian forces near Drøbak during the Nazi invasion on April 9, 1940). From there a bridge crosses over into Tjuvholmen (named for the place they hung thieves back in the 17th century). This is a planned and future-esque community, with the trendiest and costliest apartments

in town, lots of galleries, elegant shops and cafés, and the striking Astrup Fearnley Museum of Modern Art nearby. As you stroll
through Tjuvholmen, admire how each building has its own personality.

Eating: Dining here is a great idea in the evening. Choose
from many restaurants, or take advantage of the generous public
benches, lounge chairs, and picnic tables that allow people who
can't afford a fancy restaurant meal to enjoy the best seats of all
(grocery stores are a block away from the harborfront views).

▲AKERSHUS FORTRESS COMPLEX

This park-like complex of sights scattered over Oslo's fortified old
center is still a military base. (The Royal Guard is present because
the castle is a royal mausoleum.) But the public is welcome, and as
you dodge patrol guards and vans filled with soldiers, you'll see the
castle, a prison, war memorials, the Norwegian Resistance Museum, the Armed Forces Museum, and cannon-strewn ramparts
affording fine harbor views and picnic perches. There's an unim-
pressive changing of the guard daily at 13:30 (at the parade ground,
deep in the castle complex). The park is generally open daily 6:00-
21:00, but because the military is in charge here, times can change
without warning. Expect bumpy cobblestone lanes and steep hills.
To get here from the harbor, follow the stairs (which lead past the
FDR statue) to the park.

Fortress Visitors Center: Located immediately inside the
gate, the information center has an exhibit tracing the story of Oslo's fortifications from medieval times through the environmental
struggles of today. Stop here to pick up the fortress trail and site
map, quickly browse through the museum, and consider catching
a tour (see next; museum entry free, mid-June-mid-Aug Mon-Fri
10:00-17:00, Sat-Sun 11:00-17:00, shorter hours off-season, tel. 23
09 39 17, www.mil.no/felles/ak).

▲Fortress Tours

The 50-kr hour-long English walking tours of the grounds help
you make sense of the most historic piece of real estate in Oslo
(mid-June-mid-Aug 3/day, fewer off-season; depart from Fortress
Visitors Center, call center at tel. 23 09 39 17 in advance to confirm
times).

Akershus Castle

The first fortress here was built by
Norwegians in 1299. It was rebuilt
much stronger by the Danes in 1640
so the Danish king (Christian IV)
would have a suitable and safe place
to stay during his many visits. When

Oslo was rebuilt in the 17th century, many of the stones from the first Oslo cathedral were reused here, in the fortress walls.

Although it's one of Oslo's oldest buildings, the castle overlooking the harbor is mediocre by European standards; the big, empty rooms recall Norway's medieval poverty. From the old kitchen, where the ticket desk and gift shop are located, you'll follow a one-way circuit of rooms open to the public. Descend through a secret passage to the dungeon, crypt, and royal tomb. Emerge behind the altar in the chapel, then walk through echoing rooms including the Daredevil's Tower, Hall of Christian IV (with portraits of Danish kings of Norway on the walls), and Hall of Olav I. There are terrific harbor views (often filled with a giant cruise ship) from the rampart just outside.

Cost and Hours: 70 kr, includes audioguide with 45-minute tour and ghost story options; May-Aug Mon-Sat 10:00-16:00, Sun 12:30-16:00; Sept-April Sat-Sun 12:00-17:00 only, closed Mon-Fri; tel. 22 41 25 21.

▲▲Norwegian Resistance Museum (Norges Hjemmefrontmuseum)

This fascinating museum tells the story of Norway's WWII experience: appeasement, Nazi invasion (they made Akershus their headquarters), resistance, liberation, and, finally, the return of the king.

Cost and Hours: 50 kr; June-Aug Mon-Sat 10:00-17:00, Sun 11:00-17:00; Sept-May Mon-Fri 10:00-16:00, Sat-Sun 11:00-16:00; next to castle, overlooking harbor, tel. 23 09 31 38, www.forsvaretsmuseer.no.

Visiting the Museum: It's a one-way, chronological, can't-get-lost route. As you enter the museum, you're transported back to 1940, greeted by an angry commotion of rifles aimed at you. A German notice proclaiming "You will submit or die" is bayonetted onto a gun in the middle.

You'll see propaganda posters attempting to get Norwegians to join the Nazi party, and the German ultimatum to which the king gave an emphatic "No." Various displays show secret radios, transmitters, underground newspapers, crude but effective homemade weapons, and the German machine that located clandestine radio stations. Exhibits explain how the country coped with 350,000 occupying troops; how airdrops equipped a home force of 40,000 so they were ready to coordinate with the Allies when liberation was imminent; and the happy day when the resistance army came out of the forest, and peace and freedom returned to Norway.

The museum is particularly poignant because many of the patriots featured inside were executed by the Germans right outside the museum's front door; a stone memorial marks the spot. (At war's end, the traitor Vidkun Quisling was also executed at the fortress, but at a different location.) With good English descriptions, this is an inspirational look at how the national spirit can endure total occupation by a malevolent force. (Note: Copenhagen's Resistance Museum burned down and neutral Sweden didn't have a resistance.)

Armed Forces Museum (Forsvarsmuseet)

Across the fortress parade ground, a too-spacious museum traces Norwegian military history from Viking days to post-World War II. The early stuff is sketchy, but the WWII story is compelling.

Cost and Hours: Free, May-Aug Mon-Fri 10:00-16:00, Sat-Sun 11:00-17:00, shorter hours off-season, tel. 23 09 35 82.

Old Christiania

In the mid-1600s, the ruling Danes had the original Oslo leveled and built a more modern grid-planned city. They built with stone so it wouldn't burn, and located it just below the castle so it was easier to control and defend. They named it Christiania, after their king. The checkerboard zone between the castle and the cathedral today marks that original Christiania town. While Oslo didn't do a good job of protecting it through the 20th century, bits of Christiania's original Dutch Renaissance-style buildings survive. (Norwegian builders, accustomed to working with wood, lacked skill with stone, so the Danes imported Dutch builders.) The main square, Christiania Torv, is marked by a modern fountain called "The Glove." The sculpture of Christian IV's glove points as if to indicate, "This is where we'll build my city." The old City Hall, now the Gamle Raadhus restaurant, survives. If you explore this district you'll see several 17th-century buildings.

DOWNTOWN MUSEUMS

▲▲▲National Gallery (Nasjonalgalleriet)

While there are many schools of painting and sculpture displayed in Norway's National Gallery, focus on what's uniquely Norwegian. Paintings come and go in this museum (pesky curators may have even removed some of the ones listed in the self-guided tour on the next page), but you're sure to see plenty that showcase the harsh beauty of Norway's landscape and people. A thoughtful visit here gives those heading into the mountains and fjord country a chance to pack along a little of Norway's cultural soul. Tuck these images carefully away with your goat cheese—they'll sweeten your explorations.

The gallery also has several Picassos, a noteworthy Impressionist collection, a Van Gogh self-portrait, and some Vigeland statues.
Its many raving examples of Edvard Munch's work, including one

of his famous *Scream* paintings, make a trip to the Munch
Museum unnecessary for most.
It has about 50 Munch paintings in its collection, but only
about a third are on display. Be
prepared for changes, but don't
worry—no matter what the curators decide to show, you won't
have to scream for Munch's
masterpieces.

Cost and Hours: 50 kr, free on Sun, Tue-Fri 10:00-18:00,
Thu until 19:00, Sat-Sun 11:00-17:00, closed Mon, chewing
gum prohibited, Universitets Gata 13, tel. 22 20 04 04, www.
nasjonalmuseet.no. Pick up the guidebooklet to help navigate the
collection.

Eating: The richly ornamented French Salon café offers an
elegant break.

➋ Self-Guided Tour: This easy-to-handle museum gives an
effortless tour back in time and through Norway's most beautiful
valleys, mountains, and fjords, with the help of its Romantic painters (especially Johan Christian Dahl).
• *Go up the stairs into Room 24 and turn left into Room 13.*

Landscape Paintings and Romanticism

Landscape painting has always played an important role in Norwegian art, perhaps because Norway provides such an awesome and
varied landscape to inspire artists. The style reached its peak during
the Romantic period in the mid-1800s, which stressed the beauty
of unspoiled nature. (This passion for landscapes sets Norway apart
from Denmark and Sweden.) After 400 years of Danish rule, the
soul of the country was almost snuffed out. But with semi-independence and a constitution in the early 1800s, there was a national
resurgence. Romantic paintings featuring the power of Norway's
natural wonders and the toughness of its salt-of-the-earth folk
came into vogue.

➊ Johan Christian Dahl—*View from Stalheim* (1842): This
painting epitomizes the Norwegian closeness to nature. It shows
a view very similar to the one that 21st-century travelers enjoy on
their Norway in a Nutshell excursion: mountains, rivers, and farms
clinging to hillsides. Painted in 1842, it's quintessential Romantic style. Nature rules—the background is as detailed as the foreground, and you are sucked in.

OSLO

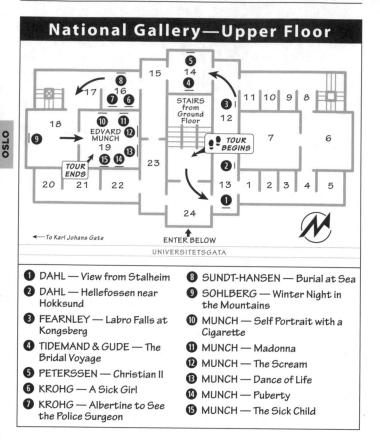

National Gallery—Upper Floor

- **1** DAHL — View from Stalheim
- **2** DAHL — Hellefossen near Hokksund
- **3** FEARNLEY — Labro Falls at Kongsberg
- **4** TIDEMAND & GUDE — The Bridal Voyage
- **5** PETERSSEN — Christian II
- **6** KROHG — A Sick Girl
- **7** KROHG — Albertine to See the Police Surgeon
- **8** SUNDT-HANSEN — Burial at Sea
- **9** SOHLBERG — Winter Night in the Mountains
- **10** MUNCH — Self Portrait with a Cigarette
- **11** MUNCH — Madonna
- **12** MUNCH — The Scream
- **13** MUNCH — Dance of Life
- **14** MUNCH — Puberty
- **15** MUNCH — The Sick Child

Johan Christian Dahl (1788-1857) is considered the father of Norwegian Romanticism. Romantics such as Dahl (and Turner, Beethoven, and Lord Byron) put emotion over rationality. They reveled in the power of nature—death and pessimism ripple through their work, though in this scene a double rainbow and a splash of sunlight give hope of a better day. The birch tree—standing boldly front and center—is a standard symbol for the politically downtrodden Norwegian people: hardy, weathered, but defiantly sprouting new branches. In the mid-19th century, Norwegians were awakening to their national identity. Throughout Europe, nationalism and Romanticism went hand in hand.

Find the farm buildings huddled near the cliff's edge, smoke rising from chimneys, and the woman in traditional dress tending her herd of goats, pausing for a moment to revel in the glory of nature. It reminds us that these farmers are hardworking, independent, small landowners. There was no feudalism in medieval

Norway. People were poor...but they owned their own land. You can almost taste goat cheese.

• *Look at the other works in Rooms 13 and 12. Dahl's paintings and those by his Norwegian contemporaries, showing heavy clouds and glaciers, repeat these same themes—drama over rationalism, nature pounding humanity. Human figures are melancholy. Norwegians, so close to nature, are fascinated by those plush, magic hours of dawn and twilight. The dusk makes us wonder: What will the future bring?*

In particular, focus on the painting to the left of the door in Room 13.

❷ **Dahl**—*Hellefossen near Hokksund* **(1838):** Another typical Dahl setting: romantic nature and an idealized scene. A fisherman checks on wooden baskets designed to catch salmon migrating up the river. In the background, a water-powered sawmill slices trees into lumber. Note another Dahl birch tree at the left, a subtle celebration of the Norwegian people and their labor.

• *Now continue into Room 12. On the right is...*

❸ **Thomas Fearnley**—*Labro Falls at Kongsberg* **(1837):** Man cannot control nature or his destiny. The landscape in this painting is devoid of people—the only sign of humanity is the jumble of sawn logs in the foreground. A wary eagle perched on one log seems to be saying, "While you can cut these trees, they'll always be mine."

• *Continue to the end of Room 12, and turn left into Room 14.*

❹ **Adolph Tidemand and Hans Gude**—*The Bridal Voyage* **(1848):** This famous painting shows the ultimate Norwegian

scene: a wedding party with everyone decked out in traditional garb, heading for the stave church on the quintessential fjord (Hardanger). It's a studio work (not real) and a collaboration: Hans Gude painted the landscape, and Adolph Tidemand painted the people. Study their wedding finery. This work trumpets the greatness of both the landscape and Norwegian culture.

• *Also in Room 14, on the opposite wall, is an example of...*

The Photographic Eye

At the end of the 19th century, Norwegian painters traded the emotions of Romanticism for more slice-of-life detail. This was the end of the Romantic period and the beginning of Realism. With the advent of photography, painters went beyond simple realism and into extreme realism.

❺ **Eilif Peterssen**—*Christian II* **(1875):** The Danish king signs the execution order for the man who'd killed the king's beloved mistress. With camera-like precision, the painter captures the whole story of murder, anguish, anger, and bitter revenge in the king's set jaw and steely eyes.

• *Go through Room 15 and into Room 16. Take time to browse the paintings.*

Vulnerability

Death, disease, and suffering were themes seen again and again in art from the late 1800s. The most serious disease during this period was tuberculosis (which killed Munch's mother and sister).

❻ **Christian Krohg—A Sick Girl (1880):** Christian Krohg (1852-1925) is known as Edvard Munch's inspiration, but to Nor-

wegians, he's famous in his own right for his artistry and giant personality. This extremely realistic painting shows a child dying of tuberculosis, as so many did in Norway in the 19th century. The girl looks directly at you. You can almost feel the cloth, with its many shades of white.

• *And just to the right of this painting, find...*

❼ **Krohg—*Albertine to See the Police Surgeon* (c. 1885-1887):** Krohg had a sharp interest in social justice. In this painting, Albertine, a sweet girl from the countryside, has fallen into the world of prostitu-

tion in the big city. She's the new kid on the Red Light block in the 1880s, as Oslo's prostitutes are pulled into the police clinic for their regular checkup. Note her traditional dress and the disdain she gets from the more experienced girls. Krohg has buried his subject in this scene. His technique requires the viewer to find her, and that search helps humanize the prostitute.

• *In Room 16 you may also find...*

❽ **Carl Sundt-Hansen—*Burial at Sea* (1890):** While Monet and the Impressionists were busy abandoning the realistic style, Norwegian artists continued to embrace it. In this painting, you're invited to participate. A dead man's funeral is attended by an ethnically diverse group of sailors and passengers, but only one is a woman—the widow. Your presence completes the half-circle at the on-deck ceremony. Notice how each person in the painting has his or her own way of confronting death. Their faces speak volumes about the life of toil here. A common thread in Norwegian art is the cycle—the tough cycle—of life. There's also an interest in everyday experiences. *Burial at Sea* may not always be on display. If it's not here, you may instead see a similar canvas, **Erik Werenskiold's** *A Peasant Burial* (1885).

• *Continue through Room 17 and into Room 18.*

Atmosphere

Landscape painters were often fascinated by the phenomena of nature, and the artwork in this room takes us back to this ideal from the Romantic Age. Painters were challenged by capturing atmospheric conditions at a specific moment, since it meant making quick sketches outdoors, before the weather changed yet again.

❾ **Harald Sohlberg—***Winter Night in the Mountains* **(1914):** Harald Sohlberg was inspired by this image while skiing in the

mountains in the winter of 1899. Over the years, he attempted to re-create the scene that inspired this remark: "The mountains in winter reduce one to silence. One is overwhelmed, as in a mighty, vaulted church, only a thousand times more so."

• *Follow the crowds into Room 19, the Munch room.*

Turmoil

Room 19 is filled with works by Norway's single most famous painter, Edvard Munch (see sidebar). Norway's long, dark winters and social isolation have produced many gloomy artists, but none gloomier than Munch. He infused his work with emotion and expression at the expense of realism. After viewing the paintings in general, take a look at these in particular (listed in clockwise order).

❿ **Edvard Munch—***Self Portrait with a Cigarette* **(1895):** In this self-portrait, Munch is spooked, haunted—an artist working, immersed in an oppressive world. Indefinable shadows inhabit the background. His hand shakes as he considers his uncertain future. (Ironic, considering he created his masterpieces during this depressed period.) After eight months in a Danish clinic, he found peace—and lost his painting power. Afterward, Munch never again painted another strong example of what we love most about his art.

⓫ **Munch—***Madonna* **(1894-1895):** Munch had a tortured relationship with women. He never married. He dreaded and struggled with love, writing that he feared if he loved too much, he'd lose his painting talent. This painting is a mystery: Is she standing or lying? Is that a red halo or some devilish accessory? Munch

Edvard Munch (1863-1944)

Edvard Munch (pronounced "moonk") is Norway's most famous and influential painter. His life was rich, complex, and sad. His father was a doctor who had a nervous breakdown. His mother and sister both died of tuberculosis. He knew suffering. And he gave us the enduring symbol of 20th-century pain, *The Scream*.

He was also Norway's most forward-thinking painter, a man who traveled extensively through Europe, soaking up the colors of the Post-Impressionists and the curves of Art Nouveau. He helped pioneer a new style—Expressionism—using lurid colors and wavy lines to "express" inner turmoil and the angst of the modern world.

After a nervous breakdown in late 1908, followed by eight months of rehab in a clinic, Munch emerged less troubled—but a less powerful painter. His late works were as a colorist: big, bright, less tormented...and less noticed.

wrote that he would strive to capture his subjects at their holiest moment. His alternative name for this work: *Woman Making Love*. What's more holy than a woman at the moment of conception?

⓬ **Munch—*The Scream* (1893):** Munch's most famous work shows a man screaming, capturing the fright many feel as the human "race" does just that. The figure seems isolated from the people on the bridge—locked up in himself, unable to stifle his scream. Munch made four versions of this scene, which has become *the* textbook example of Expressionism. On one, he graffitied: "This painting is the work of a madman." He explained that the painting "shows today's society, reverberating within me...making me want to scream." He's sharing his internal angst. In fact, this Expressionist masterpiece is a breakthrough painting; it's angst personified.

⓭ **Munch—*Dance of Life* (1899-1900):** In this scene of five dancing couples, we glimpse Munch's notion of femininity. To him, women were a complex mix of Madonna and whore. We see

Munch's take on the cycle of women's lives: She's a virgin (discarding the sweet flower of youth), a whore (a jaded temptress in red), and a widow (having destroyed the man, she is finally alone, aging, in black). With the phallic moon rising on the lake, Munch demonizes women as they turn men into green-faced, lusty monsters.

⓮ Munch—*Puberty* (1894-1895): One of the artist's most important non-*Scream* canvases reveals his ambivalence about women (see also his *Madonna,* earlier). This adolescent girl, grappling with her emerging sexuality, covers her nudity self-consciously. The looming shadow behind her—frighteningly too big and amorphous—threatens to take over the scene. The shadow's significance is open to interpretation—is it phallic, female genitalia, death, an embodiment of sexual anxiety...or Munch himself?

⓯ Munch—*The Sick Child* (1896): The death of Munch's sister in 1877 due to tuberculosis likely inspired this painting. The girl's face melts into the pillow. She's becoming two-dimensional, halfway between life and death. Everything else is peripheral, even her despairing mother saying good-bye. You can see how Munch scraped and repainted the face until he got it right.

• *Our tour is over, but there's more to see in this fine collection. Take a break from Nordic gloom and doom by visiting Rooms 15 and 23, with works by Impressionist and Post-Impressionist artists...even Munch got into the spirit with his Parisian painting, titled* Rue Lafayette. *You'll see lesser-known, but still beautiful, paintings by non-Norwegian big names such as Picasso, Modigliani, Monet, Manet, Van Gogh, Gauguin, and Cézanne.*

National Historical Museum (Historisk Museum)
Directly behind the National Gallery and just below the palace is a fine Art Nouveau building offering an easy (if underwhelming) peek at Norway's history.

Cost and Hours: 50 kr, mid-May-mid-Sept Tue-Sun 10:00-17:00, mid-Sept-mid-May Tue-Sun 11:00-16:00, closed Mon year-round; Frederiks Gate 2, tel. 22 85 99 12, www.khm.uio.no.

Visiting the Museum: The ground floor offers a walk through the local history from prehistoric times. It includes the country's top collection of Viking artifacts, displayed in low-tech, old-school exhibits with barely a word of English to give it meaning. There's also some medieval church art. The museum's highlight is upstairs: an exhibit (well-described in English) about life in the Arctic for the Sami people (previously known to outsiders as Laplanders). In this overview of the past, a few Egyptian mummies and Norwegian coins through the ages are tossed in for good measure.

Gustav Vigeland (1869-1943)

As a young man, Vigeland studied sculpture in Oslo, then supplemented his education with trips abroad to Europe's art capitals. Back home, he carved out a successful, critically acclaimed career feeding newly independent Norway's hunger for homegrown art.

During his youthful trips abroad, Vigeland had frequented the studio of Auguste Rodin, admiring Rodin's naked, restless, intertwined statues. Like Rodin, Vigeland explored the yin/yang relationship of men and women. Also like Rodin, Vigeland did not personally carve or cast his statues. Rather, he formed them in clay or plaster, to be executed by a workshop of assistants. Vigeland's sturdy humans capture universal themes of the cycle of life—birth, childhood, romance, struggle, child-rearing, growing old, and death.

A PARK AND TWO MUSEUMS
▲▲▲Vigeland Park

Within Oslo's vast Frogner Park is Vigeland Park, containing a lifetime of work by Norway's greatest sculptor, Gustav Vigeland (see sidebar). In 1921, he made a deal with the city. In return for a great studio and state support, he'd spend his creative life beautifying Oslo with this sculpture garden. From 1924 to 1943 he worked on-site, designing 192 bronze and granite statue groupings—600 figures in all, each nude and unique. Vigeland even planned the landscaping. Today the park is loved and respected by the people of Oslo (no police, no fences—and no graffiti). The Frognerbadet swimming pool is nearby in Frogner Park.

Cost and Hours: The garden is always open and free. The park is safe (cameras monitor for safety) and lit in the evening.

Getting There: Tram #12—which leaves from the central train station, Rådhusplassen in front of City Hall, Aker Brygge, and other points in town—drops you off right at the park gate (Vigelandsparken stop). Tram #19 (with stops along Karl Johans Gate) takes you to Majorstuen, a 10-minute walk to the gate (or you can change at Majorstuen to tram #12 and ride it one stop to Vigelandsparken).

Visiting the Park: Vigeland Park is more than great art: It's a city at play. Appreciate its urban Norwegian ambience.

The park is huge, but this visit is a snap. Here's a quick, four-stop, straight-line, gate-to-monolith tour:

Enter the Park from Kirkeveien: For an illustrated guide and fine souvenir, pick up the 75-kr book in the Visitors Center

(Besøkssenter) on your right as you enter. The modern cafeteria has sandwiches (indoor/outdoor seating, daily 9:00-20:30, shorter hours Sun and off-season), plus books, gifts, and WCs. Look at the statue of Gustav Vigeland (hammer and chisel in hand, drenched in pigeon poop) and consider his messed-up life. He lived with his many models. His marriages failed. His children entangled his artistic agenda. He didn't age gracefully. He didn't name his statues, and refused to explain their meanings. While those who know his life story can read it clearly in the granite and bronze, I'd forget Gustav's troubles and see his art as observations on the bittersweet cycle of life in general—from a man who must have had a passion for living.

Bridge: The 300-foot-long bridge is bounded by four granite columns: Three show a man fighting a lizard, the fourth shows a woman submitting to the lizard's embrace. Hmmm. (Vigeland was familiar with medieval mythology, where dragons represent man's primal—and sinful—nature.) But enough lizard love; the 58 bronze statues along the bridge are a general study of the human body. Many deal with relationships between people. In the middle, on the right, find the circular statue of a man and woman going round and round—perhaps the eternal attraction and love between the sexes. But directly opposite, another circle feels like a prison—

man against the world, with no refuge. From the man escaping, look down at the children's playground: eight bronze infants circling a head-down fetus.

On your left, see the famous *Sinnataggen*, the hot-headed little boy. It's said Vigeland gave him chocolate and then took it away to get this reaction. The statues capture the joys of life (and, on a sunny day, so do the Norwegians filling the park around you).

Fountain: Continue through a rose garden to the earliest sculpture unit in the park. Six giants hold a fountain, sym-

OSLO

bolically toiling with the burden of life, as water—the source of life—cascades steadily around them. Twenty tree-of-life groups surround the fountain. Four clumps of trees (on each corner) show humanity's relationship to nature and the seasons of life: childhood, young love, adulthood, and winter.

Take a quick swing through life, starting on the right with youth. In the branches you'll see a swarm of children (Vigeland called them "geniuses"): A boy sits in a tree, boys actively climb while most girls stand by quietly, and a girl glides through the branches wide-eyed and ready for life...and love. Circle clockwise to the next stage: love scenes. In the third corner, life becomes more complicated: a sad woman in an animal-like tree, a lonely child, a couple plummeting downward (perhaps falling out of love), and finally an angry man driving away babies. The fourth corner completes the cycle, as death melts into the branches of the tree of life and you realize new geniuses will bloom.

The 60 bronze reliefs circling the basin develop the theme further, showing man mixing with nature and geniuses giving the carousel of life yet another spin. Speaking of another spin, circle again and follow these reliefs.

The sidewalk surrounding the basin is a maze—life's long and winding road with twists, dead ends, frustrations, and, ultimately, a way out. If you have about an hour to spare, enter the labyrinth (on the side nearest the park's entrance gate, there's a single break in the black border) and follow the white granite path until (on the monolith side) you finally get out. (Tracing this path occupies older kids, affording parents a peaceful break in the park.) Or you can go straight up the steps to the monolith.

Monolith: The centerpiece of the park—a teeming monolith of life surrounded by 36 granite groups—continues Vigeland's cycle-of-life motif. The figures are hunched and clearly earthbound, while Vigeland explores a lifetime of human relationships. At the center, 121 figures carved out of a single block of stone rocket skyward. Three stone carvers worked daily for 14 years, cutting Vigeland's full-size plaster model into the final 180-ton, 50-foot-tall erection.

Circle the plaza, once to trace the

stages of life in the 36 statue groups, and a second time to enjoy how Norwegian kids relate to the art. The statues—both young and old—seem to speak to children.

Vigeland lived barely long enough to see his monolith raised. Covered with bodies, it seems to pick up speed as it spirals skyward. Some people seem to naturally rise. Others struggle not to fall. Some help others. Although the granite groups around the monolith are easy to understand, Vigeland left the meaning of the monolith itself open. Like life, it can be interpreted many different ways.

OSLO

From this summit of the park, look a hundred yards farther, where four children and three adults are intertwined and spinning in the Wheel of Life. Now, look back at the entrance. If the main gate is at 12 o'clock, the studio where Vigeland lived and worked—now the Vigeland Museum—is at 2 o'clock (see the green copper tower poking above the trees). His ashes sit in the top of the tower in clear view of the monolith. If you liked the park, visit the Vigeland Museum (described next), a delightful five-minute walk away, for an intimate look at the art and how it was made.

▲▲Vigeland Museum

Filled with original plaster casts and well-described exhibits on his work, this palatial city-provided studio was Gustav Vigeland's

home and workplace. The high south-facing windows provided just the right light.

Vigeland, who had a deeply religious upbringing, saw his art as an expression of his soul. He once said, "The road between feeling and execution should be as short as possible."

Here, immersed in his work, Vigeland supervised his craftsmen like a father, from 1924 until his death in 1943.

Cost and Hours: 60 kr; May-Aug Tue-Sun 10:00-17:00, Sept-April Tue-Sun 12:00-16:00, closed Mon year-round; bus #20 or tram #12 to Frogner Plass, Nobels Gate 32, tel. 23 49 37 00, www.vigeland.museum.no.

Oslo City Museum (Oslo Bymuseum)

This hard-to-be-thrilled-about little museum tells the story of Oslo. For a quick overview of the city, watch the 15-minute English video.

Cost and Hours: Free, Tue-Sun 11:00-16:00, closed Mon, borrow English description sheet, located in Frogner Park at Frogner Manor Farm across street from Vigeland Museum, tel. 23 28 41 70, www.oslomuseum.no.

OSLO

▲▲OSLO'S BYGDØY NEIGHBORHOOD

This thought-provoking and exciting cluster of sights is on a park-like peninsula just across the harbor from downtown. It provides a busy and rewarding half-day (at a minimum) of sightseeing. Here, within a short walk, are six major sights (listed in order of importance):

• **Norwegian Folk Museum,** an open-air park with traditional log buildings from all corners of the country.

• **Viking Ship Museum,** showing off the best-preserved Viking longboats in existence.

• **Fram Museum,** showcasing the modern Viking spirit with the *Fram,* the ship of Arctic-exploration fame, and the *Gjøa,* the first ship to sail through the Northwest Passage.

• **Kon-Tiki Museum,** starring the *Kon-Tiki* and the *Ra II,* in which Norwegian explorer Thor Heyerdahl proved that early civilizations—with their existing technologies—could have crossed the oceans.

• **Norwegian Maritime Museum,** interesting mostly to old salts, has a wonderfully scenic movie of Norway.

• **Norwegian Holocaust Center,** a high-tech look at the Holocaust in Norway and contemporary racism.

Getting There: Sailing from downtown to Bygdøy is fun, and it gets you in a seafaring mood. Ride the Bygdøy ferry—marked *Public Ferry Bygdøy Museums*—from pier 3 in front of City Hall (50 kr one-way; covered by Oslo Pass; mid-May-Aug daily 8:55-20:55, usually 3/hour; fewer sailings April and Sept; doesn't run Oct-March). Boats generally leave from downtown and from the museum dock at :05, :25, and :45 past each hour. In summer, avoid the nearby (much more expensive) tour boats. For a less memorable approach, you can take bus #30 (from train station or National Theater, direction: Bygdøy).

Getting Around Bygdøy: The Norwegian Folk and Viking Ship museums are a 10-minute walk from the ferry's first stop (Dronningen). The other boating museums (Fram, Kon-Tiki, and Maritime) are at the second ferry stop (Bygdøynes). The Holocaust Center is off Fredriksborgveien, about halfway between these two museum clusters. All Bygdøy sights are within a pleasant (when sunny) 15-minute walk of each other. The walk gives you a picturesque taste of small-town Norway.

City bus #30 connects the sights four times hourly in this order: Norwegian Folk Museum, Viking Ship Museum, Kon-Tiki Museum, Norwegian Holocaust Center. (For the Holocaust Center, you'll use the Bygdøyhus stop a long block away; tell the bus

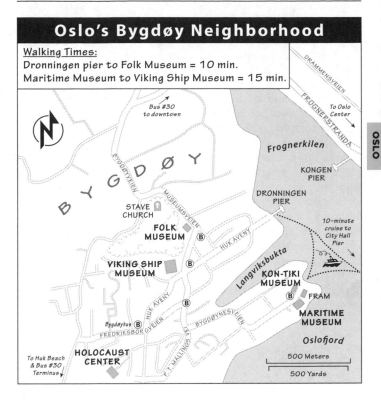

Oslo's Bygdøy Neighborhood

Walking Times:
Dronningen pier to Folk Museum = 10 min.
Maritime Museum to Viking Ship Museum = 15 min.

OSLO

driver you want the stop for the "HL-Senteret.") The bus turns around at its final stop (Huk), then passes the sights in reverse order on its way back to the city center. Note that after 17:00, bus and boat departures are sparse. If returning to Oslo by ferry, get to the dock a little early—otherwise the boat is likely to be full, and you'll have to wait for the next sailing.

Eating at Bygdøy: Lunch options near the Kon-Tiki are a sandwich bar (relaxing picnic spots along the grassy shoreline) and a cafeteria (with tables overlooking the harbor). The Norwegian Folk Museum has a decent cafeteria inside and a fun little farmers' market stall across the street from the entrance. The Holocaust Center has a small café on its second floor.

Beach at Bygdøy: A popular beach is located at Huk, on the southwest tip of the peninsula.

▲▲▲Norwegian Folk Museum (Norsk Folkemuseum)

Brought from all corners of Norway, 150 buildings have been re-assembled here on 35 acres. While Stockholm's Skansen was the first museum of this kind to open to the public, this museum is a bit older, started in 1882 as the king's private collection (and the inspiration for Skansen).

Cost and Hours: 110 kr, daily mid-May-mid-Sept 10:00-18:00, off-season park open Mon-Fri 11:00-15:00, Sat-Sun 11:00-16:00 but most historical buildings closed, free lockers, Museumsveien 10, bus #30 stops immediately in front, tel. 22 12 37 00, www.norskfolkemuseum.no.

Visiting the Museum: Think of the visit in three parts: the park sprinkled with old buildings, the re-created old town, and the folk-art museum. In peak season, the park is lively, with craftspeople doing their traditional things, barnyard animals roaming about, and costumed guides all around. (They're paid to happily answer your questions—so ask many.) The evocative Gol stave church, at the top of a hill at the park's edge, is a must-see (built in 1212 in Hallingdal and painstakingly reconstructed here). Across the park, the old town comes complete with apartments from various generations (including some reconstructions of people's actual homes) and offers an intimate look at lifestyles here in 1905, 1930, 1950, 1979, and even a modern-day Norwegian-Pakistani apartment.

The museum beautifully presents woody, colorfully painted folk art (ground floor), exquisite-in-a-peasant-kind-of-way folk

costumes (upstairs), and temporary exhibits. Everything is thoughtfully explained in English. Don't miss the best Sami culture exhibit I've seen in Scandinavia (across the courtyard in the green building, behind the toy exhibit).

Upon arrival, pick up the site map and review the list of the day's activities, concerts, and guided tours. In summer, there are two guided tours in English per day; the Telemark Farm hosts a small daily fiddle-and-dance show; and a folk music-and-dance show is held each Sunday. The folk museum is most lively June through mid-August, when buildings are open and staffed. Otherwise, the indoor museum is fine, but the park is just a walk past lots of locked-up log cabins. If you don't take a tour, pick up a guidebook and ask questions of the informative attendants stationed in buildings throughout the park.

▲▲Viking Ship Museum (Vikingskiphuset)

In this impressive museum, you'll gaze with admiration at two finely crafted, majestic oak Viking ships dating from the 9th and 10th centuries, and the scant remains of a third vessel. Along with

the two well-preserved ships, you'll see the bones of Vikings buried with these vessels and remarkable artifacts that may cause you to consider these notorious raiders in a different light. Over a thousand years ago, three things drove Vikings on their far-flung raids: hard economic times in their bleak homeland, the lure of prosperous and vulnerable communities to the south, and a mastery of the sea. There was a time when most frightened Europeans closed every prayer with, "And deliver us from the Vikings, Amen." Gazing up at the prow of one of these sleek, time-stained vessels, you can almost hear the screams and smell the armpits of those redheads on the rampage.

Cost and Hours: 80 kr, daily May-Sept 9:00-18:00, Oct-April 10:00-16:00, Huk Aveny 35, tel. 22 13 52 80, www.khm.uio.no.

Visiting the Museum: Focus on the two well-preserved ships, starting with the *Oseberg,* from A.D. 834. With its ornate carving and impressive rudder, it was likely a royal pleasure craft. It seems designed for sailing on calm inland waters during festivals, but not in the open ocean.

The *Gokstad,* from A.D. 950, is a practical working boat, capable of sailing the high seas. A ship like this brought settlers to the west of France (Normandy was named for the Norsemen). And in such a vessel, explorers such as Eric the Red hopscotched from Norway to Iceland to Greenland and on to what they called Vinland—today's Newfoundland in Canada. Imagine 30 men hauling on long oars out at sea for weeks and months at a time. In 1892, a replica of this ship sailed from Norway to America in 44 days to celebrate the 400th anniversary of Columbus *not* discovering America.

The ships tend to steal the show, but don't miss the hall displaying **jewelry and personal items** excavated along with the ships. The ships and related artifacts survived so well because they were buried in clay as part of a gravesite. Many of the finest items were not actually Viking art, but goodies they brought home after raiding more advanced (but less tough) people. Still, there are lots of actual Viking items, such as metal and leather goods, that give insight into their culture. Highlights are the cart and sleighs, ornately carved with scenes from Viking sagas.

The museum doesn't offer tours, but it's easy to eavesdrop on the many guides leading big groups through the museum. Everything is well-described in English. You probably don't need the little museum guidebook—it repeats exactly what's already posted on the exhibits.

▲▲Fram Museum (Frammuseet)

This museum holds the 125-foot, steam- and sail-powered ship that took modern-day Vikings Roald Amundsen and Fridtjof Nansen deep into the Arctic and Antarctic, farther north and south than any vessel had gone before. For three years, the *Fram*—specially designed to survive the crushing pressures of a frozen-over sea—drifted, trapped in the Arctic ice. The museum was recently enlarged to include Amundsen's *Gjøa*, the first ship to sail through the Northwest Passage.

Cost and Hours: 100 kr; June-Aug daily 9:00-18:00; May and Sept daily 10:00-17:00; Oct and March-April daily 10:00-16:00; Nov-Feb Mon-Fri 10:00-15:00, Sat-Sun 10:00-16:00; Bygdøynesveien 36, tel. 23 28 29 50, www.frammuseum.no.

Visiting the Museum: Read the ground-floor displays, check out the videos below the bow of the ship, then climb the steps to the third-floor gangway to explore the *Fram*'s claustrophobic but fascinating interior. Also featured are a tent like the one Amundsen used, reconstructed shelves from his Arctic kitchen, models of the *Fram* and the motorized sled they used to traverse the ice and snow, and a "polar simulator" plunging visitors to a 15° Fahrenheit environment. A "Northern Lights Show," best viewed from the *Fram*'s main deck, is presented every 20 minutes.

Next, take the underground passageway to the adjacent A-frame building that displays the *Gjøa*, the motor- and sail-powered ship that Amundsen and a crew of six used from 1903 to 1906 to successfully navigate the Northwest Passage. Exhibits describe their ordeal as well as other Arctic adventures, such as Amundsen's 1926 airship (zeppelin) expedition from Oslo over the North Pole to Alaska. And pop into the 100-seat cinema for a film about the polar regions (every 15 minutes).

▲▲Kon-Tiki Museum (Kon-Tiki Museet)

Next to the *Fram* is a museum housing the *Kon-Tiki* and the *Ra II*, the ships built by Thor Heyerdahl (1914-2002). In 1947, Heyerdahl and five crewmates constructed the *Kon-Tiki* raft out of balsa wood, using only pre-modern tools and techniques. They set sail from Peru on the tiny craft, surviving for 101 days on fish, coconuts, and sweet potatoes (which were native to Peru). About 4,300 miles later, they arrived in Polynesia. The point was to show that early South Americans could have settled Polynesia. (While Heyerdahl proved they could have, anthropologists doubt they did.) The *Kon-Tiki* story became a bestselling book and award-winning documentary (and helped spawn the "Tiki" culture craze in the US). In 1970, Heyerdahl's *Ra II* made a similar 3,000-mile journey from Morocco to Barbados to prove that Africans could have populated America. Both ships are well-displayed and described in English. Short clips from *Kon-Tiki*, the Oscar-winning 1950 documentary film, play in a small theater at the end of the exhibit.

Cost and Hours: 90 kr, daily June-Aug 9:30-18:00, March-May and Sept-Oct 10:00-17:00, Nov-Feb 10:00-16:00, Bygdøynesveien 36, tel. 23 08 67 67, www.kon-tiki.no.

▲Norwegian Maritime Museum (Norsk Sjøfartsmuseum)

If you like the sea, this museum is a salt lick, providing a wide-ranging look at Norway's maritime heritage. The collection was recently updated, with new exhibits such as "The Ship" ("Skipet"), tracing 2,000 years of maritime development, and "At Sea" ("Til Sjøs"), exploring what life is like on the ocean, from Viking days to the present. Don't miss the movie *The Ocean: A Way of Life,* included with your admission. It's a breathtaking widescreen film swooping you scenically over Norway's dramatic sea and fishing townscapes from here all the way to North Cape in a comfy theater (20 minutes, shown at the top and bottom of the hour, follow *Supervideografen* signs). And if you appreciate maritime art, the collection in the gallery should float your boat.

Cost and Hours: 80 kr, kids under 6 free; mid-May-Aug daily 10:00-17:00; Sept-mid-May Tue-Fri 10:00-15:00, Sat-Sun 10:00-16:00, closed Mon; Bygdøynesveien 37, tel. 24 11 41 50, www.marmuseum.no.

▲Norwegian Holocaust Center (HL-Senteret)

Located in the stately former home of Nazi collaborator Vidkun Quisling, this museum and study center offers a high-tech look at the racist ideologics that fueled the Holocaust. To show the Holocaust in a Norwegian context, the first floor displays historical documents about the rise of anti-Semitism and personal effects from Holocaust victims. Downstairs, the names of 760 Norwegian Jews killed by the Nazis are listed in a bright, white room. The *Innocent Questions* glass-and-neon sculpture outside shows an old-fashioned punch card, reminding viewers of how the Norwegian puppet government collected seemingly innocuous information before deporting its Jews. The *Contemporary Reflections* video is a reminder that racism and genocide continue today.

Cost and Hours: 50 kr, ask for free English audioguide or tablet, June-Aug daily 10:00-18:00, Sept-May Mon-Fri 10:00-16:00, Sat-Sun 11:00-16:00, Huk Aveny 56—take bus #30 to the Byg-

døyhus stop, follow signs to *HL-Senteret*, tel. 22 84 21 00, www.
hlsenteret.no.

GRÜNERLØKKA AND GRØNLAND DISTRICTS

The Grünerløkka district is trendy, and workaday Grønland is
emerging as a fun spot. The Akers Rivers bisects Grünerløkka. You
can connect the dots by taking the self-guided "Up Akers River
and Down Grünerløkka Walk." For a longer hike, start with my
"Nydalen to Grünerløkka Walk," which intersects the Akers/
Grünerløkka Walk. Everything is described in this section.

Akers River

This river, though only about five miles long, powered Oslo's early
industry: flour mills in the 1300s, sawmills in the 1500s, and Norway's Industrial Revolution in the 1800s. A walk along the river
not only spans Oslo's history, but also shows the contrast the city
offers. The bottom of the river (where this walk doesn't go)—bordered by the high-rise Oslo Radisson Blu Plaza Hotel and the "Little Pakistan" neighborhood of Grønland—has its share of drunks
and drugs, reflecting a new urban reality in Oslo. Farther up, the
river valley becomes a park as it winds past decent-size waterfalls
and red-brick factories. The source of the river (and Oslo's drinking water) is the pristine Lake Maridal, situated at the edge of the
Nordmarka wilderness. The idyllic recreation scenes along Lake
Maridal are a favorite for nature-loving Norwegians.

▲Grünerløkka

The Grünerløkka district is the largest planned urban area in Oslo.
It was built in the latter half of the 1800s to house the legions
of workers employed at the factories powered by the Akers River.
The first buildings were modeled on similar places built in Berlin.
(German visitors observe that there's now more turn-of-the-20th-
century Berlin here than in present-day Berlin.) While slummy in
the 1980s, today it's trendy. Locals sometimes refer to it as "Oslo's
Greenwich Village." Although that's a stretch, it is a bustling area
with lots of cafés, good spots for a fun meal, and few tourists.

Getting There: Grünerløkka can be reached from the center
of town by a short ride on tram #11, #12, or #13, or by taking the
short but interesting walk described next.

▲Up Akers River and Down Grünerløkka Walk

While every tourist explores the harborfront and main drag of
Oslo, few venture into this neighborhood that evokes the Industrial Revolution. Once housing poor workers, it now attracts hip
professionals. A hike up the Akers River, finishing in the stylish
Grünerløkka district, shines a truly different light on Oslo. Allow
about an hour at a brisk pace, including a fair bit of up and down.

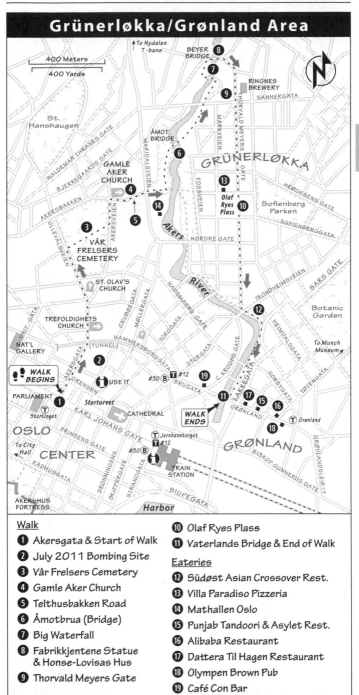

Grünerløkka/Grønland Area

OSLO

400 Meters
400 Yards

To Nydalen T-bane

BEYER BRIDGE

RINGNES BREWERY

SANNERGATA

St. Hanshaugen

ÅMOT BRIDGE

GRÜNERLØKKA

WALDEMAR THRANES GATE

BJERREGAARDS GATE

GAMLE AKER CHURCH

MARIDALSVEIEN

MARKVEIEN

THORVALD MEYERS GATE

HØGESENS GATE

FOSSVEIEN

Olaf Ryes Plass

Sofienberg Parken

SOFIENBERGGATA

AKERSBAKKEN

AKERSVEIEN

NORDRE GATE

ULLEVÅLSVEIEN

VÅR FRELSERS CEMETERY

Akers River

ST. OLAV'S CHURCH

HAUSMANNS GATE

TRONDHEIMSVEIEN

SARS GATE

Botanic Garden

TREFOLDIGHETS CHURCH

GRUBBEGATA

MØLLERGATA

TORGGATA

To Munch Museum

UNIV. GATE

NAT'L GALLERY

HAMMERSBORGGATA

(TUNNEL)

STORGATA

HEIMDALSGATA

C. KROGHS GATE

WALK BEGINS

AKERSGATA

GRENSEN

USE IT

#50 BRUGATA

NORBYGATA

TØYENGATA

PARLIAMENT

Stortinget

Stortorvet

CATHEDRAL

WALK ENDS

GRØNLAND

Grønland

OSLO CENTER

KARL JOHANS GATE

PRINSENS GATE

Jernbanetorget

GRØNLAND

BISKOP GUNNERUS GATE

GRØNLANDSLEIRET

To City Hall

RÅDHUSGATA

DRONNINGENS GATE

SKIPPERGATE

STRANDGATA

#30

TRAIN STATION

BJØRVEGATA

AKERSHUS FORTRESS

Harbor

Walk

1 Akersgata & Start of Walk
2 July 2011 Bombing Site
3 Vår Frelsers Cemetery
4 Gamle Aker Church
5 Telthusbakken Road
6 Åmotbrua (Bridge)
7 Big Waterfall
8 Fabrikkjentene Statue & Honse-Lovisas Hus
9 Thorvald Meyers Gate
10 Olaf Ryes Plass
11 Vaterlands Bridge & End of Walk

Eateries

12 Südøst Asian Crossover Rest.
13 Villa Paradiso Pizzeria
14 Mathallen Oslo
15 Punjab Tandoori & Asylet Rest.
16 Alibaba Restaurant
17 Dattera Til Hagen Restaurant
18 Olympen Brown Pub
19 Café Con Bar

In Cold Blood

Norway likes to think of itself as a quiet, peaceful nation on the edge of Europe—after all, its legislators award the Nobel Peace Prize. So the events of July 22, 2011—when an anti-immigration fanatic named Anders Behring Breivik set off a car bomb in Oslo, killing eight, and then traveled to a Labor Party summer camp where he shot and killed 69 young people and counselors—have had a profound effect on the country's psyche.

Unlike the US, Britain, or Spain, Norway had escaped 21st-century terrorism until Breivik's attack. When the public found out that the man behind the bombing and gunfire was a native Norwegian—dressed in a policeman's uniform—who hunted down his victims in cold blood, it became a national nightmare.

Though Norwegians are often characterized as stoic, there was a huge outpouring of grief. Bouquets flooded the square in front of Oslo Cathedral. Permanent memorials will eventually be built at the sites of the tragedies.

Breivik, who was arrested after the shootings, was described by police as a gun-loving fundamentalist obsessed with what he saw as the "threat" of multiculturalism and immigration to Norwegian

Navigate with the TI's free city map and the map in this chapter. This walk is best during daylight hours.

Begin the walk by leaving Karl Johans Gate at the top of the hill, and head up **Akersgata**—Oslo's "Fleet Street" (lined with major newspaper companies). After two blocks, at Apotekergata, you may see the side street blocked off and construction work to the right. They're rebuilding after the horrific bombing of July 2011 (see sidebar); the car bomb went off just a block to the right of here, on Grubbegata. Four buildings in the area suffered structural damage in the bombing. Continuing up Akersgata, the street name becomes Ullevålsveien as it passes those buildings. Norwegians are planning to build a memorial here in the near future.

Continuing past this somber site, you'll approach the massive brick Trefoldighets Church and St. Olav's Church before reaching the **Vår Frelsers (Our Savior's) Cemetery.** Enter the cemetery across from the Baby Shop store (where Ullevålsveien meets Wessels Gate).

Stop at the big metal map just inside the gate to chart your course through the cemetery: Go through the light-green Æreslunden section—with the biggest plots and highest elevation—and out the opposite end (#13 on the metal map) onto Akersveien. En

values. His targets were the Norwegian government and politically active youths—some only 14 years old—and their counselors at
an island summer camp sponsored by Norway's center-left party.

It's true that Norway has a big and growing immigrant community. More than 11 percent of today's Norwegians are not ethnic Norwegians, and a quarter of Oslo's residents are immigrants.
These "new Norwegians" have provided a much-needed and
generally appreciated labor force, filling jobs that wealthy Norwegians would rather not do.

Horrified by Breivik's actions, many Norwegians went out
of their way to make immigrants feel welcome after the attack.
But there is some resentment in a country that is disinclined to
be a melting pot. There have been scuffles between Norwegian
gangs and immigrant groups. Another source of friction is the
tough love Norwegians feel they get from their government compared to the easy ride offered to needy immigrants: "They even
get pocket money in jail!" The country recently strengthened its
immigration laws in 2014.

Norway seems determined not to let the July 22 massacre
poison its peaceful soul. Calls for police to start carrying weapons
or to reinstate the death penalty were quickly rejected. "Breivik
wanted to change Norway," an Oslo resident told me. "We're determined to keep Norway the way it was."

OSLO

route, check out some of the tomb-
stones of the illuminati and literati
buried in the honorary Æreslunden
section. They include Munch, Ibsen,
Bjørnson, and many of the painters
whose works you can see in the National Gallery (all marked on a map
posted at the entrance). Exiting on
the far side of the cemetery, walk left
100 yards up Akersveien to the church.

The Romanesque **Gamle Aker Church** (from the 1100s), the
oldest building in Oslo, is worth a look inside (free, generally Mon-
Thu 14:00-16:00, Fri 12:00-14:00). The church, which fell into
ruins and has been impressively rebuilt, is pretty bare except for a
pulpit and baptismal font from the 1700s.

From the church, backtrack 20 yards, head left at the playground, and go downhill on the steep **Telthusbakken Road** toward the huge, gray former grain silos (now student housing). The
cute lane is lined with colorful old wooden houses: The people who
constructed these homes were too poor to meet the no-wood fire-
safety building codes within the city limits, so they built in what

used to be suburbs. At the bottom of Telthusbakken, cross the busy Maridalsveien and walk directly through the park to the Akers River. The lively Grünerløkka district is straight across the river from here, but if you have 20 minutes and a little energy, detour upstream first and hook back down. Don't cross the river yet.

Walk along the riverside bike lane upstream through the river gorge park. Just above the first waterfall, cross **Åmotbrua,** the big white springy suspension footbridge from 1852 (moved here in 1958). Keep hiking uphill along the river. At the base of the next big waterfall, cross over again to the large brick buildings, hiking up the stairs to the **Beyer Bridge** (above the falls) and *Fabrikkjentene,* a statue of four women laborers. They're pondering the textile factory where they and 700 others toiled long and hard.

This gorge was once lined with the water mills that powered Oslo through its 19th-century Industrial Age boom.

Look back (on the side you just left) at the city's two biggest former textile factories. Once you could tell what color the fabric was being dyed each day by the color of the river. Just beyond them, between the two old factories, is a small white building housing the **Labor Museum** (Arbeidermuseet, free; late June-mid-Aug Tue-Sun 11:00-16:00, closed Mon; off-season Sat-Sun 11:00-16:00, closed Mon-Fri; borrow English handout). Inside you'll see old photos that humanize the life of laborers there, and an 1899 photo exhibit by Edvard Munch's sister, Inger Munch.

The tiny red house just over and below the bridge—the **Honse-Lovisas Hus** cultural center—makes a good rest-stop (Tue-Sun 11:00-18:00, closed Mon, coffee and wafels). Cross over to the red-brick Ringnes Brewery and follow **Thorvald Meyers Gate** downhill directly into the heart of Grünerløkka. The main square, called **Olaf Ryes Plass,** is a happening place to grab a meal or drink (see "Eating," later). Trams take you from here back to the center.

• *To continue exploring, you could keep going straight and continue walking until you reach a T-intersection with a busy road (Trondheims-veien). From there (passing the recommended Südøst Asian Crossover Restaurant) you can catch a tram back to the center, or drop down to the riverside path and follow it downstream to Vaterlands bridge in the* **Grønland** *district. From here the train station is a five-minute walk down Stenersgata.*

▲Nydalen to Grünerløkka Walk

For a longer hike than the "Up Akers River and Down Grüner-løkka Walk" described previously, consider this 30-minute walk, downhill and through peaceful riverside parks all the way. This walk intersects the Akers River/Grünerløkka Walk at its halfway (and highest altitude) point, Beyer Bridge, where you can choose to finish the downhill ramble following its route—either doing the first half in reverse order (visiting the Gamle Aker Church and the Vår Frelsers Cemetery on your way into the city center), or picking up the last half of the walk (through the heart of Grünerløkka and on to Grønland). Walking at a brisk pace, it'll take you 30 minutes to get from the Nydalen T-bane stop to the top of the Akers River/Grünerløkka Walk. Allow an hour from the top all the way back into town. If you follow these easy directions, I promise you won't get lost.

Ride the T-bane to **Nydalen,** where you'll be high above the city, surrounded by modern apartments and university buildings. From the T-bane stop, walk to the Akers River and head down-hill...like the water that powered the Industrial Revolution in Oslo. From here it's all downhill and along the river. Stay on the right side of the river until the second street with cars, where you'll cross the bridge to the left side of the river.

From the top, after about 15 minutes, you'll hit the first street with cars. Don't cross it: Stay right and follow the lane under an overpass and you'll once again hear the babbling sounds of the brook. Continue along the Akers River. Across the river you'll see the fine brickwork of **Lilleborg,** a huge former soap factory. Started in 1712, it was the last factory in use here (until 1997) and, ironically, infamous as a source of pollution.

Notice the lights along the path, a reminder that in the winter it gets dark early, before 16:00.

At the next big road with cars (Griffenfeldts Gate), cross the river. Pause on the bridge and consider that from 1624, wooden pipes laid from here (just upstream from the river-based industry) ran all the way to the center, providing drinking water to Oslo. This remained Oslo's water source until 1879, when encroaching industry forced its relocation upstream to higher ground.

Soon you'll arrive at **Beyer Bridge,** with the statue of four female factory workers on it. Across the bridge, between what used to be the city's two biggest textile factories, stands the little Labor Museum.

At Beyer Bridge, you hit the Akers River/Grünerløkka Walk" (described previously) and need to decide which leg of the walk you'd like to take (or you could head left a block or so and hop on any tram heading downhill). And, as mentioned earlier, you could walk through the core of Grünerløkka to the suburb of...

Grønland

With the Industrial Revolution, Oslo's population exploded. The city grew from an estimated 10,000 in 1850 to 250,000 in 1900. The T-bane's Grønland stop deposits you in the center of what was the first suburb to accommodate workers of Industrial Age Oslo. If you look down side streets, you'll see fine 19th-century facades from this period. While the suburb is down-and-dirty like working-class and immigrant neighborhoods in other cities, Grønland is starting to emerge as a trendy place for eating out and after-dark fun. Locals know you'll get double the food and lots more beer for the kroner here (see "Eating in Oslo," later). If you'd enjoy a whiff of Istanbul, make a point to wander through the underground commercial zone at the Grønland station (easy to visit even if you're not riding the T-bane).

OUTER OSLO
▲▲Holmenkollen Ski Jump and Ski Museum

The site of one of the world's oldest ski jumps (from 1892), Holmenkollen has hosted many championships, including the 1952 Winter Olympics. To win the privi-
lege of hosting the 2011 World Ski Jump Championship, Oslo built a bigger jump to match modern ones built elsewhere. This futuristic, can-tilevered, Olympic-standard **ski jump** has a tilted elevator that you can ride to the top (on a sunny day, you may have to wait your turn for

the elevator). Stand right at the starting gate, just like an athlete, and get a feel for this daredevil sport. The jump empties into a 30,000-seat amphitheater, and if you go when it's clear, you'll see one of the best possible views of Oslo. While the view is exciting from the top, even more exciting is watching thrill-seekers rocket down the course on a zip-line from the same lofty perch (600 kr per trip).

As you ponder the jump, consider how modern athletes continually push the boundaries of their sport. The first champion here in 1892 jumped 21 meters (nearly 69 feet). In 1930 it took a 50-meter jump to win. In 1962 it was 80 meters, and in 1980 the champ cracked 100 meters. And, most recently, a jump of 140 meters (459 feet) took first place.

The **ski museum,** a must for skiers, traces the evolution of the sport, from 4,000-year-old rock paintings to crude 1,500-year-old wooden sticks to the slick and quickly evolving skis of modern times, including a fun exhibit showing the royal family on skis. You'll see gear from Roald Amundsen's famous trek to the South

Pole, including the stuffed remains of Obersten (the Colonel), one of his sled dogs.

Cost and Hours: 120-kr ticket includes museum and viewing platform at top of jump; daily June-Aug 9:00-20:00, May and Sept 10:00-17:00, Oct-April 10:00-16:00; tel. 22 92 32 64, www. holmenkollen.com or www.skiforeningen.no.

Simulator: To cap your Holmenkollen experience, step into the simulator and fly down the ski jump and ski in a virtual downhill race. My legs were exhausted after the five-minute terror. This simulator (or should I say stimulator?) costs 60 kr. It's located at the lower level of the complex, near the entry of the ski museum. Outside, have fun watching a candid video of those shrieking inside.

Getting There: T-bane line #1 gets you out of the city, through the hills, forests, and mansions that surround Oslo, and to the jump (direction: Frognerseteren). From the Holmenkollen station, you'll hike steeply up the road 15 minutes to the ski jump. (Getting back is just 5 minutes. Note T-bane departure times before you leave.)

Nearby: For an easy downhill jaunt through the Norwegian forest, with a woodsy coffee or meal break in the middle, stay on the T-bane past Holmenkollen to the end of the line (Frognerseteren) and walk 10 minutes downhill to the recommended **Frognerseteren Hovedrestaurant,** a fine traditional eatery with a sod roof, reindeer meat on the griddle, and a city view. Continue on the same road another 20 minutes downhill to the ski jump, and then to the Holmenkollen T-bane stop. The **Holmenkollen Restaurant** is just a few steps above the T-bane stop and offers a similar view and better food and prices, but without the pewter-and-antlers folk theme.

▲Ekeberg Sculpture Park and Ruins of Medieval Oslo

The buzz in Oslo is its modern sculpture park (opened in 2013), with striking art sprinkled through a forest with grand city views. There's lots of climbing. The park has a long story, from evidence of the Stone Age people who chose to live here 7,000 years ago to the memory of its days as a Nazi military cemetery in World War II.

Getting There: The park, always open and free, is a 10-minute tram ride southeast of the center (catch tram #18 or #19 from station, platform E). From the Ekebergparken tram stop, climb uphill to the visitors center with its small museum (30 kr), where you can join a guided walk in English (150 kr, 90 minutes, Mon-Sat at 13:00, Sun at 14:00), or just pick up a map and start your hike.

Background: Ekeberg Park is the big project and gift to the city from real estate tycoon Christian Ringnes (grandson of Norwegian brewery tycoons, who—like Coors in Denver and Carlsberg in Copenhagen—have lots of money for grand city projects). Norwegians tend to be skeptical of any fat cat giving something to the city. What's the real motive? They note that the park's popularity will bring lots more business to the fancy Ringnes-owned restaurant within the park. But critics are getting over that, and today the people of Oslo are embracing this lovely 63-acre mix of forest and contemporary art. Art collector Ringnes loves women and wanted to the park to be a celebration of femininity. While that vision was considered a bit ill-advised and scaled back, the park is plenty feminine and organic.

Nearby: The faint **medieval remains of Oslo** (free, always open) are immediately below Ekeberg Park. While a bit obscure for most, history buffs can spend a few minutes wandering a park with the ruins of the 11th-century town—back when it was 3,000 people huddled around a big stone cathedral, seat of the Norwegian bishop. The arcade of a 13th-century Dominican monastery still stands (office of today's Lutheran bishop). To get there, hop off at the St. Halvards Plass stop on your way to the Ekebergparken tram stop (note when the next tram is due). The ruins are across the street from the bus stop.

▲Edvard Munch Museum (Munch Museet)

The only Norwegian painter to have had a serious impact on European art, Munch (pronounced "moonk") is a surprise to many who visit this fine museum, located one mile east of Oslo's center. The emotional, disturbing, and powerfully Expressionistic work of this strange and perplexing man is arranged chronologically. You'll see an extensive collection of paintings, drawings, lithographs, and photographs. (Note that Oslo's centrally located National Gallery, which also displays many of Munch's most popular works, is a better alternative for those who just want to see a dozen great Munch paintings, including "The Scream," without leaving the city center.)

The Munch Museum was in the news in August of 2004, when two Munch paintings, *Madonna* and a version of his famous *Scream,* were brazenly stolen right off the walls in broad daylight. Two men in black hoods simply entered through the museum café, waved guns at the stunned guards and tourists, ripped the paintings off the wall, and sped off in a black Audi station wagon. Happily, in 2006, the thieves were caught and the stolen paintings recovered. Today they are on display again, behind glass and with heightened security.

Cost and Hours: 95 kr; mid-June-Sept daily 10:00-17:00; Oct-mid-June Wed-Mon 11:00-17:00, closed Tue; 25-kr audioguide, guided tours in English daily July-Aug at 13:00, T-bane or bus #60 to Tøyen, Tøyengata 53, tel. 23 49 35 00, www.munch.museum.no.

ESCAPES FROM THE CITY

Oslo is surrounded by a vast forest dotted with idyllic little lakes, huts, joggers, bikers, and sun-worshippers. Mountain-biking possibilities are endless (as you'll discover if you go exploring without a good map). Consider taking your bike on the T-bane (free outside of rush hour, otherwise half the normal adult fare) to the end of line #1 (Frognerseteren, 30 minutes from National Theater) to gain the most altitude possible. Then follow the gravelly roads (mostly downhill but with some climbing) past several dreamy lakes to Sognsvann at the end of T-bane line #6. Farther east, from Maridalsvannet, a bike path follows the Akers River all the way back into town. (The TI has details.) While Oslo isn't much on bike rentals, you can rent quality bikes at Viking Biking.

For plenty of trees and none of the exercise, ride T-bane line #6 to its last stop, Sognsvann (with a beach towel rather than a bike), and join the lakeside scene. A pleasant trail leads around the lake.

Oslofjord Island Beaches

On a hot day it seems the busy ferry scene at Oslo's harborfront is primarily designed to get locals out of their offices and onto the cool, green islands across the harbor so they can take a dip in the fjord, enjoy a little beach time, or simply stroll and enjoy views of the city. The larger Hovedøya offers good beaches, the ruins of a Cistercian monastery from 1147, some old cannons from the early 1800s, a marina, and a café. Little Gressholmen has good swimming, easy wandering to a pair of connected islands, and Gressholmen Kro, a rustic café dating to the 1930s.

Getting to the Islands: Take bus #60 to Vippetangen and catch ferry #92 or #93 to Hovedøya or ferry #93 to Gressholmen (both covered by city transit passes). Ferry #92 takes you directly to Hovedøya in five minutes, while ferry #93 takes a slightly longer, scenic route past several islands (including Gressholmen) on its way to Hovedøya. For schedules and fare info, check www.ruter.no.

Beach at Bygdøy: Remember there's also a beach at Huk on the Bygdøy peninsula; take the direct boat from pier 3 in front of City Hall or bus #30.

Tusenfryd

This giant amusement complex just out of town offers a world of family fun. It's sort of a combination Norwegian Disneyland/Viking Knott's Berry Farm, with more than 50 rides, plenty of entertainment, and restaurants.

Cost and Hours: Admission is based on your height: under 95 centimeters (3 feet)—free, under 1.2 meters (4 feet)—315 kr, over 1.2 meters (4 feet)—389 kr. Daily July-mid-Aug 10:30-19:00, shorter hours April-June and mid-Aug–Sept, closed in winter, tel. 64 97 66 99, www.tusenfryd.no.

Getting There: Bus #541 takes fun-seekers to the park from behind Oslo's train station (50 kr, 2/hour, 20-minute ride).

Wet Fun

Oslo offers a variety of water play. Located near Vigeland Park, the **Frognerbadet** has three outdoor pools, a waterslide, high dives, a cafeteria, and lots of young families (100 kr, students-70 kr, mid-May-late Aug Mon-Fri 7:00-19:30, Sat-Sun 10:00-18:00, last entry 30 minutes before closing, closed late Aug-mid-May, Middelthunsgate 28, tel. 23 27 54 50).

Tøyenbadet, a modern indoor/outdoor pool complex with a 330-foot-long waterslide, also has a gym and sauna (100 kr, children-50 kr, Mon-Fri 7:00-19:00, Sat-Sun 9:00-19:00, sometimes closed mornings for school events, 10-minute walk from Edvard Munch Museum, Helgengate 90, tel. 23 30 44 70). Oslo's free botanical gardens are nearby.

NEAR OSLO

▲Eidsvoll Manor

During the Napoleonic period, control of Norway changed from Denmark to Sweden. This ruffled the patriotic feathers of Norway's Thomas Jeffersons and Ben Franklins, and on May 17, 1814, Norway's constitution was written and signed in this stately mansion (in the town of Eidsvoll Verk, north of Oslo). While Sweden still ruled, Norway had more autonomy than ever.

To get ready for the bicentennial of Norway's constitution, the manor itself was restored to how it looked in 1814. A visitors center in the nearby Wergeland House tells the history of Norway's march to independence with 21st-century high-tech touches.

Cost and Hours: 100 kr, includes Eidsvoll Manor, Wergeland House, and guided tour; May-Aug daily 10:00-17:00; Sept Mon-Fri 10:00-16:00, Sat-Sun 11:00-16:00; Oct-April Tue-Fri 10:00-16:00, Sat-Sun 11:00-16:00, closed Mon; tel. 63 92 22 10, www.eidsvoll1814.no.

Getting There: Eidsvoll is 45 minutes from Oslo by car (take road E-6 toward Trondheim, turn right at *Eidsvolls Bygningen* sign, free parking) or bus (direct bus #854 runs hourly from Oslo Airport). You can also take the train to Eidsvoll (hourly, 45 minutes plus 15-minute walk). If you're driving from Oslo to Lillehammer and the Gudbrandsdal Valley, it's right on the way and worth a stop.

Drøbak

This delightful fjord town is just an hour from Oslo by bus (70 kr one-way if bought in advance, 90 kr on board, 2/hour, bus #541 or

#542 from behind the train station) or ferry (70 kr one-way, sporadic departures usually Wed and Fri-Sun, check at pier 1 or ask at Oslo TI). Consider taking the 1.25-hour boat trip down, exploring the town, having dinner, and taking the bus back.

For holiday cheer year-round, stop into **Tregaarden's Julehuset** Christmas shop, right off Drøbak's main square (generally Mon-Fri 10:00-17:00, Sat 10:00-15:00, Sun 12:00-16:00, longer hours in Dec, closed Jan-Feb, tel. 64 93 41 78, www.julehus.no). Then wander out past the church and cemetery on the north side of town to a pleasant park. Looking out into the fjord, you can see the old **Oscarsborg Fortress,** where Norwegian troops fired cannons and torpedoes to sink Hitler's warship, *Blücher.* The attack bought enough time for Norway's king and parliament to escape capture and eventually set up a government-in-exile in London during the Nazi occupation of Norway (1940-1945). Nearby, a monument is dedicated to the commander of the fortress, and one of *Blücher's* anchors rests aground (the other is at Aker Brygge in Oslo). A 100-kr round-trip summer ferry shuttles visitors from the town harbor.

If you want to spend the night, the **TI** can recommend accommodations (June-Aug Mon-Fri 8:30-16:00, Sat-Sun 10:00-14:00; Sept-May Mon-Fri 8:30-16:00, closed Sat-Sun; tel. 64 93 50 87, www.visitdrobak.no). **Restaurant Skipperstuen** is a good option for dinner, with outdoor seating that overlooks the fjord and all the Oslo-bound boat traffic (entrées from 300 kr, Mon-Sat 12:00-22:00, Sun 12:00-20:00, tel. 64 93 07 03).

Shopping in Oslo

Shops in Oslo are generally open 10:00-18:00 or 19:00. Many close early on Saturday and all day Sunday. Shopping centers are open Monday through Friday 10:00-21:00, Saturday 9:00-18:00, and are closed Sunday. Remember, when you make a purchase of 315 kr or more, you can get the 25 percent tax refunded when you leave the country if you hang on to the paperwork. Here are a few favorite shopping opportunities many travelers enjoy, but not on Sunday, when they're all closed.

Norway Designs, just outside the National Theater, shows off the country's sleek, contemporary designs in clothing, kitchenware, glass, textiles, jewelry—and high prices (Stortingsgata 12, T-bane: Nationaltheatret, tel. 23 11 45 10).

Paleet is a mall in the heart of Oslo, with 30 shops on three levels and a food court in the basement (Karl Johans Gate 37, tel. 23 08 08 11).

Dale of Norway, considered Norway's biggest and best maker of traditional and contemporary sweaters, offers its complete collection at this "concept store" (Karl Johans Gate 45, tel. 97 48 12 07).

Heimen Husflid has a superb selection of authentic Norwegian sweaters, *bunads* (national costumes), traditional jewelry, and other Norwegian crafts (top quality at high prices, Rosenkrantz Gate 8, tel. 23 21 42 00).

GlasMagasinet is one of Oslo's oldest and fanciest department stores (top end, good souvenir shop, near the cathedral at Stortorvet 9, tel. 22 82 23 00).

The Husfliden Shop, in the basement of the GlasMagasinet department store (listed previously), is popular for its Norwegian-made sweaters, yarn, and colorful Norwegian folk crafts (tel. 22 42 10 75).

The Oslo Sweater Shop has competitive prices for Norwegian-made sweaters (in Radisson Blu Scandinavia Hotel at Tullinsgate 5, tel. 22 11 29 22).

Byporten, the big, splashy mall adjoining the central train station, is filled with youthful and hip shops, specialty stores, and eateries (Jernbanetorget 6, tel. 23 36 21 60).

The street named **Bogstadveien** is considered to have the city's trendiest boutiques and chic, high-quality shops (stretches from behind the Royal Palace to Majorstuen near Vigeland Park).

Oslo's Flea Market makes Saturday morning a happy day for those who brake for garage sales (at Vestkanttorvet, March-Nov only, two blocks east of Frogner Park at the corner of Professor Dahl's Gate and Neubergsgate).

Oslo Flaggfabrikk sells quality flags of all shapes and sizes, including the long, pennant-shaped *vimpel,* seen fluttering from flagpoles all over Norway (875 kr for 11.5-foot *vimpel*—dresses up a boat or cabin wonderfully, near City Hall at Hieronymus Heyerdahlsgate 1, entrance on Tordenskioldsgate—on the other side of the block, tel. 22 40 50 60).

Vinmonopolet stores are the only places where you can buy wine and spirits in Norway. The most convenient location is at the central train station. Another location, not far from Stortinget, is at Rosenkrantzgate 11. The bottles used to be kept behind the counter, but now you can actually touch the merchandise. Locals say it went from being a "jewelry store" to a "grocery store." (Light beer is sold in grocery stores, but strong beer is still limited to Vinmonopolet shops.)

Sleeping in Oslo

In Oslo, like in many other big cities, supply and demand dictate hotel room prices. And yet, some hotels may still offer lower rates on weekends and during some parts of the summer. The only way to

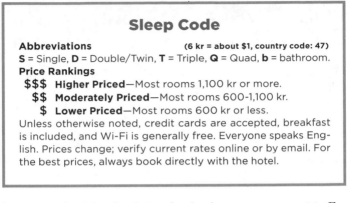

know is to check hotel websites for the dates you want to visit. For convenience and modern comfort, I like the Thon Budget Hotels. For lower prices, consider a cheap hotel or a hostel.

If you arrive without a reservation, the TI can try to sort through all of the confusing hotel specials and get you the best deal going on fancy hotel rooms on the push list. With "dynamic pricing," it's tough to get a hotel to give a firm rate. If booking on your own and on a budget, check hotel websites far in advance to see who's willing to offer the most aggressive discount.

The TI's **Oslo Package** offers business-class rooms plus an Oslo Pass for around 800 kr per person (based on double occupancy); prices vary depending on the hotel you choose. This special offer may be discontinued in the future; check with the TI at www.visitoslo.com before your trip to find out if it is still available. It may be a good deal for couples and for families with young children. Two kids under 16 sleep free, breakfast is included, and up to four family members get free Oslo Passes, covering admission to sights and all public transportation. These passes are valid for four days, even if you only stay one night at the hotel (allowing you to squeeze two days of sightseeing out of a one-night stay—for example, if you take an overnight train or boat out of town on your second evening). Buy the Oslo Package through your travel agent at home or, simpler and quicker, upon arrival in Oslo at the TI. Even if you show up late in the day when prices may be deeply discounted, you still get the Oslo Pass along with your room.

NEAR THE TRAIN STATION AND KARL JOHANS GATE

These accommodations are within a 15-minute walk of the station. While evidence of an earlier, shadier time survives nearest the station, the hotels feel secure and comfortable. Parking in a central garage will run you about 250-300 kr per day.

OSLO

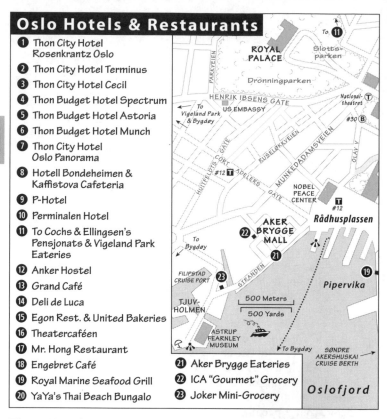

Oslo Hotels & Restaurants

❶ Thon City Hotel Rosenkrantz Oslo

❷ Thon City Hotel Terminus

❸ Thon City Hotel Cecil

❹ Thon Budget Hotel Spectrum

❺ Thon Budget Hotel Astoria

❻ Thon Budget Hotel Munch

❼ Thon City Hotel Oslo Panorama

❽ Hotell Bondeheimen & Kaffistova Cafeteria

❾ P-Hotel

❿ Perminalen Hotel

⓫ To Cochs & Ellingsen's Pensjonats & Vigeland Park Eateries

⓬ Anker Hostel

⓭ Grand Café

⓮ Deli de Luca

⓯ Egon Rest. & United Bakeries

⓰ Theatercaféen

⓱ Mr. Hong Restaurant

⓲ Engebret Café

⓳ Royal Marine Seafood Grill

⓴ YaYa's Thai Beach Bungalo

㉑ Aker Brygge Eateries

㉒ ICA "Gourmet" Grocery

㉓ Joker Mini-Grocery

Thon Hotels

This chain of business-class hotels (found in big cities throughout Norway) knows which comforts are worth paying for and which are not. They offer little character, but provide maximum comfort per krone in big, modern, conveniently located buildings. Each hotel has a cheery staff and lobby, tight but well-designed rooms, free Wi-Fi, and a big buffet breakfast. All are non-smoking.

Thon Hotels come in categories: Their "City Hotels" are a cut above their "Budget Hotels" and are generally more expensive. But depending on demand, you may be able to find a City Hotel that's discounted below the cost of the Budget Hotels. Both Budget and City Hotels are usually cheaper during the summer. Most City Hotels offer free juice and coffee all day. In Budget Hotels, all rooms lack phones and mini-fridges; also, rooms with double beds are a bit bigger than twin-bedded rooms for the same price.

Because Thon Hotels base their prices on demand, their rates vary wildly, so the following prices are roughly the midpoint of a huge range: **Thon City Hotels**—Sb-1,525, Db-1,825 kr; **Thon**

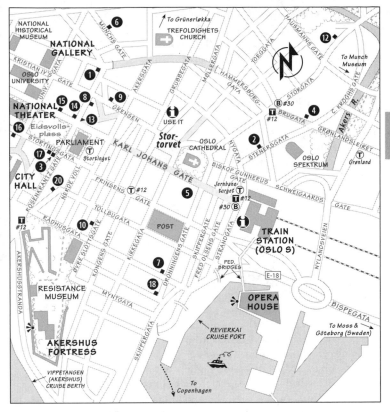

Budget Hotels—Sb-795 kr, Db-1,100 kr. Extra beds are 200 kr for an adult and 100 kr for a child under 13. Book by phone or online (central booking tel. 81 55 24 00, www.thonhotels.no).

For the best prices, check the "price calendar" on the Thon Hotels website. Booking via the Thon website gets you a 12 percent "Thon WebDeal" discount (with some exceptions) if you prepay, with no option to change or cancel your reservation 24 hours after booking. My price ratings for Thon Hotels are based on their average summer rates. Of the 14 Thon Hotels in Oslo, I find the following most convenient:

$$$ Thon City Hotel Rosenkrantz Oslo offers 151 modern, comfortable rooms in a classy and central location two blocks off Karl Johans Gate. Its eighth-floor lounge offers views of the Royal Palace park. If you want to splurge, this is the place to do it (Rosenkrantz Gate 1, tel. 23 31 55 00, www.thonhotels.no/rosenkrantzoslo, rosenkrantzoslo@thonhotels.no).

$$$ Thon City Hotel Terminus is similar but closer to the station (Steners Gate 10, tel. 22 05 60 00, www.thonhotels.no/terminus, terminus@thonhotels.no).

$$$ Thon City Hotel Cecil is near the Parliament building a block below Karl Johans Gate (Stortingsgata 8, tel. 23 31 48 00, www.thonhotels.no/cecil, cecil@thonhotels.no, manager Livanne loves my readers).

$$ Thon Budget Hotel Spectrum is four blocks from the station near the Grønland Torg shopping street. A quarter of its rooms are plagued by disco noise on weekends (leave station out north entrance toward bus terminal, go across footbridge toward tall glass Radisson Blu Plaza Hotel, and pass through Grønland Torg, Brugata 7; tel. 23 36 27 00, www.thonhotels.no/spectrum, spectrum@thonhotels.no).

$$ Thon Budget Hotel Astoria has the least charm of my recommended Thon Hotels, but it's well-located and perfectly serviceable (3 blocks in front of station, 50 yards off Karl Johans Gate, Dronningens Gate 21, tel. 24 14 55 50, www.thonhotels.no/astoria, astoria@thonhotels.no).

$$ Thon Budget Hotel Munch, a few blocks from the National Gallery, is like its sisters. Of all the Thon Budget hotels listed, this one has the most upscale location (Munchs Gate 5, tel. 23 21 96 00, www.thonhotels.no/munch, munch@thonhotels.no).

$$ Thon City Hotel Oslo Panorama is a 15-story attempt at a downtown condominium building (the condos didn't work, so now it's a budget hotel). While higher rooms are more expensive, even those reserving a cheap room often get bumped up. If you request anything higher than the fourth floor, you'll likely enjoy a bigger room, perhaps with a balcony (just off Dronningens Gate at Rådhusgata 7, about 6 blocks from station, tel. 23 31 08 00, www.thonhotels.no/oslopanorama, oslopanorama@thonhotels.no).

More Hotels near the Train Station

$$$ Hotell Bondeheimen ("Farmer's Home") is a historic hotel run by the farmers' youth league, *Bondeungdomslaget*. It once housed the children of rural farmers attending school in Oslo. Now a Best Western, its 127 rooms have all the comforts of a modern hotel (Db-1,195-1,990 kr, prices can vary wildly—check website for best deals, lower prices in July; non-smoking, elevator, Rosenkrantz Gate 8, tel. 23 21 41 00, www.bondeheimen.com, bookingoffice@bondeheimen.com). This almost-100-year-old building is also home to the Kaffistova cafeteria (see "Eating in Oslo") and the Heimen Husflid shop (see "Shopping in Oslo").

$$$ P-Hotel rents 93 comfortable rooms—some with hardwood-slick floors—for the same price every day of the year. You get a boxed breakfast delivered each morning, as well as a guest computer and Wi-Fi. Avoid late-night street noise by requesting a room high up or in the back (Db-895-1,250 kr, bigger rooms add 200 kr per person up to five, some sixth-floor rooms have balconies, pay by credit card—no cash accepted, Grensen 19, T-bane: Stortinget, tel. 23 31 80 00, www.p-hotels.com, oslo@p-hotels.no).

$$ Perminalen Hotel, a place for military personnel on leave, is perfectly central, spartan, inexpensive, and welcoming to civvies. They have the same fair prices all year. Spliced invisibly into a giant office block on a quiet street, it has sleek woody furniture and a no-nonsense reception desk (Sb-620 kr, twin Db-860 kr, some seventh-floor rooms have balconies, entirely non-smoking, elevator, pay guest computer, Wi-Fi in lobby, tram #12 from station to Øvre Slottsgate 2, tel. 23 09 30 81, www.perminalen.com, post.perminalen@iss.no). Single beds in shared quads segregated by sexes (with lockers and breakfast) rent for 380 kr each. Its cheap mess hall is open all day.

THE WEST END

$$ Cochs Pensjonat has 89 characteristic rooms (20 remodeled doubles), many with kitchenettes. It's on the far side of the Royal Palace (S-510 kr, Sb-610-660 kr, D-720 kr, Db-840-900 kr, Q-1,180 kr, Qb-1,340 kr, July usually cheaper, discounts for breakfast at nearby cafés, non-smoking rooms, elevator; T-bane: Nationaltheatret, exit to Parkveien, and 10-minute walk through park; or more-convenient trams #11, #17, or #18 to Welhavens Gate; Parkveien 25; tel. 23 33 24 00, www.cochspensjonat.no, booking@cochs.no, three generations of the Skram family).

$$ Ellingsen's Pensjonat rents 18 clean, bright rooms with fluffy down comforters. It's in a residential neighborhood four blocks behind the Royal Palace (S-500 kr, Sb-600 kr, D-800 kr, Db-990 kr, extra bed-350 kr, breakfast-85 kr, lower prices Sept-Feb, non-smoking, back rooms have less street noise, tram #19 from central station to Rosenborg stop, near Uranienborg church at Holtegata 25, tel. 22 60 03 59, www.ellingsenspensjonat.no, post@ellingsenspensjonat.no).

PRIVATE HOMES

To find a room in a private home, which can save you money but at the cost of being farther from the center, try Airbnb or www.bbnorway.com. The TI does not offer a booking service for private homes, but they do list B&Bs and pensions on their website, www.visitoslo.com.

HOSTELS

$ Anker Hostel, a huge student dorm open to travelers of any age, offers 250 of Oslo's best cheap doubles. Though it comes with the ambience of a bomb shelter, each of its rooms is spacious, simple, and clean. There are kitchens and elevators (bed in 6-bed room-240-260 kr, bed in quad-270-290 kr, Db-620-640 kr, Tb-810-870 kr, higher prices are weekend rates, sheets-50 kr, towel-20 kr, no breakfast, self-serve laundry, parking-230 kr/day; tram #12 or #13, or bus #30 or #31 from central station, bus and tram stop: Hausmannsgate; or 10-minute walk from station; Storgata 55, tel. 22 99 72 00, www.ankerhostel.no, hostel@anker.oslo.no).

$ Haraldsheim Youth Hostel (IYHF), a huge, modern hostel open all year, comes with a grand view, laundry, self-service kitchen, 315 beds—most of them in four-bed rooms...and a long commute (2.5 miles out of town). Beds in the fancy quads with private showers and toilets are 280 kr per person (bed in simple quad with bathroom down the hall-255 kr). They also offer private rooms (S-455 kr, Sb-510 kr, D-610 kr, Db-690 kr, bunk-bed D-540 kr, Db-625 kr; all include breakfast, members get 10 percent off, sheets-50 kr, catch bus #31 or tram #17 or T-bane lines #4 or #6 from Oslo's central train station to Sinsenkrysset, then 5-minute uphill hike to Haraldsheimveien 4, tel. 22 22 29 65, www.haraldsheim.no, oslo. haraldsheim@hihostels.no). Eurailers can train to the hostel with their rail pass (2/hour, to Grefsen and walk 10 minutes).

SLEEPING ON THE TRAIN OR BOAT

Norway's trains and ferries offer ways to travel while sleeping. The eight-hour night train between Bergen and Oslo leaves at about 23:00 in each direction (nightly except Sat). The overnight cruise between these Nordic capitals is a clever way to avoid a night in a hotel and to travel while you sleep, saving a day in your itinerary (see "Oslo Connections," later).

Eating in Oslo

EATING CHEAPLY

How do the Norwegians afford their high-priced restaurants? They don't eat out much. This is one city in which you might just settle for simple or ethnic meals—you'll save a lot and miss little. Many menus list small and large plates. Because portions tend to be large, choosing a small plate or splitting a large one makes some otherwise pricey options reasonable. You'll notice many locals just drink free tap water, even in fine restaurants. For a description of Oslo's classic (and expensive) restaurants, see the TI's *Oslo Guide* booklet.

Splurge for a hotel that includes breakfast, or pay for it if it's

Oslo's One-Time Grills

Norwegians are experts at completely avoiding costly restaurants. "One-time grills," or *engangsgrill*, are the rage for locals on a budget. For about 25 kr, you get a disposable outdoor cooker consisting of an aluminum tray, easy-to-light charcoal, and a flimsy metal grill. All that's required is a sunny evening, a grassy park, and a group of friends. During balmy summer evenings, the air in Oslo's city parks is thick with the smell of disposable (and not terribly eco-friendly) grills. It's fun to see how prices for this kind of "dining" aren't that bad in the supermarket: Norwegian beer-28 kr/half-liter, potato salad-30 kr/tub, cooked shrimp-50 kr/half kilo, "ready for grill" steak-two for 120 kr, *grill polse* hot dogs-75 kr per dozen, *lomper* (Norwegian tortillas for wrapping hot dogs)-20 kr per stack, and the actual grill itself.

Bars are also too expensive for the average Norwegian. Young night owls drink at home before *(forspiel)* and after *(nachspiel)* an evening on the town, with a couple of hours, generally around midnight, when they go out for a single drink in a public setting. A beer in a bar costs about $12 for a half-liter (compared to $6 in Ireland and $2 in the Czech Republic), while they can get a six-pack for about twice that price in a grocery store.

optional. At around 80 kr, a Norwegian breakfast fit for a Viking is a good deal. Picnic for lunch or dinner. Basements of big department stores have huge, first-class supermarkets with lots of alternatives to sandwiches for picnic dinners. The little yogurt tubs with cereal come with collapsible spoons. Wasa crackers and meat, shrimp, or cheese spread in a tube are cheap and pack well. The central station has a Joker supermarket with long hours (Mon-Fri 6:00-23:00, Sat 8:00-23:00, Sun 9:00-23:00). Some supermarkets have takeout food that is discounted just before closing—showing up just before 20:00 or so to buy some roast chicken could be your cheapest meal in Oslo. My favorite meals in Oslo are picnic dinners harborside.

You'll save 12 percent by getting takeaway food from a restaurant rather than eating inside. (The VAT on takeaway food is 12 percent; restaurant food is 24 percent.) Fast-food restaurants ask if you want to take away or not before they ring up your order on the cash register. Even McDonald's has a two-tiered price list.

Oslo is awash with little budget eateries (modern, ethnic, fast food, pizza, department-store cafeterias, and so on). **Deli de Luca,** a cheery convenience store chain, notorious for having a store on every key corner in Oslo, is a step up from the similarly ubiquitous 7-Elevens. Most are open 24/7, selling sandwiches, pastries, sushi, and to-go boxes of warm pasta or Asian noodle dishes. You can fill your belly here for about 80 kr. Some outlets (such as the one at the corner of Karl Johans Gate and Rosenkrantz Gate) have seating on the street or upstairs. Beware: Because this is still a *convenience* store, not everything is well-priced. Convenience stores—while convenient—charge double what supermarkets do.

OSLO

KARL JOHANS GATE STRIP

Strangely, **Karl Johans Gate** itself—the most Norwegian of boulevards—is lined with a strip of good-time American chain eateries and sports bars where you can get ribs, burgers, and pizza, including T.G.I. Fridays and the Hard Rock Cafe. **Egon Restaurant** offers a daily 110-kr all-you-can-eat pizza deal (available Tue-Sat 11:00-18:00, Sun-Mon all day). Each place comes with great sidewalk seating and essentially the same prices.

Grand Café is perhaps the most venerable place in town. At lunchtime, they set up a sandwich buffet (150-kr single-sandwich, 315-kr all-you-like). Lunch plates are 150-200 kr, and dinner plates run about 250-300 kr. Reserve a window, and if you hit a time when there's no tour group, you're suddenly a posh Norwegian (daily 11:00-23:00, Karl Johans Gate 31, tel. 23 21 20 18).

Deli de Luca, just across from the Grand Café, offers good-value food and handy seats on Karl Johans Gate. For a fast meal with the best people-watching view in town, you may find yourself dropping by here repeatedly (for 60 kr you can get a calzone, or a portion of chicken noodles, beef noodles, or chicken vindaloo with rice—ask to have it heated up, open 24/7, Karl Johans Gate 33, tel. 22 33 35 22).

United Bakeries, next to the Paleet mall, is a quiet bit of Norwegian quality among sports bars, appreciated for its salads, light lunches, and fresh pastries (seating inside and out, Mon-Fri 7:00-20:00, Sat 9:00-20:00, Sun 9:00-16:00).

Kaffistova, a block off the main drag, is where my thrifty Norwegian grandparents always took me. And it remains almost unchanged since the 1970s. This alcohol-free cafeteria still serves simple, hearty, and typically Norwegian (read: bland) meals for a good price (140-kr daily specials, Mon-Fri 10:00-21:00, Sat-Sun 11:00-19:00, Rosenkrantz Gate 8, tel. 23 21 42 10).

Theatercaféen, since 1900 the place for Norway's illuminati to see and be seen (note the celebrity portraits adorning the walls), is a swanky splurge steeped in Art Nouveau elegance (175-195-kr starters, 200-375-kr main dishes, 655-kr three-course meal,

Norwegian Cuisine

Traditionally Norwegian cuisine doesn't rank very high in terms of excitement value. But the typical diet of meat, fish, and potatoes is definitely evolving to incorporate more diverse products, and the food here is steadily improving. Fresh produce, colorful markets, and efficient supermarkets abound in Europe's most expensive corner.

In this land of farmers and fishermen, you'll find raw ingredients like potatoes, salmon, or beef in traditional recipes. Norway's national dish is *Fårikål,* a lamb or mutton stew with cabbage, peppercorns, and potatoes. It's served with lingonberry jam and lefse—a soft flatbread made from potatoes, milk, and flour. This dish is so popular that the last Thursday in September is *Fårikål* day in Norway. Norwegian grandmothers prepare this hearty stew by throwing together the basic ingredients with whatever leftovers are lying around the kitchen. There's really no need for a recipe, so every stew turns out differently—and every grandma claims hers is the best.

Because of its long, cold winters, Norway relies heavily on the harvesting and preservation of fish. Smoked salmon, called *røkt laks,* is prepared by salt-curing the fish and cold-smoking it, ensuring the temperature never rises above 85°F. This makes the texture smooth and almost raw. *Bacalao* is another favorite: salted and dried cod that is soaked in water before cooking. You'll often find *bacalao* served with tomatoes and olives.

Some Norwegians serve lutefisk around Christmas time, but you'll rarely see this salty, pungent dish on the menu. Instead, try the more pleasant *fiskekake,* a small white fish cake made with cream, eggs, milk, and flour. You can find these patties year-round. For a break from the abundance of seafood, try local specialties such as reindeer meatballs, or pork-and-ground beef meat cakes called *kjøttkaker.* True to Scandinavian cuisine, *kjøttkaker* are usually slathered in a heavy cream sauce.

Dessert and coffee after a meal are essential. *Bløtkake,* a popular delight on Norway's Constitution Day (May 17), is a layered cake drizzled with strawberry juice, covered in whipped cream, and decorated with fresh strawberries. The cloudberry *(multe),* which grows in the Scandinavian tundra, makes a unique jelly that tastes delicious on vanilla ice cream, or even whipped into a rich cream topping for heart-shaped waffles. Norwegians are proud of their breads and pastries, and you'll never be too far from a bakery that sells an almond-flavored *kringle* or a cone-shaped *krumkake* cookie filled with whipped cream.

Mon-Sat 11:00-23:00, Sun 15:00-22:00, in Hotel Continental at Stortingsgata 24, across from National Theater, tel. 22 82 40 50).

Mr. Hong Restaurant is a busy Asian eatery serving fish, duck, chicken, pork, and beef dishes and an all-day, all-you-can-eat grill buffet (165-240-kr main dishes, 200-kr buffet, Mon-Fri 14:00-23:00, Sat 13:00-23:30, Sun 14:00-22:00, Stortingsgata 8, entrance on Rosenkrantz Gate, right next to recommended Hotel Cecil, tel. 22 42 20 08).

EATING IN THE SHADOW OF THE FORTRESS

Engebret Café is a fine old restaurant in a 17th-century building in the Christiania section of town below the fortress. Since 1857 it's been serving old-fashioned Norse food (reindeer is always on the menu) in a classic old Norwegian setting, with outdoor dining in spring and summer (250-350-kr main dishes, Mon-Fri 11:30-23:00, Sat in summer 13:00-23:00, closed Sun and July, Bankplassen 1, tel. 22 82 25 25).

Royal Marine Seafood Grill is a good bet for affordable dining on the harborfront on a balmy evening. All seats are outside, where you'll enjoy nice views and sunsets on the Oslofjord. In contrast to the Aker Brygge scene, this is a casual place under the castle with nothing trendy about it (150-180-kr salads, burgers, fish-and-chips, 200-kr seafood dishes, daily May-Aug 14:00-22:00, closed Sept-April, Akershusstranda 5, tel. 22 08 03 00).

YaYa's Thai Beach Bungalow is a welcome change from Norwegian bland. The tiki-bar decor is infectious, the menu is fun and accessible, and the food is surprisingly authentic—I slurped up every morsel of my green curry pork. Don't be surprised if your dinner is accompanied by the sounds and lights of an hourly tropical thunderstorm (100-kr starters, 170-kr main dishes, vegetarian options, daily 16:00-22:00, Fri-Sat until 23:00, between the Parliament building and City Hall at Øvre Vollgate 13, tel. 22 83 71 10).

HARBORSIDE DINING IN AKER BRYGGE

Aker Brygge, the harborfront mall, is popular with businesspeople and tourists. While it isn't cheap, its inviting cafés and restaurants with outdoor, harborview tables make for a memorable waterfront meal. Before deciding where to eat, you might want to walk the entire lane (including the back side), considering both the regular places (some with second-floor view seating) and the various floating options. Nearly all are open for lunch and dinner.

Lekter'n Lounge, right on the water, offers the best harbor view (rather than views of strolling people). This trendy bar has a floating dining area open only when the weather is warm. It serves hamburgers, fish-and-chips, 150-180-kr salads, mussels, and shrimp buckets. Budget eaters can split a 160-kr pizza (all outdoors, Stranden 3, tel. 22 83 76 46). If you go just for drinks, the sofas make you feel right at home and a DJ adds to the ambience.

Rorbua, the "Fisherman's Cabin," is a lively yet cozy eatery tucked into this mostly modern stretch of restaurants. The specialty is food from Norway's north, such as whale and reindeer. Inside, it's extremely woody with a rustic charm and candlelit picnic tables surrounded by harpoons and old B&W photos. Grab a stool at one of the wooden tables, and choose from a menu of meat-and-potato dishes (200-300 kr). A hearty daily special with coffee for 165 kr is one of the best restaurant deals in the city (daily 12:30-23:00, Stranden 71, tel. 22 83 64 84).

Lofoten Fiskerestaurant serves fish amid a dressy yacht-club atmosphere at the end of the strip. While it's beyond the people-watching action, it's comfortable even in cold and blustery weather because of its heated atrium, which makes a meal here practically outdoor dining. Reservations are a must, especially if you want a harborside window table (lunch-200 kr, dinner from 300 kr, open daily, Stranden 75, tel. 22 83 08 08, www.lofoten-fiskerestaurant. no).

Budget Tips: If you're on a budget, try a hotdog from a *pølse* stand or get a picnic from a nearby grocery store and grab a bench along the boardwalk. The **ICA "Gourmet"** grocery store—in the middle of the mall a few steps behind all the fancy restaurants—has salads, warm takeaway dishes (sold by the weight), and more (turn in about midway down the boardwalk, Mon-Fri 8:00-22:00, Sat 9:00-20:00, closed Sun). Farther down, the **Joker mini-grocery** (just over the bridge and to the right on Lille Stranden in Tjuvholmen) is open until 22:00.

DINING NEAR VIGELAND PARK

Lofotstua Restaurant feels transplanted from the far northern islands it's named for. Kjell Jenssen and his son, Jan Hugo, proudly serve up fish Lofoten-style. Evangelical about fish, they will patiently explain to you the fine differences between all the local varieties, with the help of a photo-filled chart. They serve only the freshest catch, perfectly—if simply—prepared. If you want meat, they've got it—whale or seal (170-290-kr plates, Mon-Fri 15:00-22:00, generally closed in July, 5-minute walk from gate of Vigeland statue garden, tram #12, in Majorstuen at Kirkeveien 40, tel. 22 46 93 96). This place is packed daily in winter for their famous lutefisk.

Curry and Ketchup Indian Restaurant is filled with in-the-know locals enjoying tasty and hearty meals for about 100 kr. This happening place requires no reservations and feels like an Indian market. If you want a reasonable Indian meal in Oslo, this is hard to beat (daily 14:00-23:00, cash only, a 5-minute walk from gate of Vigeland statue garden, tram #12, in Majorstuen at Kirkeveien 51, tel. 22 69 05 22).

TRENDY DINING AT THE BOTTOM OF GRÜNERLØKKA

Südøst Asian Crossover Restaurant, once a big bank, now fills its vault with wine (which makes sense, given Norwegian alcohol prices). Today it's popular with young Norwegian professionals as a place to see and be seen. It's a fine mix of Norwegian-chic woody ambience inside with a trendy menu, and a big riverside terrace outdoors with a more casual menu. Diners enjoy its chic setting, smart service, and modern creative Asian-fusion cuisine (200-kr dinner plate, 300-kr dinner menu, daily 16:00-24:00, at bottom of Grünerløkka, tram #11, #12, or #17 to Trondheimsveien 5, tel. 23 35 30 70).

Olaf Ryes Plass, Grünerløkka's main square (and the streets nearby), is lined with inviting eateries and has a relaxed, bohemian-chic vibe. The top side of the square (near Villa Paradiso Pizzeria) has several pubs selling beer-centric food to a beer-centric crowd. To get here, hop on tram #11, #12, or #13 to Olaf Ryes Plass.

Villa Paradiso Pizzeria serves Oslo's favorite pizza. Youthful and family-friendly, it has a rustic interior and a popular terrace overlooking the square and people scene (120-180-kr pizza, Olaf Ryes Plass 8, tel. 22 35 40 60).

Mathallen Oslo is a former 19th-century factory, spiffed up and morphed into a neighborhood market with a mix of produce stalls and enticing eateries all sharing food-circus-type seating in the middle (Tue-Sun until late, closed Mon, on the river, 5-minute walk from Olaf Ryes Plass).

EATING CHEAP AND SPICY IN GRØNLAND

The street called Grønland leads through this colorful immigrant neighborhood (a short walk behind the train station or T-bane: Grønland). After the cleanliness and orderliness of the rest of the city, the rough edges and diversity of people here can feel like a breath of fresh air. Whether you eat here or not, the street is fun to explore. In Grønland, backpackers and immigrants munch street food for dinner. Cheap and tasty *börek* (feta, spinach, mushroom) is sold hot and greasy to go for 25 kr.

Punjab Tandoori is friendly and serves hearty meals (70-100-kr, lamb and chicken curry, tandoori specials). I like eating outside here with a view of the street scene (daily 11:00-23:00, Grønland 24).

Alibaba Restaurant is clean, simple, and cheap for Turkish food. They have good indoor or outdoor seating (139-kr fixed-price meal Mon-Thu only, open daily 12:30-22:30, corner of Grønland-sleiret and Tøyengata at Tøyengata 2, tel. 22 17 22 22).

Asylet is more expensive and feels like it was here long before Norway ever saw a Pakistani. This big, traditional eatery—like a Norwegian beer garden—has a rustic, cozy interior and a cobbled backyard filled with picnic tables (150-240-kr plates and hearty dinner salads, daily 11:00-24:00, Grønland 28, tel. 22 17 09 39).

Dattera Til Hagen feels like a college party. It's a lively scene filling a courtyard with picnic tables and benches under strings of colored lights. If it's too cold, hang out inside. Locals like it for the tapas, burgers, salads, and Norwegian microbrews on tap (180-kr plates, Grønland 10, tel. 22 17 18 61). On weekends after 22:00, it becomes a disco.

Olympen Brown Pub is a dressy dining hall that's a blast from the past. You'll eat in a spacious, woody saloon with big dark furniture, faded paintings of circa-1920 Oslo lining the walls, and huge chandeliers. It's good for solo travelers, because sharing the long dinner tables is standard practice. They serve hearty 200-kr plates and offer a huge selection of beers. Traditional Norwegian cuisine is served downstairs, while upstairs on the rooftop, the food is grilled (daily 11:00-2:00 in the morning, Grønlandsleiret 15, tel. 22 17 28 08).

Café Con Bar is a trendy yuppie eatery on the downtown edge of Grønland. Locals consider it to have the best burgers in town (150 kr). While the tight interior seating is very noisy, the sidewalk tables are great for people-watching (160-kr daily specials, 150-190-kr main dishes, Mon-Sat 10:00-late, Sun 12:00-late, kitchen closes at 23:00, where Grønland hits Brugata).

NEAR THE SKI JUMP, HIGH ON THE MOUNTAIN

Frognerseteren Hovedrestaurant, nestled high above Oslo (and 1,400 feet above sea level), is a classy, sod-roofed old restaurant. Its terrace, offering a commanding view of the city, is a popular stop for famous apple cake and coffee. The café is casual and less expensive, with indoor and outdoor seating (90-kr sandwiches and cold dishes, 140-190-kr entrées, Mon-Sat 11:00-22:00, Sun 11:00-21:00, reservations unnecessary). The elegant view restaurant is pricier (375-395-kr plates, Mon-Fri 12:00-22:00, Sat 13:00-22:00, Sun 13:00-21:00, reindeer specials, reserve for evening dining, tel. 22 92 40 40).

The **Holmenkollen** restaurant, just below the ski jump and a few steps above the Holmenkollen T-bane stop, is a practical alternative to the Frognerseteren restaurant. It serves better food at better prices with a similarly grand Oslo fjord view, but without the folk charm.

You can combine a trip into the forested hills surrounding the city with lunch or dinner and get a chance to see the famous Holmenkollen Ski Jump up close.

Oslo Connections

BY TRAIN, BUS, OR CAR

For train information, call 81 50 08 88 and press 9 for English. For international trains, press 3. Even if you have a rail pass, reservations are required for long rides (free with first-class pass, 50 kr for second-class; SJ InterCity reservation fee for tickets to Stockholm in costs about 35 kr regardless of class). First class often comes with a hot meal, fruit bowl, and unlimited juice and coffee.

Be warned that international connections from Oslo are often in flux. Schedules can vary depending on the day of the week, so carefully confirm the specific train you need and purchase any required reservations in advance. Aside from the occasional direct train to Stockholm, most trips from Oslo to Copenhagen or Stockholm require a change in Sweden.

From Oslo by Train to Bergen: Oslo and Bergen are linked by a spectacularly scenic train ride (3-5/day, 7 hours, overnight possible daily except Sat). Many travelers take it as part of the **Norway in a Nutshell** route, which combines train, ferry, and bus travel in an unforgettably beautiful trip. For information on times and prices, see the next chapter.

By Train to: Lillehammer (almost hourly, 2.25 hours), **Kristiansand** (5/day, 4.5 hours, overnight possible), **Stavanger** (4/day, 8-8.5 hours, overnight possible), **Copenhagen** (2/day, 8.5 hours, transfer at Göteborg, more with multiple changes), **Stockholm** (2/day direct InterCity trains, 5.75 hours; 2/day with change in Göteborg, 6-7.5 hours).

By Bus to Stockholm: Taking the bus to Stockholm is cheaper but slower than the train (3/day, 8 hours, www.swebus.se).

BY CRUISE SHIP

Oslo has three cruise ports, described next. For more in-depth cruising information, pick up my *Rick Steves Northern European Cruise Ports* guidebook.

Getting Downtown: To varying degrees, all of Oslo's cruise ports are within walking distance of the city center—but from the farthest-flung port, Filipstad, your best option is probably to take advantage of your cruise line's shuttle bus, even if you have to pay for it (most drop off by the Nobel Peace Center, near City Hall on the harborfront). No public transit serves the ports, but Open Top Sightseeing's hop-on, hop-off bus tours meet arriving cruise ships at or near all ports (pricey but convenient). A taxi into town from any of the ports costs a hefty 150 kr.

Once you arrive at the City Hall/harbor area, you can simply walk up the street behind City Hall to find Karl Johans Gate, and the National Gallery; hop on tram #12 (ride it toward Majorstuen to reach Vigeland Park—use the Vigelandsparken stop; or ride it toward Disen to reach the train station—use the Jernbanetorget stop); or take the shuttle boat across the harbor to the museums at Bygdøy.

Port Details: Akershus, right on the harbor below Akershus Fortress, has two berths: **Søndre Akershuskai,** a bit closer to town, and **Vippetangen,** a bit farther out (at the tip of the peninsula). Both are within an easy 10-minute walk of City Hall (just stroll with the harbor on your left).

Revierkai, around the east side of the Akershus Fortress peninsula, faces Oslo's can't-miss-it, cutting-edge Opera House. From the Opera House, a pedestrian overpass takes you directly to the train station and the start of my self-guided "Welcome to Oslo" walk, or you can head up the street called Rådhusgata to City Hall.

Filipstad is just west of downtown, next to the brand-new Tjuvholmen development (around the far side of Aker Brygge from City Hall). From here, it's a dull 20-minute walk into town: Walk out of the port, turn right at the roundabout, then head to the busy highway and follow the path to the right and signs to *sentrum.* When construction around Filipstad and Tjuvholmen is finally finished (years from now), it will be possible to cross directly from the port to Tjuvholmen and then it will be a quick walk along Aker Brygge to the city center. Your ship's upper deck provides the perfect high-altitude vantage point for scouting your options before disembarking.

BY OVERNIGHT BOAT TO COPENHAGEN

Consider connecting Oslo and Copenhagen by cruise ship. The boat leaves daily from Oslo at 16:30 (arrives in Copenhagen at 9:45 the following morning; going the other way, it departs Copenhagen at 16:30 and arrives in Oslo at 9:45; about 17 hours sailing each way). The boat leaves Oslo from the far (non-City Hall) side of the Akershus Fortress peninsula (get there via bus #60 from the train station, 2-3/hour, get off at Vippetangen stop and follow signs to DFDS ticket office). Boarding is from 15:00 to 16:15. From Oslo, you'll sail through the Oslofjord—not as dramatic as Norway's western fjords, but impressive if you're not going to Bergen. On board are gourmet restaurants, dinner and breakfast buffets, cafés, nightclubs, shops, a sauna, hot tub, and swimming pool. This is fun and convenient, but more expensive and not as swanky as the Stockholm-Helsinki cruise.

You can take this cruise one-way or do a round-trip from either city. Book online or by phone (from Norway, call DFDS Seaways' Denmark office: Mon-Fri 9:00-16:30, closed Sat-Sun, tel. 00 45 33 42 30 10, www.dfdsseaways.us). Book in advance for the best prices.

OSLO

NORWAY IN A NUTSHELL

A Scenic Journey to the Sognefjord

While Oslo and Bergen are the big draws for tourists, Norway is first and foremost a place of unforgettable natural beauty. There's a certain mystique about the "land of the midnight sun," but you'll get the most scenic travel thrills per mile, minute, and dollar by going west from Oslo rather than north.

Norway's greatest claims to scenic fame are her deep, lush fjords. Three million years ago, an ice age made this land as inhabitable as the center of Greenland. As the glaciers advanced and cut their way to the sea, they gouged out long grooves—today's fjords.

The entire west coast is slashed by stunning fjords, and the Sognefjord—Norway's longest (120 miles) and deepest (1 mile)—is tops. The seductive Sognefjord has tiny but tough ferries, towering canyons, and isolated farms and villages marinated in the mist of countless waterfalls.

A series of well-organized and spectacular bus, train, and ferry connections—appropriately nicknamed "Norway in a Nutshell"—lays Norway's beautiful fjord country before you on a scenic platter. With the Nutshell, you'll delve into two offshoots of the Sognefjord, which make an upside-down "U" route: the Aurlandsfjord and the Nærøyfjord. You'll link the ferry ride to the rest of Norway with two trains and a bus: The main train is an express route that takes you through stark and icy scenery above the tree line. To get from the express train down to the ferry, you'll catch an old-fashioned slow train one way (passing waterfalls and forests) and a bus the other way (offering fjord views and more waterfalls). All connections are designed for tourists, explained in English, convenient, and easy. At the start of the fjord, you'll go through the town of Flåm (a transit hub), then pass briefly by the workaday town of

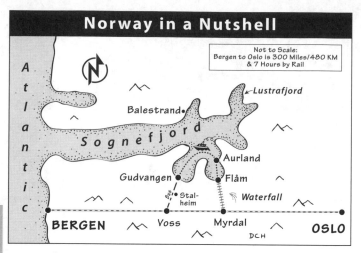

Norway in a Nutshell

Not to Scale:
Bergen to Oslo is 300 Miles/480 KM
& 7 Hours by Rail

Atlantic

Lustrafjord

Balestrand•

S o g n e f j o r d

Aurland

Gudvangen   •Flåm

Bus •Stal-heim   Waterfall

BERGEN   Voss   Myrdal   OSLO

DCH

Aurland and the hamlet of Undredal (by taking the Nutshell trip segments at your own pace, you can visit the latter two fjord towns on your own; all are described in this chapter).

This region enjoys mild weather for its latitude, thanks to the warm Gulf Stream. (When it rains in Bergen, it just drizzles here.) But if the weather is bad—don't fret. I've often arrived to gloomy weather, only to enjoy sporadic splashes of brilliant sunshine all day long.

Recently the popularity of the Nutshell route has skyrocketed. And the 2005 completion of the longest car tunnel in the world (15 miles between Flåm and Lærdal) rerouted the main E-16 road between Bergen and Oslo through this idyllic fjord corner. All of this means that July and August come with a crush of crowds, dampening some of the area's magic. Unfortunately, many tourists are overcome by Nutshell tunnel-vision, and spend so much energy scurrying between boats, trains, and buses that they forget to simply enjoy the fjords. Relax—you're on vacation.

PLANNING YOUR TIME

Even the blitz tourist needs a day for the Norway in a Nutshell trip. With more time, sleep in a town along the fjord, and customize your fjord experience to include sights outside the Nutshell.

Day 1: The Nutshell works well as a single day (one-way between Oslo and Bergen in either direction, or as a long day trip from either city). Those with a car and only one day can leave the car in Oslo and do the Nutshell by train, bus, and boat. If you're using public transportation and want to make efficient use of your time, organize your trip so that it ends in Bergen, or return to Oslo on a night train (sleeping through all the scenery you saw west-bound).

Day 2: If you have enough time, spend the night somewhere on the Sognefjord—either along the Nutshell route itself (in Flåm

or Aurland; accommodations listed later), or in another, even more appealing fjordside town (such as Balestrand or Solvorn, both described in the next chapter).

With More Time: The Sognefjord deserves more than a day. If you can spare the time, venture off the Nutshell route. You can easily connect to some non-Nutshell towns (such as Balestrand) via ferry or express boat. Drivers can improve on the Nutshell by taking a northern route: From Oslo, drive through the Gudbrandsdal Valley, go over the Jotunheimen Mountains, then along Lustrafjord to Balestrand; from there, you can cross the Sognefjord on a car ferry (such as Kaupanger-Gudvangen) and drive the Nutshell route on to Bergen. (Most of these sights, and the car ferry connection, are covered in the next two chapters.) For more tips, see the "Beyond the Nutshell" sidebar.

Orientation to the Nutshell

The most exciting single-day trip you could make from Oslo or Bergen is this circular train/boat/bus/train jaunt through fjord country.

Local TIs (listed throughout this chapter) are well-informed about your options, and they sell tickets for various segments of the trip. At TIs, train stations, and hotels, look for souvenir-worthy brochures with photos, descriptions, and exact times (see sample schedules later in this chapter).

Route Overview: The basic idea is this: Take a train halfway across the mountainous spine of Norway, make your way down to the Sognefjord for a boat cruise, then climb back up out of the fjord to rejoin the main train line. Each of these steps is explained in the self-guided "Nutshell Tour" in this chapter. Transportation along the Nutshell route is carefully coordinated. If any segment of your journey is delayed, the transportation for the next segment

"Norway in a Nutshell" in a Nutshell

The essential five Nutshell segments (all described in detail in this chapter) are:

Norwegian State Railways (NSB) Oslo to Myrdal Train: Five hours, two departures each morning—6:43 (recommended) and 8:05 (for sleepyheads), www.nsb.no. Confirm times online or locally.

Private Train from Myrdal to Flåm (Flåmsbana): One hour, hourly departures, generally timed for arrival of Oslo train.

Boat Through the Fjords: Flåm to Gudvangen, 2 hours, about hourly departures, two boat companies, same route and cost.

Bus from Gudvangen to Voss: 25 miles, one hour, departures timed with boat arrivals.

Train from Voss to Bergen: One hour, hourly departures.

Nutshell travelers originating in Bergen can use this route in reverse. Check schedules at www.scandinavianrail.com and ruteinfo.net.

will wait for you (because everyone on board is catching the same connection).

The route works round-trip from Oslo or Bergen, or one-way between those two cities (going in either direction). Doing the Nutshell one-way between Oslo and Bergen (or vice versa) is most satisfying—you'll see the whole shebang, and it's extremely efficient if you're connecting the two cities anyway. Doing the Nutshell as a round-trip from Bergen is cheaper, but it doesn't include the majestic train ride between Myrdal and Oslo. Conversely, even though the round-trip from Oslo doesn't go all the way to Bergen, it still includes all the must-sees (the Voss-Bergen leg is the least thrilling, anyway).

When to Go: The Nutshell trip is possible all year. In the summer (late June-late Aug), the connections are most convenient, the weather is most likely to be good...and the route is at its most crowded. Outside of this time, sights close and schedules become more challenging. Some say the Nutshell is most beautiful in winter, though schedules are severely reduced (and you can't do it as a day trip from Oslo). It's easy to confirm schedules, connections, and prices locally or online (www.ruteinfo.net).

Sample Oslo-Bergen Schedule: You must take one of two morning departures (6:43 or 8:05) to do the entire trip from Oslo to Bergen in a day. I recommend the earlier departure to enjoy an hour more free time in Flåm and generally fewer crowds. This itinerary shows typical sample times for summer travel; confirm exact times before your trip (www.nsb.no for trains and www.ruteinfo. net for boats and buses):

- Oslo to Myrdal—6:43-12:05
- Myrdal to Flåm—12:13-13:10
- Free time in Flåm—13:10-15:10
- Boat from Flåm to Gudvangen—15:10-17:30
- Bus from Gudvangen to Voss—17:45-19:00
- Train from Voss to Bergen—19:41-21:08
- Free time in Bergen—21:08-22:59
- Overnight train from Bergen to Oslo—22:59-6:27

If you leave Oslo on the 8:05 train, you'll have only one hour of free time on the fjord in Flåm and arrive in Bergen at the same time (21:08). If overnighting in Flåm, you have nearly hourly boats, buses, and trains the next day to continue on into Bergen. Doing the Nutshell route round-trip from Bergen, or from Bergen to Oslo, requires leaving Bergen at 8:40.

Reservations: While reservations are possible for most of the legs, they're only really worth considering for two: The Oslo-Myrdal train (essential), and the Flåmsbana train between Myrdal and Flåm (less critical, but worth having—especially at times when cruise passengers docked in Flåm can jam up the train). Fortunately, both of these legs can be reserved at www.nsb.no or at the Oslo train station; to avoid disappointment, you may as well book both trains at once. The other legs—the boat trip, the bus ride, and the Voss-Bergen train—are less crowded and it's easy to just wing it (though it's wise to book your specific boat departure in Flåm once you know which one you'd like to take).

Buying Tickets: Without a rail pass, you'll save about 100 kr by purchasing Norwegian State Railways tickets in advance. If you have a Eurail pass, the train connections from Oslo-Myrdal and Voss-Bergen are free, and you get a 30 percent discount on the Myrdal-Flåm ride (no rail pass discounts on boat or bus). Standard ticket prices for the Nutshell legs are 320 kr for Myrdal-Flåm (220 kr with rail pass, same price in advance, at station, or on train from conductor); 300 kr on either line for the Flåm-Gudvangen boat; and 100 kr for the Gudvangen-Voss bus (buy from driver).

Dealing with Your Luggage: Many travelers connect Oslo and Bergen with the Nutshell trip and are therefore carrying their luggage. Luckily, the connections require almost no walking: At Myrdal, you just cross the platform; in Flåm, you walk 50 yards from the train to the dock; in Gudvangen, the bus meets the ferry at the dock (look for buses marked *Norway in a Nutshell*); in Voss, the bus drops you at the train station. On the three train segments, simply put your bag in the overhead rack. If you want to check your bag during your free time in Flåm, use the baggage-check cabin at the head of the train track, across the lane from the boat dock.

On the ferry, leave your bag with the stack of bags on the car deck. And on the bus (which meets the boat), the driver will help you stow your bag underneath, or you can take it on board. The biggest chore is getting your bags to and from the train stations in Oslo and Bergen.

MORE SAMPLE NUTSHELL ITINERARIES

Here are non-Oslo-Bergen one-day options for doing the Nutshell in the summer. Confirm specific times before your trip (www.ruteinfo.net).

Bergen-Oslo: Train departs Bergen-8:40, arrives Voss-9:56; bus departs Voss-10:10, arrives Gudvangen-11:20; boat departs Gudvangen-11:45, arrives Flåm-14:10; Flåmsbana train departs Flåm-16:05, arrives Myrdal-17:03; train departs Myrdal-17:53, arrives Oslo-22:45.

Day Trip from Oslo: Train departs Oslo-6:43, arrives Myrdal-12:01; Flåmsbana train departs Myrdal-12:13; arrives Flåm-13:10; boat departs Flåm-13:20, arrives Gudvangen-15:30; bus departs Gudvangen-15:40, arrives Voss-16:55; train departs Voss-17:08, arrives Oslo-22:45.

Day Trip from Bergen: Train departs Bergen-8:40, arrives Voss-9:56; bus departs Voss-10:10, arrives Gudvangen-11:20; boat departs Gudvangen-11:45, arrives Flåm-14:10; Flåmsbana train departs Flåm-14:40, arrives Myrdal-15:40; train departs Myrdal-17:01, arrives Bergen-19:05.

Express Boat to Balestrand and Bergen: If you don't want to do the entire Nutshell route, take note of the very handy and speedy express boat connecting this area (Aurland and Flåm) with two other worthwhile destinations: Balestrand (on the Sognefjord's northern bank) and Bergen. While this boat misses the best fjord (Nærøyfjord), many travelers use it to craft their own itinerary that escapes the Nutshell rut.

Eating: Options along the route aren't great—on the Nutshell I'd consider food just as a source of nutrition and forget about fine dining. You can buy some food on the fjord cruises (50-75-kr hot dogs, burgers, and pizza) and the Oslo-Bergen train (50-100-kr hot meals, 150-kr daily specials). Depending on the timing of your layovers, Myrdal, Voss, or Flåm are your best lunch-stop options (the Myrdal and Flåm train stations have decent cafeterias, and other eateries surround the Flåm and Voss stations)—although you won't have a lot of time there if you're making the journey all in one day. Your best bet is to pack picnic meals and munch en route. If catching an early train in Oslo, the station has several handy grocery stores open at 6:00.

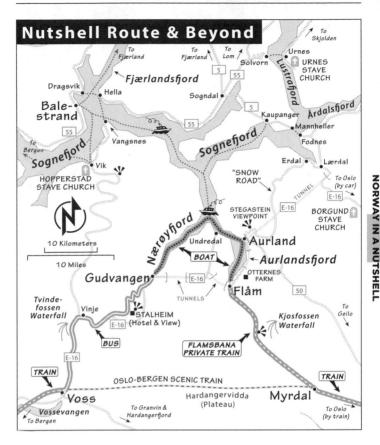

WITH A PACKAGE DEAL OR ON YOUR OWN?

The Fjord Tours package deals are easy to book—they'll save you time as well as a little money. If you have a rail pass, or if you're a student or a senior (and therefore eligible for discounts), you'll save money doing the Nutshell on your own. Just buy tickets as you go (described on the next page).

Package Deals

Fjord Tours sells the Nutshell package and other package trips at all Norwegian State Railways stations, including Oslo and Bergen, or through their customer-service line in Norway (tel. 81 56 82 22, www.fjordtours.no). With these packages, your train departures are fixed and you can catch whichever boat and bus you like.

The costs of the Nutshell packages are as follows:
- One-way from Bergen or Oslo-1,630 kr
- Round-trip from Oslo via Voss (but not Bergen)-2,205 kr
- Round-trip from Oslo via Bergen-2,490 kr

- Round-trip from Bergen via Myrdal (but not Oslo)-1,220 kr
- Round-trip from Flåm-840 kr

They also sell a "Sognefjord in a Nutshell" tour, which takes an express boat from Bergen to Flåm, then picks up the Nutshell route from there (round-trip back to Bergen-1,465 kr; one-way to Oslo-1,865 kr; runs only May-Sept).

On Your Own

Unless you have a rail pass or are eligible for student or senior discounts, you'll pay roughly the same to do the Nutshell on your own as you would with a package tour (see prices above).

Rail Pass Discounts: If you have any rail pass that includes Norway, the Oslo-Bergen train is covered (except a 50-kr reservation fee for second class; free for first-class passholders); you also get a 30 percent discount on the Myrdal-Flåm Flåmsbana train. You still have to pay full fare for the boat cruise and the Gudvangen-Voss bus. Your total one-way cost between Oslo and Bergen: about 600 kr with a first-class pass, 650 kr with a second-class pass.

Buying Train Tickets: You can get Nutshell train tickets (Oslo-Flåm and Flåm-Bergen) at the NSB train stations in Oslo or Bergen. In summer, it's smart to reserve the Oslo-Myrdal segment in advance (see below). You can also get your Flåmsbana ticket at the Flåmsbana station in Flåm or Myrdal if you didn't book it through NSB; purchase your fjord-cruise ticket on the boat or from the TI in Flåm; and buy the tickets for the Gudvangen bus on board from the driver. If you're a student or senior, always ask about discounts.

Reservations: At peak season (July-Aug), the train from Oslo to Myrdal can fill up in advance. You can get a reservation (free with first-class rail pass) at any Norwegian train station (including at the Oslo airport) or at the Oslo TI. To reserve further in advance, book your seat online at www.nsb.no. You'll be given a choice of picking up your ticket at the train station, sending it to your smartphone, or printing it out. If you have any difficulty paying for your ticket with a US credit card online, call 81 50 08 88 or 23 62 00 00; press 9 for English, and you'll be given a Web link where you can finish processing your credit-card payment.

The **Flåmsbana train** is usually no problem to just hop on, but certain departures are greatly affected by cruise ships docked in Flåm. Morning departures from Flåm to Myrdal can sell out, and late-morning or early-afternoon trains from Myrdal back to Flåm can be jammed. If you're booking ahead for your Oslo-Myrdal leg, you may as well book a Flåmsbana seat at the same time. At other times, you can just buy your ticket on the spot at either the Myrdal or Flåm stations, or from the conductor on the train (same price).

Beyond the Nutshell

The Sognefjord is the ultimate natural thrill Norway has to offer, and there's no doubt that the Nutshell route outlined in this chapter is the most efficient way to see it quickly. Unfortunately, its trains, buses, and boats are thronged with other visitors who have the same idea.

Travelers with a bit more time, and the willingness to chart their own course, often have a more rewarding Sognefjord experience. It's surprisingly easy to break out of the Nutshell and hit the northern part of the Sognefjord (for example, using the Bergen-Vik-Balestrand-Aurland-Flåm express boat, described on page 128).

In the next chapter, you'll find some tempting stopovers on the north bank of the Sognefjord, including adorable fjordside villages (such as Balestrand and Solvorn), evocative stave churches (including Hopperstad and Urnes), and a chance to get up close to a glacier (at the Nigard Glacier).

Read up on your options, then be adventurous about mixing and matching the fjordside attractions that appeal to you most. Ideally, use the Nutshell as a springboard for diving into the Back Door fjords of your travel dreams.

NORWAY IN A NUTSHELL

While you may be told in Oslo that the Flåmsbana train is sold out, you most likely can still catch it at the time you wanted (or an hour later, since it runs about hourly).

You don't need to reserve the **Flåm-Gudvangen fjord** boat trip, but it's smart to buy your boat ticket upon arrival in Flåm. You don't need a reservation for the **Gudvangen-Voss bus.**

Tips for Cruise-Ship Passengers Arriving in Flåm

Tiny Flåm—in the heart of Nutshell country—is an increasingly popular destination for huge cruise ships. If your cruise is stopping in Flåm, you can do the middle part of the Nutshell loop in a day, but it helps to know a few pointers:

• Plan your day in advance (using this chapter), disembark as early as possible, and head straight for the train station (a short walk from the dock). Many ships arrive around 8:00; Flåm's TI and train-station ticket office both open at 8:15; and the first Nutshell fjord boat sets sail at 9:00—leaving you a narrow window of time to confirm schedules and book tickets. Stragglers may get stuck in long lines and (literally) miss the boat.

• The Nutshell loop is practical for cruisers only if done counterclockwise: Flåm-Gudvangen boat, 9:00-11:25; Gudvangen-Voss bus, 11:40-12:55; Voss-Myrdal train, 13:10-14:00; Flåmsbana train from Myrdal to Flåm, 14:40-15:40 (these are 2014 times; confirm locally). The opposite direction (Flåm-Myrdal-Voss-Gudvangen-Flåm) returns to Flåm too late for most cruise ships.

• The same "package vs. on your own" considerations, explained earlier, apply to cruisers. Unless you're eligible for student, senior, or rail pass discounts, book the Flåm round-trip package (at the Flåm TI).

• If you'd rather not do the Nutshell loop on your day in port, you could do one or two legs: For example, cruise to Gudvangen, then take a bus straight back to Flåm (skipping the train rides); or simply go for a round-trip ride on the Flåmsbana train to Myrdal and back (this popular-with-cruisers option often sells out—get your tickets as quickly as possible on arrival in Flåm).

Nutshell Tour

If you only have one day for this region, it'll be a thrilling day—worth ▲▲▲. The following self-guided segments of the Nutshell route are narrated from Oslo to Bergen. If you're going the other way, hold the book upside down.

▲▲Oslo-Bergen Train

This is simply the most spectacular train ride in northern Europe. The scenery crescendos as you climb over Norway's mountainous spine. After a mild three hours of deep woods and lakes, you're into the barren, windswept heaths and glaciers. These tracks were begun in 1894 to link Stockholm and Bergen, but Norway won its independence from Sweden in 1905, so the line served to link the two main cities in the new country—Oslo and Bergen. The entire railway, an amazing engineering feat completed in 1909, is 300 miles long; peaks at 4,266 feet, which, at this Alaskan latitude, is far above the tree line; goes under 18 miles of snow sheds; trundles over 300 bridges; and passes through 200 tunnels in just under seven hours.

Here's what you'll see traveling westward from Oslo: Leaving Oslo, you pass through a six-mile-long tunnel and stop in Drammen, Norway's fifth-largest town. The scenery stays low-key and woodsy up Hallingdal Valley until you reach Geilo, a popular ski resort. Then you enter a land of big views and tough little cabins. Finse, at about 4,000 feet, is the highest stop on the line. At several towns, the conductor may announce how many minutes the train will be stopped there. This gives you a few fun moments to get out, stretch, take a photograph, and look around.

Before Myrdal, you enter the longest high-mountain stretch of railway in Europe. Much of the line is protected by snow tunnels. The scenery gets more dramatic as you approach Myrdal (MEER-doll). Just before Myrdal, look to the right and down into the Flåm

Valley, where the Flåmsbana branch line winds its way down to the fjord. Nutshell travelers get off at Myrdal.

Cost: Note that the Nutshell route includes only part of this train ride (as a day trip from Oslo, for instance, you take the Oslo-Myrdal and Voss-Oslo segments). Here are the one-way fares for various segments: Oslo-Bergen-815 kr, Oslo-Myrdal-660 kr, Myrdal-Voss-117 kr, Myrdal-Bergen-286 kr, Voss-Bergen-200 kr. You can save money on these fares if you book in advance at www.nsb.no.

Remember, second-class rail-pass holders pay just 50 kr to reserve, and first-class passholders pay nothing. If you have a second-class rail pass or ticket, you can pay 90 kr to upgrade to "Komfort" class, with more legroom, reclining seats, free coffee and tea, and an electrical socket for your laptop (just ask the conductor when you board).

Schedule: This train runs three to five times per day (overnight possible daily except Sat). The segment from Oslo to Myrdal takes about 5 hours; going all the way to Bergen takes about 7 hours.

Reservations: In peak season, get reservations for this train at least a week in advance.

▲▲Myrdal-Flåm Train (Flåmsbana)

The little 12-mile spur line leaves the Oslo-Bergen line at Myrdal (2,800 feet), which is nothing but a scenic high-altitude train junction with a decent cafeteria. From Myrdal, the Flåmsbana train winds down to Flåm (sea level) through 20 tunnels (more than three miles' worth) in 55 thrilling minutes. It's party time on board, and the engineer even stops the train for photos at the best waterfall, Kjosfossen. According to a Norwegian legend, a tempt-

ress lives behind these falls and tries to lure men to the rocks with her singing...look out for her...and keep a wary eye on your partner.

The train line is an even more impressive feat of engineering when you realize it's not a cogwheel train—it's held to the tracks only by steel wheels, though it does have five separate braking systems. Before boarding, pick up the free, multilingual souvenir pamphlet with lots of info on the trip (or see www.flaamsbana.

no). Video screens onboard and sporadic English commentary on the loudspeakers explain points of interest, but there's not much to say—it's all about the scenery.

If you're choosing seats, you'll enjoy slightly more scenery if you sit on the left going down.

Cost: 320 kr one-way (rail-pass holders pay 220 kr), 420 kr round-trip. You can buy tickets at the Flåmsbana stations in Myrdal or Flåm or on the train (same price). Train-information staff in Oslo may tell you that the Mrydal-Flåm train is booked—don't worry, it very rarely fills up. Simply get to Myrdal and hop on that train.

Schedule: The train departs in each direction nearly hourly.

Reservations: On trains going from Myrdal down to Flåm, you can always squeeze in, even if it's standing-room only. However, morning trains ascending from Flåm to Myrdal (when there are several cruise ships in port) can sell out. This is a concern only for those wanting to leave Flåm to Myrdal in the morning. If that's you, try to buy your ticket the night before or right when the Flåm ticket office opens (at 8:15).

▲▲▲Flåm-Gudvangen Fjord Cruise

The Flåmsbana train deposits you at **Flåm,** a scenic, functional transit hub at the far end of the Aurlandsfjord. If you're doing the Nutshell route nonstop, follow the crowds and hop on the sightseeing boat that'll take you to **Gudvangen.** With minimal English narration, the boat takes you close to the goats, sheep, waterfalls, and awesome cliffs.

There are two boat companies to choose from: Fjord 1 and Sogne-fjorden. Between them, there are departures about hourly from Flåm to Gudvangen. Beware: The first ticket desk you hit in Flåm's visitors center is the Sognefjorden boat desk, and they'll sell you a boat ticket implying it's your only option.

Fjord 1 is the public ferry with cars and lots of open space. It stops at Aurland and Undredal, which is handy if you want to hop off and on along the way—though you'll need to buy separate tickets for each leg of your trip, and it'll end up costing you at least

The Facts on Fjords

The process that created the majestic Sognefjord began during an ice age about three million years ago. A glacier up to 6,500 feet thick slid downhill at an inch an hour, following a former river valley on its way to the sea. Rocks embedded in the glacier gouged out a steep, U-shaped valley, displacing enough rock material to form a mountain 13 miles high. When the climate warmed up, the ice age came to an end. The melting glaciers retreated and the sea level rose nearly 300 feet, flooding the valley now known as the Sognefjord. The fjord is more than a mile deep, flanked by 3,000-foot mountains—for a total relief of 9,300 feet. Waterfalls spill down the cliffs, fed by runoff from today's glaciers. Powdery sediment tinges the fjords a cloudy green, the distinct color of glacier melt.

Why are there fjords on the west coast of Norway, but not, for instance, on the east coast of Sweden? The creation of

a fjord requires a setting of coastal mountains, a good source of moisture, and a climate cold enough for glaciers to form and advance. Due to the earth's rotation, the prevailing winds in higher latitudes blow from west to east, so chances of glaciation are ideal where there is an ocean to the west of land with coastal mountains. When the winds blow east over the water, they pick up a lot of moisture, then bump up against the coastal mountain range, and dump their moisture in the form of snow—which feeds the glaciers that carve valleys down to the sea.

You can find fjords along the northwest coast of Europe—including western Norway and Sweden, Denmark's Faroe Islands, Scotland's Shetland Islands, Iceland, and Greenland; the northwest coast of North America (from Puget Sound in Washington state north to Alaska); the southwest coast of South America (Chile); the west coast of New Zealand's South Island; and on the continent of Antarctica.

As you travel through Scandinavia, bear in mind that, while we English-speakers use the word "fjord" to mean only glacier-cut inlets, Scandinavians often use it in a more general sense to include bays, lakes, and lagoons that weren't formed by glacial action.

85 kr more (be sure to notify the ticket-seller where you want to get off, to make certain they'll stop).

The Sognefjorden boat (same price, route, and journey time) is more of a sightseeing boat rather than a public car and post boat—but it's mostly closed in.

I much prefer the Fjord 1 boat because I like to be in the open air, I enjoy hanging out on the car deck, and the Gudvangen-Voss Nutshell bus connection in Gudvangen is immediate and reliable.

You'll cruise up the lovely **Aurlandsfjord,** motoring by the town of **Aurland** (a good home base, but your boat may not stop

here unless you ask), pass the town of **Undredal** (or stop here if you request it), and hang a left at the stunning **Nærøy-fjord.** The cruise ends at the apex of the Nærøyfjord, in **Gudvangen.**

The trip is breathtaking in any weather. For the last hour, as you sail down the Nærøyfjord, camera-clicking tourists scurry around struggling to get a photo that will catch the magic. Waterfalls turn the black cliffs into bridal veils, and you can nearly reach out and touch the cliffs of the Nærøyfjord. It's the world's narrowest fjord: six miles long and as little as 820 feet wide and 40 feet deep. On a sunny day, the ride is one of those fine times—like when you're high on the tip of an Alp—when a warm camaraderie spontaneously combusts between the strangers who've come together for the experience.

Cost: For the whole route (Flåm-Gudvangen), you'll pay 300 kr one-way (150 kr for students with ISIC cards; 450 kr round-trip).

Schedule: In summer (May-Sept), boats run four to five times each day in both directions. Specific departure times can vary, but generally boats leave Flåm at 9:00, 13:20, 15:10, and 18:00 (with an additional 11:00 departure from late June to late August) and leave Gudvangen at 10:30, 11:45, 15:45, and 17:40 (with an additional 13:30 departure from late June to late August). Frequency drops off-season. The trip takes about two hours and 15 minutes. Your only concern is that the Nutshell bus may not meet the last departure of day (check locally); the worst-case scenario is that you'd need to catch the regular commuter bus to Voss, which makes more stops and doesn't take the razzle-dazzle Stalheimskleiva corkscrew road.

Reservations: Don't bother. Just buy your ticket in Flåm as soon as you know which boat you want.

Other Ways to Cruise Nærøyfjord: If staying in Flåm, you could take a thrilling ride on a little inflatable FjordSafari speed-boat.

▲Gudvangen-Voss Bus

Nutshellers get off the boat at Gudvangen and take the 25-mile bus ride to Voss. Gudvangen is little more than a boat dock and giant tourist kiosk. If you want, you can browse through the grass-roofed souvenir stores and walk onto a wooden footbridge—then catch your bus. Buses meet each ferry, or will show up soon. (Confirm this in advance if you plan to take the last boat of the day—the ferry crew can call ahead to be sure the bus waits for you.) While some buses—designed for commuters rather than sightseers—take the direct route to Voss, buses tied to the Nutshell schedule take a super-scenic detour via Stalheim (described below). If you're a waterfall junkie, sit on the left.

First the bus takes you up the **Nærøydal** and through a couple of long tunnels. Then you'll take a turnoff to drive past the landmark **Stalheim Hotel** for the first of many spectacular views back

into fjord country. Though the hotel dates from 1885, there's been an inn here since about 1700, where the royal mailmen would change horses. The hotel is geared for tour groups (genuine trolls sew the pewter buttons on the sweaters), but the priceless view from the backyard is free. Drivers should be sure to stop here for the view and peruse the hotel's living room to survey the art showing this perch in the 19th century.

Leaving the hotel, the bus wends its way down a road called **Stalheimskleiva,** with a corkscrew series of switchbacks flanked by a pair of dramatic waterfalls. With its 18 percent grade, it's the steepest road in Norway.

After winding your way down into the valley, you're back on the same highway. The bus goes through those same tunnels again, then continues straight on the main road through pastoral countryside to Voss. You'll pass a huge lake, then follow a crystal-clear, surging river. Just before Voss, look to the right for the wide **Tvindefossen waterfall,** tumbling down its terraced cliff. Drivers will find the grassy meadow and flat rocks at its base ideal for letting the mist fog their glasses and enjoying a drink or snack (be discreet, as "picnics are forbidden").

Cost: 100 kr, pay on board, no rail pass discounts.

Reservations: Not necessary.

Voss

The Nutshell bus from Gudvangen drops you at the Voss train station, which is on the Oslo-Bergen train line. This connection is generally not well-coordinated; you'll likely have 40 minutes or so to kill before the next train to Bergen.

A plain town in a lovely lake-and-mountain setting, Voss lacks the striking fjordside scenery of Flåm, Aurland, or Undredal, and is

NORWAY IN A NUTSHELL

basically a home base for summer or winter sports (Norway's Winter Olympics teams often practice here). Voss surrounds its fine, 13th-century church with workaday streets—busy with both local shops and souvenir stores—stretching in several directions. Fans of American football may want to see the humble monument to player and coach Knute Rockne, who was born in Voss in 1888; look for the metal memorial plaque on a rock near the train station.

Voss' helpful **TI** is a five-minute walk from the train station—just head toward the church (June-Aug daily 8:00-19:00; Sept-May Mon-Sat 8:30-17:00, closed Sun; facing the church in the center of town at Vangsgatan 20, mobile 40 61 77 00, www.visitvoss.no).

Drivers should zip right through Voss, but two miles outside town, you can stop at the **Mølstertunet Folk Museum,** which has 16 buildings showing off farm life in the 17th and 18th centuries (70 kr; mid-May-Aug daily 10:00-17:00; Sept-mid-May Mon-Fri 10:00-15:00, Sun 12:00-15:00, closed Sat; Mølstervegen 143, tel. 47 47 97 94, www.vossfolkemuseum.no).

▲Voss-Bergen Train

The least exciting segment of the trip—but still pleasantly scenic—this train chugs 60 miles along the valley between the midsize town of Voss (described above) and Bergen. For the best scenery, sit on the right side of the train if coming from Oslo/Voss, or the left side if coming from Bergen. Between Voss and Dale, you'll pass several scenic lakes; near Bergen, you'll go along the Veafjord.

Cost: The train costs 200 kr between Voss and Bergen and is fully covered by rail passes that include Norway.

Schedule and Reservations: Unlike the long-distance Oslo-Bergen journey, this line is also served by more frequent commuter trains (about hourly, 75 minutes), and reservations aren't necessary.

Voss-Oslo Train: Note that if you're doing the Nutshell round-trip from Oslo, you should catch the train from Voss (rather than Bergen) back to Oslo. The return trip takes 6 hours and costs 747 kr; reservations are strongly recommended in peak season.

Flåm

Flåm (pronounced "flome")—
where the boat and Flåmsbana
train meet, at the head of the
Aurlandsfjord—feels more like
a transit junction than a village. But its striking setting,
easy transportation connections, and touristy bustle make
it appealing as a home base for
exploring the nearby area.

NORWAY IN A NUTSHELL

Orientation to Flåm

Most of Flåm's services are in a modern cluster of buildings in and
around the train station, including the TI (see below), train ticket
desk, public WC, cafeteria, and souvenir shops. Just outside the
station, the little red shed at the head of the tracks serves as a left-
luggage desk (40 kr, daily 8:00-19:45, on your right as you depart
the train, ring bell if nobody's there), and displays a chart of the
services you'll find in the station. The boat dock for fjord cruises
is just beyond the end of the tracks. Surrounding the station are a
Co-op Marked grocery store (with a basic pharmacy and post office inside, Mon-Sat 9:00-20:00, shorter hours off-season, closed
Sun year-round) and a smattering of hotels, travel agencies, and
touristy restaurants. Aside from a few scattered farmhouses and
some homes lining the road, there's not much of a town here. (The
extremely sleepy old town center—where tourists rarely venture,
and which you'll pass on the Flåmsbana train—is a few miles up
the river, in the valley.)

TOURIST INFORMATION

At the TI inside the train station, you can purchase your boat tickets (for Fjord 1 but not Sognefjorden) and load up on handy brochures (daily May and late Sept 8:15-16:00, June-mid-Sept 8:15-
20:00, closed Oct-April, tel. 57 63 21 06, www.visitflam.com or
www.alr.no). The TI hands out a variety of useful items: an excellent flier with a good map and up-to-date schedules for public transit options; a diagram of the train-station area, identifying services
available in each building; and a map of Flåm and the surrounding
area, marked with suggested walks and hikes. Answers to most of
your questions can be found posted on the walls and from staff at
the counter. Bus schedules, boat and train timetables, maps, and

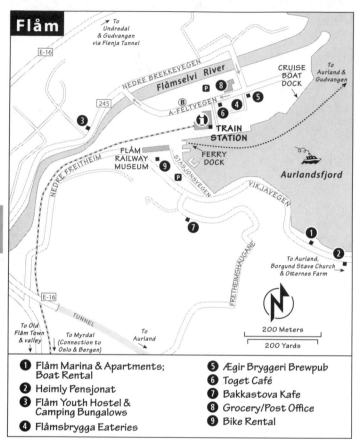

Flåm

To Undredal & Gudvangen via Flenja Tunnel

E-16

NEDRE BREKKEVEGEN

Flåmselvi River

CRUISE BOAT DOCK

To Aurland & Gudvangen

245

A-FELTVEGEN

TRAIN STATION

FLÅM RAILWAY MUSEUM

FERRY DOCK

Aurlandsfjord

NEDRE FREITHEIM

STASJONSVEGEN

VIKJAVEGEN

FRETHEIMSHAUGANE

To Aurland, Borgund Stave Church & Otternes Farm

E-16

TUNNEL

To Old Flåm Town & valley

To Myrdal (Connection to Oslo & Bergen)

To Aurland

N

200 Meters

200 Yards

❶ Flåm Marina & Apartments; Boat Rental
❷ Heimly Pensjonat
❸ Flåm Youth Hostel & Camping Bungalows
❹ Flåmsbrygga Eateries
❺ Ægir Bryggeri Brewpub
❻ Toget Café
❼ Bakkastova Kafe
❽ Grocery/Post Office
❾ Bike Rental

NORWAY IN A NUTSHELL

more are photocopied and available for your convenience. You can pick up Bergen or Oslo information as well.

Sights in and near Flåm

ALONG THE WATERFRONT

Flåm's village activities are all along or near the pier.

The **Flåm Railway Museum** (Flåmsbana Museet), sprawling through the long old train station building alongside the tracks, has surprisingly good exhibits about the history of the train that connects Flåm to the main line up above. You'll find good English explanations, artifacts, re-creations of historic interiors (such as a humble schoolhouse), and an old train car. It's the only real museum in town and a good place to kill time while waiting for your boat or train (free, daily 9:00-17:00, until 20:00 in summer).

A pointless and overpriced **tourist train** does a 45-minute loop around Flåm (95 kr).

The pleasantly woody **Ægir Bryggeri,** a microbrewery designed to resemble an old Viking longhouse, offers tastes of its five beers (135 kr; also restaurant meals in evening with a matching beer menu).

The TI hands out a map suggesting several **walks and hikes** in the area, starting from right in town.

Consider renting a **boat** to go out on the peaceful waters of the fjord. You can paddle near the walls of the fjord and really get a sense of the immensity of these mountains. You can rent rowboats, motorboats, and paddleboats at the little marina across the harbor. If you'd rather have a kayak, Njord does kayak tours, but won't rent you one unless you're certified (tel. 91 32 66 28, www.njord.as).

But the main reason people come to Flåm is to leave it—see some options below. Because Aurland and Flåm are close together (10 minutes away by car or bus, or 20 minutes by boat), I've also listed attractions near Aurland, below.

▲▲▲Cruising Nærøyfjord

The most scenic fjord I've seen anywhere in Norway is about an hour from Flåm (basically the last half of the 2-hour Flåm-Gudvangen trip). There are several ways to cruise it: You can take the Fjord 1 ferry, described earlier as part of the Norway in a Nutshell trip (4.5-hour round-trips departing Flåm in peak season at 9:00, 11:00, and 13:20, 400 kr; these should also stop in Aurland and Undredal—make sure the crew knows that you want to get off, and that the cruise ends in Gudvangen). Or you can consider two other Flåm-based options:

Sognefjorden Sightseeing & Tours: This private company runs trips from Flåm to Gudvangen and back to Flåm, using their own boats and buses (rather than the public ones on the "official" Nutshell route). If the Nutshell departures don't work for you, consider these trips as an alternative. Their main offering, the World Heritage Cruise, is a boat trip up the Nærøyfjord with a return by bus (365 kr, 3 hours, multiple departures daily mid-May-mid-Sept). They also do a variation on this trip with a 45-minute stop in the village of Undredal for lunch and a goat-cheese tasting (495 kr, June-Aug only); a bus trip up to the Stalheim Hotel for the view (290 kr, or combined with return from Gudvangen by boat for 510 kr); a bus ride up to the thrilling Stegastein viewpoint (a concrete-and-wood viewing pier sticking out from a mountainside high above Aurland, 190 kr, mid-May-mid-Sept); and more. For details, drop by their office inside the Flåm train station, call 57 66 00 55, or visit www.visitflam.com/sognefjorden.

▲▲FjordSafari to Nærøyfjord: FjordSafari takes little

groups out onto the fjord in small, open Zodiac-type boats with an English-speaking guide. Participants wear full-body weather suits, furry hats, and spacey goggles (making everyone on the boat look like crash-test dummies). As the boat rockets across the water, you'll be thankful for the gear, no matter what the weather. Their two-hour Flåm-Gudvangen-Flåm tour focuses on the Nærøyfjord, and gets you all the fjord magnificence you can imagine (610 kr). Their three-hour tour is the same as the two-hour tour, except that it includes a stop in Undredal, where you can see goat cheese being made, taste the finished product, and wander that sleepy village (720 kr, several departures daily June-Aug, fewer off-season, kids get discounts, tel. 99 09 08 60, www.fjordsafari.no, Maylene). Their 1.5-hour "mini" tour costs 510 kr and just barely touches on the Nærøyfjord...so what's the point?

▲Flåm Valley Bike Ride or Hike

For the best single-day, non-fjord activity from Flåm, take the Flåmsbana train to Myrdal, then hike or mountain-bike along the

road (half gravel, half paved) back down to Flåm (2-3 hours by bike, gorgeous waterfalls, great mountain scenery, and a cute church with an evocative graveyard, but no fjord views).

Walkers can just hike the best two hours from Myrdal to Blomheller, and catch the train from there into the valley. Or, without riding the train, you can simply walk up the valley 2.5 miles to the church and a little farther to a waterfall. Whenever you get tired hiking up or down the valley, you can hop on the next train. Pick up the helpful map with this and other hiking options (ranging from easy to strenuous) at the Flåm TI.

Bikers can rent good mountain bikes from the bike-rental cabin next to the Flåm train station (daily June-Sept 8:00-20:00, 50 kr/hour, 250 kr/day, includes helmet). It costs 100 kr to take a bike to Myrdal on the train.

▲▲Otternes Farms

This humble but magical cluster of four centuries-old farms is about three miles from Flåm (easy for drivers; a decent walk or bike ride otherwise). It's perched high on a ridge, up a twisty gravel road midway

between Flåm and Aurland. Laila Kvellestad runs this low-key sight, valiantly working to save and share traditional life as it was back when butter was the farmers' gold. (That was before emigration decimated the workforce, coinage replaced barter, and industrialized margarine became more popular than butter—all of which left farmers to eke out a living relying only on their goats and the cheese they produced.) Until 1919 the only road between Aurland and Flåm passed between this huddle of 27 buildings, high above the fjord. First settled in 1522, farmers lived here until the 1990s. Laila gives 45-minute English tours through several time-warp houses and barns at 10:00, 12:00, 14:00, and 16:00 (50-kr entry plus 30 kr for guided tour, June-mid-Sept daily 10:00-17:00, tel. 48 12 51 38, www.otternes.no). It's wise to call first to confirm tour times and that it's open. For an additional 70 kr, Laila serves a traditional snack of pancakes and coffee or tea with your tour. Or book in advance for a 175-kr full lunch featuring locally sourced specialties such as *rømmegrøt* (porridge) and meatballs.

OVER (OR UNDER) THE MOUNTAINS, TO LÆRDAL AND BORGUND

To reach these sights, you'll first head along the fjord to Aurland. Of the sights below, the Lærdal Tunnel, Stegastein viewpoint, and Aurlandsvegen "Snow Road" are best for drivers. The Borgund Stave Church can be reached by car, or by bus from Flåm or Aurland.

For more specifics on driving through the Lærdal Tunnel or on the Aurlandsvegen "Snow Road," see below.

Lærdal Tunnel

Drivers find that this tunnel makes connecting Flåm and Lærdal a snap. It's the world's longest road-vehicle tunnel, stretching 15 miles between Aurland and Lærdal as part of the E-16 highway. It also makes the wonderful Borgund Stave Church (described on the next page) less than an hour's drive from Aurland. The downside to the tunnel is that it goes beneath my favorite scenic drive in Norway (the Aurlandsvegen "Snow Road," described next). But with about two hours, you can drive through the tunnel to Lærdal and then return via the "Snow Road," with the Stegastein viewpoint as a finale, before dropping back into Aurland.

▲▲Stegastein Viewpoint and Aurlandsvegen "Snow Road"

With a car, clear weather, and a little nerve, consider twisting up the mountain behind Aur-

land on route 243 for about 20 minutes to a magnificent view over the Aurlandsfjord. A viewpoint called Stegastein—which looks like a giant, wooden, sideways number "7"—provides a platform from which you can enjoy stunning views across the fjord and straight down to Aurland. Immediately beyond the viewpoint, you leave the fjord views and enter the beautifully desolate mountain-top world of the Aurlandsvegen "Snow Road." When this narrow ribbon of a road finally hits civilization on the other side, you're a mile from the Lærdal tunnel entrance and about 30 minutes from the fine Borgund Stave Church.

▲▲Borgund Stave Church

About 16 miles east of Lærdal, in the village of Borgund, is Norway's most-visited and one of its best-preserved stave churches.

Borgund's church comes with one of this country's best stave-church history museums, which beautifully explains these icons of medieval Norway. Dating from around 1180, the interior features only a few later additions, including a 16th-century pulpit, 17th-century stone altar, painted decorations, and crossbeam reinforcements.

The oldest and most authentic item in the church is the stone baptismal font. In medieval times, priests conducting baptisms would go outside to shoo away the evil spirits from an infant before bringing it inside the church for the ritual. (If infants died before being baptized, they couldn't be buried in the churchyard, so parents would put their bodies in little coffins and hide them under the church's floorboards to get them as close as possible to God.)

Explore the dimly lit interior, illuminated only by the original, small, circular windows up high. Notice the X-shaped crosses of St. Andrew (the church's patron), carvings of dragons, and medieval runes.

Cost and Hours: 75 kr, buy tickets in museum across street, daily June-Aug 8:00-20:00, May and Sept 10:00-17:00, closed Oct-April. The museum has a shop and a fine little cafeteria serving filling and tasty lunches (70-kr soup with bread, tel. 57 66 81 09, www.stavechurch.com).

Getting There: It's about a 30-minute **drive** east of Lærdal, on E-16 (the road to Oslo—if coming from Aurland or Flåm, consider taking the scenic route via the Stegastein viewpoint, described above). There's also a convenient **bus** connection: The bus departs Flåm and Aurland around midday (direction: Lillehammer) and heads for the church, with a return bus departing Borgund in mid-

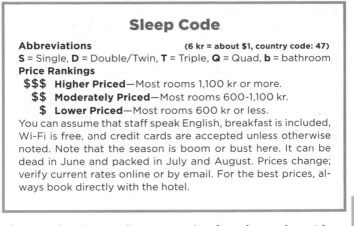

Sleep Code

Abbreviations   **(6 kr = about $1, country code: 47)**
S = Single, **D** = Double/Twin, **T** = Triple, **Q** = Quad, **b** = bathroom
Price Rankings
  $$$ **Higher Priced**—Most rooms 1,100 kr or more.
    $$ **Moderately Priced**—Most rooms 600-1,100 kr.
     $ **Lower Priced**—Most rooms 600 kr or less.
You can assume that staff speak English, breakfast is included, Wi-Fi is free, and credit cards are accepted unless otherwise noted. Note that the season is boom or bust here. It can be dead in June and packed in July and August. Prices change; verify current rates online or by email. For the best prices, always book directly with the hotel.

NORWAY IN A NUTSHELL

afternoon (170-kr round-trip, get ticket from driver, about 1 hour each way with about 1 hour at the church, bus runs daily May-Sept, tell driver you want to get off at the church).

Sleeping in Flåm

My recommended accommodations are away from the tacky train-station bustle, but a close enough walk to be convenient. The first two places are located along the waterfront a quarter-mile from the station: Walk around the little harbor (with the water on your left) for about 10 minutes. It's more enjoyable to follow the level, waterfront dock than to hike up the main road.

$$$ Flåm Marina and Apartments, perched right on the fjord, is ideal for families and longer stays. They offer 10 new-feeling, self-catering apartments that each sleep 2-5 people. All units offer views of the fjord with a balcony, kitchenette, and small dining area (Db-1,198 kr May-mid-Sept, less off season, 450 kr more for each additional adult, check online or ask about specials for longer stays, no breakfast, café open during high season, boat rental, laundry facilities, next to the guest harbor just below Heimly Pensjonat—see next listing, tel. 57 63 35 55, www.flammarina.no, booking@flammarina.no).

$$ Heimly Pensjonat, with 22 straightforward rooms, is clean, efficient, and the best small hotel in town. Sit on the porch with new friends and watch the clouds roll down the fjord (Sb-895 kr, Db-1,095 kr, view Db costs 100 kr more in summer, extra bed-395 kr for adult or 295 kr for child, cheaper Oct-May, Db rooms are mostly twins, try to reserve a room with a view at the standard price, car rental, tel. 57 63 23 00, www.heimly.no, post@heimly.no).

$-$$ Flåm Youth Hostel and Camping Bungalows, voted

Scandinavia's most beautiful campground, is run by the friendly Håland family, who rent the cheapest beds in the area (hostel: bunk in 4-bed room-240 kr, S-390 kr, D-620-650 kr; newer, fancier building: bunk in 4-bed room-260-315 kr, Db-800-865 kr; hostel prices include sheets and towels; cabins-700-1,300 kr; sheets and towels-50 kr, showers-10 kr, 10 percent discount for members, no meals but kitchen access, laundry, apple grove, tel. 57 63 21 21, www.flaam-camping.no, camping@flaam-camping.no). It's a five-minute walk toward the valley from the train station: Cross the bridge and turn left up the main road; then look for the hostel on the right.

Eating in Flåm

Dining options beyond your hotel's dining room or kitchenette are expensive and touristy. Don't aim for high cuisine here—go practical. Almost all eateries are clustered near the train station complex. Hours can be unpredictable, flexing with the season, but you can expect these to be open daily in high season. Places here tend to close pretty early (especially in shoulder season)—don't wait too long for dinner.

The **Flåmsbrygga** complex, sprawling through a long building toward the fjord from the station, includes a hotel, the affordable **Furukroa Caféteria** (daily 8:00-20:00 in season, cafeteria with 50-65-kr cold sandwiches, 100-150-kr fast-food meals, and 200-225-kr pizzas), and the pricey **Flåmstova Restaurant** (235-kr lunch buffet, 325-kr dinner buffet, plus other menu options at dinner). Next door is their fun, Viking-longhouse-shaped brewpub, **Ægir Bryggeri** (daily 17:00-22:00, local microbrews, 200-300-kr Viking-inspired meals). **Toget Café,** with seating in old train cars, prides itself on using as many locally sourced and organic ingredients as possible (65-75-kr sandwiches, 160-195-kr main dishes). **Bakkastova Kafe,** at the other end of town, feels cozier; it's in a traditional Norwegian red cabin just above the Fretheim Hotel, with a view terrace, and serves sandwiches, salads, and authentic Norwegian fare (daily 10:00-18:00).

Aurland

A few miles north of Flåm, Aurland is more of a real town and less of a tourist depot. While it's nothing exciting (Balestrand is more lively and appealing, and Solvorn is cuter—see next chapter), it's a good, easygoing fjordside home base. And thanks to its lo-

cation—on the main road and boat lines, near Flåm—it's relatively handy for those taking public transportation.

Getting There: Aurland is an easy 10-minute drive or bus trip from Flåm. If you want to stay overnight in Aurland, note that every train (except the late-night one) arriving in Flåm connects with a bus or boat to Aurland. Eleven buses and at least four ferries link the towns daily in summer (bus-40 kr, 10 minutes; boat-100 kr, 20 minutes). The Flåm-Gudvangen boat doesn't always have a scheduled stop at Aurland, but they're willing to stop there if you ask—so it's possible to continue the Nutshell route from Aurland without backtracking to Flåm. Boat tickets bought at the Aurland TI come with a reservation (helpful on the busiest days in July and August, when the boats can fill up in Flåm). The Bergen-Balestrand-Flåm express boat stops in Aurland.

Orientation to Aurland

From Aurland's dingy boat dock area, walk one block up the paved street into the heart of town. On your right are the Matkroken and Spar supermarkets (handy for picnic supplies) and Marianne Bakeri and Café (at the bridge). To your left is the Vangsgården Guest House and, behind it, Aurland Fjordhotel. To reach the TI, go straight ahead and bear right, then look behind the white church (800 years old and worth a peek). The bus stop, with buses to Flåm, is in front of the TI.

TOURIST INFORMATION

The TI stocks English-language brochures about hikes and day trips from the area, offers free Internet terminals, and hosts a small history exhibit (June-Aug Mon-Fri 9:00-17:00, Sat-Sun 10:30-17:00, Sept-May Mon-Fri 9:00-16:00, closed Sat-Sun; behind the white church—look for green-and-white *i* sign; tel. 57 63 33 13, www.alr.no).

Sleeping in Aurland

$$$ Aurland Fjordhotel is big, modern, and centrally located. While it has a business-hotel vibe, most of its 30 rooms come with gorgeous fjord-view balconies (Sb-995 kr, Db-1,490 kr, Tb-1,580, prices lower off-season, check website for deals, Wi-Fi, tel. 57 63

NORWAY IN A NUTSHELL

35 05, www.aurland-fjordhotel.com, post@aurland-fjordhotel.com, Steinar Kjerstein).

$$$ Vangsgården Guest House, closest to the boat landing, is a complex of old buildings dominating the old center of Aurland and run from one reception desk (Wi-Fi in main building, tel. 57 63 35 80, www.vangsgaarden.no, vangsgaarden@alb.no, open all year, Astrid). The main building is a simple, old guesthouse offering basic rooms and a fine old-timey living room (Sb-830 kr, Db-1,250 kr). Their old-fashioned **Aabelheim Pension** is Aurland's best *koselig* (cozy)-like-a-farmhouse place (same prices). And lining the waterfront are their six adorable wood cabins, each with a kitchen, bathroom, and two bedrooms (1,250 kr for 2-6 people, sheets-65 kr/person, book 2 months in advance). The owners also run the Duehuset Pub (see "Eating in Aurland," below) and rent bikes for 200 kr/day.

NEAR AURLAND

$$ Skahjem Gard is an active farm run by Aurland's former deputy mayor, Nils Tore. He's converted his old sheep barn into seven spic-and-span family apartments with private bathrooms and kitchenettes, each sleeping up to four people (750-800 kr for studio, 900 kr with separate bedroom; sheets and towels-60 kr/person, Wi-Fi, two miles up the valley—road #50, follow *Hol* signs, tel. 57 63 33 29, mobile 95 17 25 67, www.skahjemgard.com, nskahjem@online.no). It's a 25-minute walk from town, but Nils will pick up and drop off travelers at the ferry. This is best for families and foursomes with cars.

$ Winjum Huts, about a half-mile from Aurland's dock, rents 14 basic cabins on a peaceful perch overlooking the majestic fjord. The washhouse/kitchen is where you'll find the toilets and showers. Follow the road uphill past the Aurland Fjordhotel; the huts are after the first hairpin curve (450-500 kr for up to 4 people, 2-bed apartment-900-1,200 kr, sheets-50 kr/person, showers-10 kr/5 minutes, no food available—just beer, tel. 57 63 34 61, mobile 41 47 47 51).

Eating in Aurland

Marianne Bakeri and Café is a basic little bakery/café serving the best-value food in town. It's a block from the main square, at the bridge over the river. Sit inside or on its riverside terrace (55-95-kr sandwiches, 155-kr pizza, 165-kr quiche, daily 10:00-17:00, tel. 57 63 36 66).

Duehuset Pub ("The Dove's House"), run by Vangsgården Guest House, serves up decent food in the center of town (190-240-kr pizzas big enough for four, 160-240-kr main dishes; June-

Sept daily 15:00-23:00; Oct-May Fri-Sun 18:00-23:00, closed Mon-Thu).

The **Aurland Fjordhotel** is your only alternative for splurges (200-kr main dishes, 70-kr starters, 250-300-kr dinner buffet, daily 19:00-22:00, shorter hours off-season, bar open later, tel. 57 63 35 05).

For cheap eats on dockside benches, gather a picnic at the **Spar** or **Matkroken** supermarkets (both open Mon-Fri 9:00-20:00, Sat 9:00-18:00, closed Sun).

Undredal

This almost impossibly remote community is home to about 80 people and 400 goats. A huge percentage of the town's former population (300 people) emigrated to the US between 1850 and 1925. Undredal was accessible only by boat until 1988, when the road from Flåm opened. There's not much in the town, which is famous for its church and its goat cheese, but I'll never forget the picnic I had on the ferry wharf. While appeal-

ing, Undredal is quiet (some say better from the boat) and difficult to reach—you'll have to be patient to connect to other towns. For more information on the town, see www.undredal.no.

Undredal has Norway's smallest still-used **church,** seating 40 people for services every fourth Sunday. The original church was built in 1147 (look for the four original stave pillars inside). It was later expanded, pews added, and the interior painted in the 16th century in a way that resembles the traditional Norwegian *rosemaling* style (which came later). You can get in only with a 30-minute tour (60 kr, June-mid-Aug daily 10:00-17:00, less in shoulder season, closed Oct-April, tel. 95 29 76 68).

Undredal's farms exist to produce cheese. The beloved local cheese comes in two versions: brown and white. The brown version is unaged and slightly sweet, while the white cheese has been aged and is mild and a bit salty. For samples, visit the Undredalsbui grocery store at the harbor (Mon-Sat 9:00-17:00, Sun 12:00-16:00, shorter hours and closed Sun off-season).

The 15-minute drive from Flåm is mostly through a tunnel. By sea, you'll sail past Undredal on the Flåm-Gudvangen boat (you can request a stop). To get the ferry to pick you up in Undredal, turn on the blinking light (though some express boats will not stop).

This sleepy town can accommodate maybe a dozen visitors a night. **$$ Undredal Overnatting** rents four modern, woody, comfortable rooms and two apartments. The reception is at the café on the harbor, while the accommodations are at the top of town (Db-795 kr, D-645-695 kr in guesthouse with shared kitchen, apartments start at 1,290 kr, includes sheets, breakfast-110 kr, tel. 57 63 30 80 or 57 63 31 00, www.visitundredal.no, visit@undredal.no).

MORE ON THE SOGNEFJORD

Balestrand • The Lustrafjord • Scenic Drives

Norway's world of fjords is decorated with medieval stave churches, fishing boats, cascading waterfalls, dramatic glaciers, and brightly painted shiplap villages. Travelers in a hurry zip through the fjords on the Norway in a Nutshell route (see previous chapter). Their heads spin from all the scenery, and most wish they had more time on the Sognefjord. If you can linger in fjord country, this chapter is for you.

Snuggle into the fjordside village of Balestrand, which has a variety of walking and biking options and a fun local arts scene. Balestrand is also a handy jumping-off spot for adventures great and small, including a day trip up the Fjærlandsfjord to gaze at a receding tongue of the Jostedal Glacier, or across the Sognefjord to the truly medieval-feeling Hopperstad Stave Church. Farther east is the Lustrafjord, a tranquil branch of the Sognefjord offering drivers an appealing concentration of visit-worthy sights. On the Lustrafjord, you'll enjoy enchanting hamlets with pristine fjord views (such as Solvorn), historic churches (including Norway's oldest stave church at Urnes and the humble village Dale Church in Luster), an opportunity to touch and even hike on a glacier (the Nigard), and more stunning fjord views.

This region is important to the people of Norway. After four centuries under Danish rule, the soul of the country was nearly lost. With semi-independence and its own constitution in the early 1800s, the country experienced a resurgence of national pride. Urban Norwegians headed for the fjord country here in the west. Norway's first Romantic painters and writers were drawn to Balestrand, inspired by the unusual light and dramatic views of mountains plunging into the fjords. The Sognefjord, with its many

Sognefjord Overview

MORE SOGNEFJORD

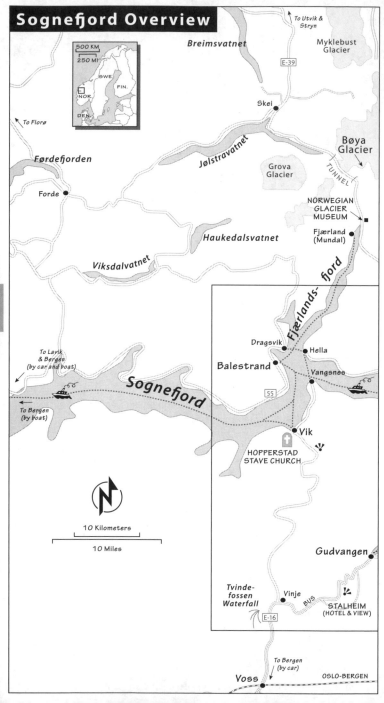

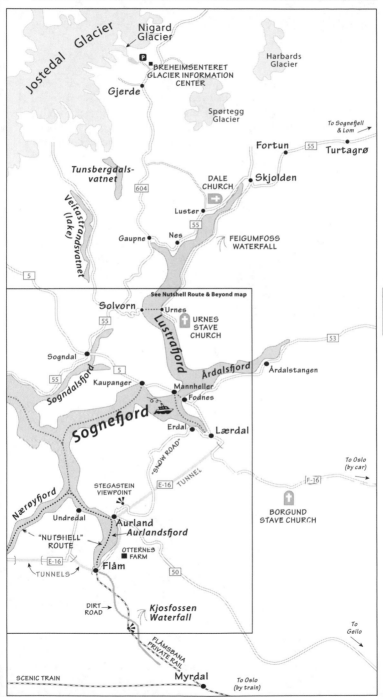

branches, is featured in more Romantic paintings than any other fjord.

PLANNING YOUR TIME

If you can spare a day or two off the Norway in a Nutshell route, spend it here. Balestrand is the best home base, especially if you're

relying on public transportation (it's well-connected by express boat both to the Nutshell scene and to Bergen). If you have a car, consider staying in the heart of the Lustrafjord region in sweet little Solvorn (easy ferry connection to the Urnes Stave Church and a short drive to the Nigard Glacier). As fjord home bases go, Balestrand and Solvorn are both better—but less convenient—than Flåm or Aurland on the Nutshell route (see previous chapter).

With one night in this area, you'll have to blitz the sights on the way between destinations; with two nights, you can slow your pace (and your pulse) to enjoy the fjord scenery and plenty of day-trip possibilities.

Balestrand

The pleasant fjord town of Balestrand (pop. 2,000) has a long history of hosting tourists, thanks to its landmark Kviknes Hotel. But it also feels real and lived-in, making Balestrand a nice mix of cuteness and convenience. The town

is near, but not *too* near, the Nutshell bustle is across the fjord—and yet it's an easy express-boat trip away if you'd like to dive into the Nuttiness. In short, consider Balestrand a worthwhile detour from the typical fjord visit—allowing you to dig deeper into the Sognefjord, just like the glaciers did during the last ice age.

With two nights, you can relax and consider some day trips: Cruise up the nearby Fjærlandsfjord for a peek at a distant tongue of the ever-less-mighty Jostedal Glacier, or head across the Sognefjord to the beautiful Hopperstad Stave Church in Vik. Balestrand also has outdoor activities for everyone, from dreamy fjordside strolls and strenuous mountain hikes to wildly scenic bike rides. For dinner, splurge on the memorable *smörgåsbord*-style *store koldt bord* dinner in the Kviknes Hotel dining room, then sip coffee from its balcony as you watch the sun set (or not) over the fjord.

PLANNING YOUR TIME

Balestrand's key advantage is its easy express-boat connection to Bergen, offering an alternative route to the fjord from the typical Nutshell train-bus combo. Consider zipping here on the Bergen boat, then continuing on via the Nutshell route.

One night is enough to get a taste of Balestrand. But two nights buy you some time for day trips. Note that the first flurry of day trips departs early, around 7:30-8:05 (includes the boat to Vik/Hopperstad Stave Church or the full-day Fjærlandsfjord glacier excursion), and the next batch departs around noon (the half-day Fjærlandsfjord glacier excursion and the boat to Flåm). If you wait until after 12:00 to make your choice, you'll miss the boat...literally.

Balestrand pretty much shuts down from mid-September through mid-May—when most of the activities, sights, hotels, and restaurants listed here likely are closed.

Orientation to Balestrand

Most travelers arrive in Balestrand on the express boat from Bergen or Flåm. The tidy harbor area has a TI, two grocery stores, a couple of galleries, a town history museum, and a small aquarium devoted to marine life found in the fjord. The historic wooden Kviknes Hotel and its ugly modern annex dominate Balestrand's waterfront.

Even during tourist season, Balestrand is quiet. How quiet? The police station closes on weekends. And it's tiny—from the harbor to the Balestrand Hotel is a five-minute stroll, and you can walk from the aquarium to Kviknes Hotel in less time than that.

Balestrand became accessible to the wider world in 1858 when an activist minister (from the church you see across the fjord from town) brought in the first steamer service. That put Balestrand on the Grand Tour map of the Romantic Age. Even the German *Kaiser* chose to summer here. Today, people from around the world come here to feel the grandeur of the fjord country and connect with the essence of Norway.

TOURIST INFORMATION

At the TI, located next to the Joker supermarket at the harbor, pick up the free, helpful *Outdoor Activities in Balestrand* brochure.

MORE SOGNEFJORD

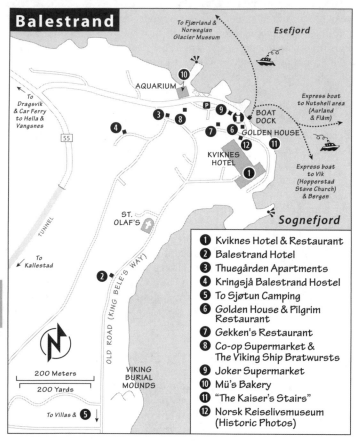

Balestrand

To Fjærland &
Norwegian
Glacier Museum

Esefjord

AQUARIUM

To
Dragsvik
& Car Ferry
to Hella &
Vangsnes

55

Express boat
to Nutshell area
(Aurland
& Flåm)

BOAT
DOCK

GOLDEN HOUSE

KVIKNES
HOTEL

Express boat
to Vik
(Hopperstad
Stave Church)
& Bergen

ST.
OLAF'S

Sognefjord

To
Kallestad

TUNNEL

OLD ROAD (KING BELE'S WAY)

N

200 Meters

200 Yards

VIKING
BURIAL
MOUNDS

To Villas & ❺

MORE SOGNEFJORD

❶ Kviknes Hotel & Restaurant
❷ Balestrand Hotel
❸ Thuegården Apartments
❹ Kringsjå Balestrand Hostel
❺ To Sjøtun Camping
❻ Golden House & Pilgrim
   Restaurant
❼ Gekken's Restaurant
❽ Co-op Supermarket &
   The Viking Ship Bratwursts
❾ Joker Supermarket
❿ Mü's Bakery
⓫ "The Kaiser's Stairs"
⓬ Norsk Reiselivsmuseum
   (Historic Photos)

If you're planning on a longer hike, consider buying the good 70-kr hiking map. The TI has numerous brochures about the Sognefjord area and detailed information on the more challenging hikes. It offers terminals with Internet access (1 kr/minute) and pay Wi-Fi, rents bikes (70 kr/hour, 270 kr/day), sells day-trip excursions to the glacier, and more (late June-late Aug Mon-Fri 9:00-17:30, Sat-Sun 10:00-17:30, shorter hours in spring and fall, closed Oct-April, tel. 57 69 12 55—answered all year).

Local Guide: Bjørg Bjøberg, who runs the Golden House (Det Gylne Hus) art gallery, knows the town well and is happy to show visitors around (1,000-1,500 kr/2 hours per group—gather several people and divvy up the cost, mobile 91 56 28 42).

Car Rental: The **Balholm Car Rental** agency will deliver a car to your Balestrand hotel, and they'll pick it up, too (daily 8:00-20:00, tel. 41 24 82 53, www.rentacarbalholm.com, post@

rentacarbalholm.com). Also, the Kviknes Hotel can arrange a one-day car rental for you (tel. 57 69 42 00).

Sights in Balestrand

Balestrand Harborfront Stroll

The tiny harbor stretches from the aquarium to the big, old Kviknes Hotel. Stroll its length, starting at the aquarium (described later) and little marina. Across the street, at The Viking Ship shack, a German woman named Carola sells German sausages with an evangelical zeal (see "Eating in Balestrand," later). A couple of doors down, the Spindelvev ("Spider's Web") shop sells handicrafts made by people with physical and mental disabilities. A local home for the disabled was closed in the 1980s, but many of its former residents stayed in Balestrand because the government gave them pensions and houses in town.

Then, in the ugly modern strip mall, you'll find the TI, supermarket, and a community bulletin board with the schedule for the summer cinema (the little theater, 800 yards away, runs films nightly in their original language). On the corner is the Golden House art gallery and museum (described later). Behind it—and built into solid rock—is the boxy new moss-covered home of the Norwegian Travel Museum (Norsk Reiselivsmuseum), featuring photos showing this part of Norway over the past 150 years, interactive exhibits, and souvenirs. And just beyond that is the dock where the big Bergen-Sognefjord express catamaran ties up.

Across the street is a cute white house (at #8), which used to stand at the harborfront until the big Joker supermarket and Kviknes Hotel, with its modern annex, partnered to ruin the town center. This little house was considered historic enough to be air-lifted 100 yards to this new spot. It's flanked by two other historic buildings, which house a gallery and an artisans' workshop.

Farther along, find the rust-red building that was the waiting room for the 19th-century steamer that first brought tourism to town. Walk a few steps farther, and stop at the tall stone monument erected to celebrate the North Bergen Steamship Company. Its boats first connected Balestrand to the rest of the world in 1858. In front of the monument, some nondescript concrete steps lead into the water. These are "The Kaiser's Stairs," built for the German emperor, Kaiser Wilhelm II, who made his first summer visit (complete with navy convoy) in 1899 and kept returning until the outbreak of World War I.

Behind the monument stands one of the largest old wooden buildings in Norway, Kviknes Hotel. It was built in the 1870s and faces the rare little island in the fjord, which helped give the town its name: "Balestrand" means the strand or promenade in front of an island. (The island is now connected to the hotel's front yard and is part of a playground for its guests.) Hike up the black driveway that leads from the monument to the hotel's modern lobby. Go inside and find (to your left) the plush old lounge, a virtual painting gallery. All the pieces are by artists from this area, celebrating the natural wonder of the fjord country—part of the trend that helped 19th-century Norway reconnect with its heritage. (While you're here, consider making a reservation and choosing a table for a *smörgåsbord* dinner tonight.) Leave the hotel lobby (from the door opposite to the one you entered), and head up to St. Olaf's Church (300 yards, described next). To continue this stroll, take King Bele's Way (described later) up the fjord.

St. Olaf's Church

This distinctive wooden church was built in 1897. Construction was started by Margaret Sophia Kvikne, the wife of Knut Kvikne

(of the Kviknes Hotel family; her portrait is in the rear of the nave), but she died in 1894, before the church was finished. This devout Englishwoman wanted a church in Balestrand where English services were held...and to this day, bells ring to announce services by British clergy. St. Olaf, who brought Christianity to Norway in the 11th century, was the country's patron saint in Catholic times. The church was built in a "Neo-stave" style, with lots of light from its windows and an altar painting inspired by the famous *Risen Christ* statue in Copenhagen's Cathedral of Our Lady. Here, Christ is flanked by fields of daisies (called "priests' collars" in Norwegian) and peace lilies. From the door of the church, enjoy a good view of the island in the fjord.

Cost and Hours: Free, open daily, services in English every Sun from late May through August.

Golden House (Det Gylne Hus)

This golden-colored house facing the ferry landing was built as a general store in 1928. Today it houses an art installation called "Golden Memories" and a quirky museum created by local watercolorist and historian Bjørg Bjøberg, and her husband, Arthur Adamson.

On the ground floor, you'll find Bjørg's gallery, with her watercolors celebrating the beauty of Norway, and Arthur's paintings, celebrating the beauty of women. Upstairs is the Pilgrimage Balestrand room, focusing on their local nature pilgrimage program, along with a free exhibit of historical knickknacks, contributed by locals wanting to preserve treasures from their families' past. You'll see a medicine cabinet stocked with old-fashioned pills, an antiquated tourist map, lots of skis, and WWII-era mementos. A wheel in the wall once powered a crane that could winch up goods from the fjord below (back when this store was actually on the waterfront). While there are no written English explanations, Bjørg is happy to explain things.

Unable to contain her creative spirit, Bjørg has paired an eccentric wonderland experience with her private tour of the Golden House's hidden rooms. The tour includes a 30-minute movie (at 17:00 and 18:00), either about her art and local nature, or about Balestrand in winter. Bjørg and Arthur also run the recommended on-site restaurant, Pilgrim. Diners have free access to the glass dome on top of the building, with a telescope and lovely views.

Cost and Hours: Free entry; optional private one-hour tour-50/kr person, 100-kr minimum, 200-kr maximum; May-Aug daily 10:00-22:00, shorter hours late April and Sept, mobile 91 56 28 42, www.detgylnehus.no.

Strolling King Bele's Way up the Fjord

For a delightful walk (or bike ride), head west out of town up the "old road"—once the main road from the harbor—for about a mile. It follows the fjord's edge, passing numerous "villas" from the late 1800s. At the time, this Swiss style was popular with some locals, who hoped to introduce a dose of Romanticism into Norwegian architecture. Look for the dragons' heads (copied from Viking-age stave churches) decorating the gables. Along the walk, you'll pass a swimming area, a campground, and two burial mounds from the Viking age, marked by a ponderous statue of the Viking King Bele. Check out the wooden shelters for the mailboxes; some give the elevation (*m.o.h.* stands for "meters over *havet*"—the sea)—not too high, are they? The walk is described in the *Outdoor Activities in Balestrand* brochure (free at the TI or your hotel).

Aquarium

The tiny aquarium gives you a good look at marine life in the Sognefjord. For descriptions, borrow the English booklet at the front desk. While not thrilling, the well-explained place is a decent rainy-day option. A 15-minute slide show starts at the top and bottom of each hour. The last room is filled with wood carvings depicting traditional everyday life in the fjordside village of Munken. The fish-filled tanks on the dock outside are also worth a look.

Cost and Hours: 70 kr, May-Aug daily 9:00-19:00, closed Sept-April, tel. 57 69 13 03.

Biking
You can cycle around town, or go farther by circling the scenic Esefjord (north of town, en route to the ferry landing at Drags-vik—about 6 miles each way). Or pedal west up Sognefjord along the scenic King Bele's Way (described above). The roads here are relatively flat. Rental bikes are available at the TI and through Kviknes Hotel.

NEAR BALESTRAND
These two side-trips are possible only if you've got the better part of a day in Balestrand. With a car, you can see Hopperstad Stave Church on the drive to Bergen.

▲▲Hopperstad Stave Church (Hopperstad Stavkyrkje) in Vik
The most accessible stave church in the area—and perhaps the most scenically situated in all Norway—is located just a 15-minute express-boat ride across the Sognefjord,  in the town of Vik. Hopperstad Stave Church boasts a breathtaking exterior, with several tiers of dragon heads overlooking rolling fields between fjord cliffs. The interior is notable for its emptiness. Instead of being crammed full of later additions, the church is blissfully unclut-tered, as it was when it was built in the mid-12th century.

Cost and Hours: 60 kr, good 30-kr color booklet in English, daily mid-May-mid-Sept 10:00-17:00, mid-June-mid-Aug opens at 9:00, closed mid-Sept-mid-May, tel. 57 69 52 70, www.stavechurch.com.

Tours: The attendant will give you a free tour at your request, provided she's not too busy. (Ask where the medieval graffiti is, and she'll grab her flashlight and show you.)

Location: The church is a 20-minute walk up the valley from Vik's harbor. From the boat landing, walk up the main street from the harbor about 200 yards (past the TI, a grocery store, and hotel). Take a right at the sign for *Hopperstad Stavkyrkje*, walk 10 minutes, and you'll see the church perched on a small hill in the distance.

Getting There: Pedestrians can ride the express passenger boat between Balestrand and Vik (78 kr each way, 15 minutes). The only way to get to the church and back in one day (only possible Mon-Sat) is to take the 7:50 departure from Balestrand, then re-turn on the 11:30 departure from Vik, arriving back in Balestrand at 11:50—just in time to join a 12:00 glacier excursion (described next). Because schedules can change, be sure to double-check these times at the TI or www.norled.no. Since cars can't go on this express boat, **drivers** must go around the small Esefjord to the town of Dragsvik, then catch the ferry across the Sognefjord to Vangsnes (a 20-minute drive from Vik and the church).

Visiting the Church: Originally built around 1140 and retaining most of its original wood, Hopperstad was thoroughly restored and taken back to basics in the 1880s by renowned archi-

tect Peter Blix. Unlike the famous stave church at Urnes (described later), whose interior has been rejiggered by centuries of engineers and filled with altars and pews, the Hopperstad church looks close to the way it did when it was built. You'll see only a few non-original features, including the beautifully painted canopy that once covered a side altar (probably dating from around 1300), and a tombstone from 1738. There are only a few colorful illustrations and some very scant medieval "graffiti" carvings and runic inscriptions. Notice the intact chancel screen (the only one surviving in Norway), which separates the altar area from the congregation. As with the iconostasis (panel of icons) in today's Orthodox faith, this screen gave priests privacy to do the spiritual heavy lifting. Because Hopperstad's interior lacks the typical adornments, you can really grasp the fundamentally vertical nature of stave church architecture, leading your gaze to the heavens. Follow that impulse and look up to appreciate the Viking-ship rafters. Imagine the comfort this ceiling brought the church's original parishioners, whose seafaring ancestors had once sought refuge under overturned boats. For a unique angle on this graceful structure, lay your camera on the floor and shoot the ceiling.

▲Excursion to Fjærland and the Jostedal Glacier

From Balestrand, cruise up the Fjærlandsfjord to visit the Norwegian Glacier Museum in Fjærland and to see a receding tongue of the Jostedal Glacier (Jostedalbreen). Half-day and full-day (685 kr for either tour) excursions are sold by Balestrand's TI or onboard the boat. Reservations are smart (tours offered daily June-Aug only, tel. 57 63 32 00, www.visitflam.com/sognefjorden and follow links for "Fjærlandsfjord").

While the museum and the glacier's tongue are underwhelming, it's a pleasant excursion with a dreamy fjord cruise (80 minutes each way). To take the all-day trip, catch the 8:05 ferry; for the shorter trip, hop on the 11:55 boat. They both return on the same boat, getting you back in Balestrand at 16:50 (in time to catch the fast boat back to Bergen). Both tours offer the same fjord ride, museum visit, and trip to the glacier. The all-day version, however, gives you a second glacier viewing point and 2.5 hours to hang out in the town of Fjærland. (This sleepy village, famous for its secondhand book shops, is about as exciting as Walter Mondale, the US vice president whose ancestors came from here.)

The ferry ride (no stops, no narration) is just a scenic glide with the gulls. Bring a picnic, as there's almost no food sold onboard, and some bread to toss to the gulls (they do acrobatics to catch whatever you loft into the air). You'll be met at the ferry dock (labeled *Mundal*) by a bus—and your guide, who reads a script about the glacier as you drive up the valley for about 15 minutes. You'll stop for an hour at the **Norwegian Glacier Museum** (Norsk Bremuseum). After watching an 18-minute aerial tour of the dramatic Jostedal Glacier in the theater, you'll learn how glaciers were formed, experiment with your own hunk of glacier, weigh evidence of the woolly mammoth's existence in Norway, and learn about the effect of global climate change on the fjords (way overpriced at 120 kr, included in excursion price, daily June-Aug 9:00-19:00, April-May and Sept-Oct 10:00-16:00, closed Nov-March, tel. 57 69 32 88, www.bre.museum.no). From the museum, the bus runs you up to a café near a lake, at a spot that gives you a good look at the Bøyabreen, a tongue of the Jostedal Glacier. Marvel at how far the glacier has retreated—10 years ago, the visit was more dramatic. With global warming, glacier excursions like this become more sad than majestic. I wonder how long they'll even be able to bill this as a "glacier visit."

Considering that the fjord trip is the highlight of this journey, you could save time and money by just riding the ferry up and back (8:05-11:30). At 390 kr for the round-trip boat ride, it's much cheaper than the 685-kr tour.

Note that if you're into glaciers, a nearby arm of the Jostedal, called the **Nigard Glacier,** is a more dramatic and boots-on experience. It's easy for drivers to reach.

Sleeping in Balestrand

$$$ Kviknes Hotel is the classy grande dame of Balestrand, dominating the town and packed with tour groups. The picturesque wooden hotel—and five generations of the Kvikne family—have welcomed tourists to Balestrand since the late 19th century. The hotel has two parts: a new wing, and the historic wooden section, with 25 older, classic rooms, and no elevator. All rooms come with balconies. The elegant Old World public spaces in the old section make you want to just sit there and sip tea all afternoon (Db-1,720

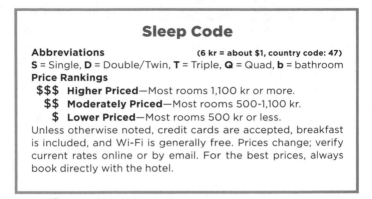

Sleep Code

Abbreviations **(6 kr = about $1, country code: 47)**
S = Single, **D** = Double/Twin, **T** = Triple, **Q** = Quad, **b** = bathroom
Price Rankings
  $$$ **Higher Priced**—Most rooms 1,100 kr or more.
   $$ **Moderately Priced**—Most rooms 500-1,100 kr.
    $ **Lower Priced**—Most rooms 500 kr or less.
Unless otherwise noted, credit cards are accepted, breakfast is included, and Wi-Fi is generally free. Prices change; verify current rates online or by email. For the best prices, always book directly with the hotel.

kr in new building, about 350 kr more with view, Db-2,270 kr in old building, non-smoking, Wi-Fi, family rooms available, closed Oct-April, tel. 57 69 42 00, www.kviknes.no, booking@kviknes.no).  Part of the Kviknes ritual is gorging on the *store koldt bord* buffet dinner—open to non-guests, and a nice way to soak in the hotel's old-time elegance without splurging on an overnight (see "Eating in Balestrand," later; cheaper if you stay at the hotel for 2 or more nights).

$$ Balestrand Hotel, family-run by Unni-Marie Kvikne, her California-born husband Eric Palmer, and their three children, is your best fjordside home. Open mid-May through early September, this cozy, welcoming place has 30 well-appointed, comfortable, quiet rooms; a large, modern common area with lots of English paperbacks; laundry service, Wi-Fi, balconies (in some rooms), and outdoor benches for soaking in the scenery. The waterfront yard has inviting lounge chairs and a mesmerizing view. When reserving, let them know your arrival time, and they'll pick you up at the harborfront (non-view Sb-750 kr, view Sb-890 kr, non-view Db-1,090 kr, view Db-1,390 kr, 5-minute walk from dock, past St. Olaf's Church—or free pick-up, tel. 57 69 11 38, www.balestrand.com, info@balestrand.com).

$$ Thuegården offers five clean, bright, modern doubles with mini-kitchens, conveniently located near the ferry dock and just up the street from the Co-op grocery store. Some rooms have balconies and some come with a fjord view (Db-850-950 kr, discount if staying more than 3 nights, no breakfast, Wi-Fi, office inside ground-floor hair salon, tel. 57 69 15 95, mobile 97 19 92 63, www.thuegaarden.com, thuegaarden@gmail.com).

$-$$ Kringsjå Balestrand Hostel, a camp school for sixth-graders, rents beds and rooms to budget travelers from mid-June to mid-August. Three-quarters of their 58 beds are in doubles. All the rooms have private bathrooms and most have view balconies (bunk in 4-bed dorm-295 kr, Sb-690 kr, Db-890-990 kr, Qb-1,090 kr, extra bed-120 kr, discount for hostel members, includes sheets and towels, game room, Wi-Fi, tel. 57 69 13 03, www.kringsja.no, kringsja@kringsja.no).

$ Sjøtun Camping rents the cheapest beds around, in rustic huts (4-person hut-300 kr, sheets-60 kr/person, no breakfast, a mile west of town, mobile 95 06 72 61, www.sjotun.com, camping@ sjotun.com).

Eating in Balestrand

Balestrand's dining options are limited, but good.

Kviknes Hotel offers a splendid, spendy *store koldt bord* buffet dinner in a massive yet stately old dining room. For a memorable fjordside *smörgåsbord* experience, it doesn't get any better than this. Don't rush. Consider taking a preview tour—surveying the reindeer meat, lingonberries, and fjord-caught seafood—before you dive in, so you can budget your stomach space. Get a new plate with each course and save room for dessert. Each dish is labeled in English (545 kr/person, May-Sept daily 19:00-21:00, closed Oct-April). They also  offer a four-course, locally sourced dinner for 645 kr. After dinner, head into the rich lounge to pick up your cup of coffee or tea (included), which you'll sip sitting on classy old-fashioned furniture and basking in fjord views.

Pilgrim, inside the Golden House at the harbor, dishes up Norwegian home cooking and a variety of salads. Sit outside or inside, in a dining area built to resemble a traditional Norwegian kitchen. The restaurant upstairs shows off part of owner Bjørg's antique collection. They serve 100-130-kr lunches and pricier meals for dinner, such as 150-220-kr meat and fish dishes (May-Sept Mon-Sat 13:00-21:00, Sun 16:00-21:00, closed Oct-April, mobile 91 56 28 42).

Gekken's is an informal summer restaurant serving good-value meat, fish, and vegetarian dishes, along with burgers, fish-and-chips, and other fried fare. Sit in the simply decorated interior, or out on the shaded little terrace. Geir Arne "Gekken" Bale can trace his family's roots back 400 years in Balestrand. He has filled his walls with fascinating historic photos and paintings, making his dining hall an art gallery of sorts (light dishes-60-100 kr, daily dinner plates-100-200 kr, May-Aug daily 12:00-22:00, closed Sept-April, above and behind the TI from the harbor, tel. 57 69 14 14).

The Viking Ship, the hot-dog stand facing the harbor, is proudly run by Carola. A bratwurst missionary from Germany, she claims it took her years to get Norwegians to accept the tastier bratwurst over their beloved *pølser* weenies. Eat at her picnic tables or across the street on the harbor park (fine sausages, fish-and-chips, May-Sept daily 11:00-20:00, closed Oct-April).

Picnic: The delightful waterfront park next to the aquarium has benches and million-dollar fjord views. The Co-op and Joker **supermarkets** at the harbor have basic grocery supplies, including bread, meats, cheeses, and drinks; the Co-op is bigger and has a wider selection (Co-op open Mon-Fri 8:00-20:00, Sat 8:00-18:00; Joker open Mon-Fri 9:00-18:00—until 20:00 in summer, Sat 9:00-15:00; both closed Sun). **Mü's Bakery** offers a healthy assortment of sandwiches and fresh-baked goodies (Mon-Sat 9:30-18:00, Sun 9:30-15:00, closed mid-Sept-early May, just inside the aquarium entrance).

Balestrand Connections

Because Balestrand is separated from the Lustrafjord by the long Fjærlandsfjord, most Balestrand connections involve a boat trip.

BY EXPRESS PASSENGER BOAT

The easiest way to reach Balestrand is on the handy express boat, which connects to **Bergen, Vik** (near Hopperstad Stave Church), **Aurland,** and **Flåm** (see sidebar on next page for schedules). Note that you can also use this boat to join the Nutshell trip in Flåm. From here, continue on the Nutshell boat down the Nærøyfjord to Gudvangen, where you'll join the crowd onward to Voss, then Bergen or Oslo. As you're making schedule and sightseeing decisions, consider that the Balestrand-Flåm boat skips the Nærøyfjord, the most dramatic arm of the Sognefjord.

BY CAR FERRY

Balestrand's main car-ferry dock is at the village of **Dragsvik,** a six-mile, 15-minute drive around the adorable little Eselfjord. From Dragsvik, a car ferry makes the short crossing east to **Hella** (a 30-minute drive from Sogndal and the Lustrafjord), then crosses the Sognefjord south to **Vangsnes** (a 20-minute drive to Hopperstad Stave Church and onward to Bergen). The ferry goes at least once per hour (2/hour in peak times, fewer boats Sun, 87 kr for car and driver).

MORE SOGNEFJORD

Express Boat Between Bergen and the Sognefjord

The made-for-tourists express boat makes it a snap to connect Bergen with Balestrand and other Sognefjord towns (for foot passengers only—no cars). In summer, the boat links Bergen, Vik, Balestrand, Aurland, and Flåm. You can also use this boat to connect towns on the Sognefjord, such as zipping from quiet Balestrand to busy Flåm, in the heart of the Nutshell action (reservations are smart—call 51 86 87 00 or visit www. norled.no; discounts for students and seniors, tickets also sold on boat and at TI). The following times were good for 2014—confirm them locally.

Between Bergen and the Sognefjord: The boat trip between Bergen and **Balestrand** takes four hours (545 kr, departs Bergen May-Sept daily at 8:00, also Mon-Fri at 16:30, Sat at 14:15, some Sun at 16:30—but not mid-June–mid-Aug; Oct-April Sun-Fri at 16:30, Sat at 14:15; departs Balestrand May-Sept daily at 16:55, Mon-Sat also at 7:50, some Sun at 11:30—but not mid-June–mid Aug; Oct-April Mon-Sat at 7:50, Sun at 16:25). In summer, the 8:00 boat from Bergen continues to Flåm.

Between Flåm and Balestrand: Going by boat between Flåm and Balestrand takes about 1.5 hours (250 kr, departs Flåm May-Sept daily at 15:30, stops at Aurland, arrives in Balestrand at 16:55; departs Balestrand daily at 11:50 arriving Flåm at 13:25; no express boats between Flåm and Balestrand Oct-April).

From Oslo to Balestrand via the Nutshell: This variation on the standard Norway in a Nutshell route is called "Sognefjord in a Nutshell" (Oslo-Myrdal-Flåm-Balestrand-Bergen). From Oslo, you can take an early train to Flåm (no later than the 8:05 train as part of the Norway in a Nutshell route—see previous chapter), then catch the 15:30 express boat to Balestrand. After your visit, you can continue on the express boat to Bergen, or return to the Nutshell route by taking the express boat to Flåm, and transferring to the next boat to Gudvangen.

Note that you can also drive through Sogndal to catch the **Kaupanger-Gudvangen** or **Mannheller-Fodnes** ferries (described under "Lustrafjord Connections," near the end of this chapter).

BY BUS

A local bus links Balestrand to **Sogndal** (Mon-Fri only, 1/day, maybe more in summer, 1.25 hours, includes ride on Dragsvik-Hella ferry, get details at TI).

The Lustrafjord

This arm of the Sognefjord is rugged country—only 2 percent of the land is fit to build on or farm. The Lustrafjord is ringed with

tiny villages where farmers sell cherries and giant raspberries. A few interesting attractions lie along the Lustrafjord: the village Dale Church at Luster; the impressive Nigard Glacier (a 45-minute drive up a valley); the postcard-pretty village of Solvorn; and, across the fjord, Norway's oldest stave church at Urnes. While a bit trickier to explore by public transportation, this beautiful region is easy by car, but still feels remote. There are no ATMs between Lom and Gaupne—that's how remote this region is.

SUGGESTED ROUTE FOR DRIVERS

The Lustrafjord can be seen either coming from the north (over the Sognefjell pass from the Jotunheimen region—see next chapter) or from the south (from Balestrand or the Norway in a Nutshell route—see previous chapter). Note that public buses between Lom and Sogndal follow this same route (see "Lustrafjord Connections," later).

Here's what you'll see if you're driving from the north (if you're coming from the south, read this section backward): Descending from Sognefjell, you'll hit the fjord at the village of Skjolden (decent TI in big community center, mobile 99 23 15 00). Follow Route 55 along the west bank of the fjord. In the town of Luster, consider visiting the beautifully decorated Dale Church (described next). Farther along, near the hamlet of Nes, you'll have views across the fjord of the towering Feigumfoss waterfall. Drops and dribbles come from miles around for this 650-foot tumble. Soon Route 55 veers along an inlet to the town of Gaupne, where you can choose to detour about an hour to the Nigard Glacier (up Route 604; described under "Sights on the Lustrafjord," next). After Gaupne, Route 55 enters a tunnel and cuts inland, emerging at a long, fjord-like lake at the town of Hafslo. Just beyond is the turnoff for Solvorn, a fine home-base town with the ferry across to Urnes and its stave church (Solvorn and Urnes Stave Church both described under "Sights on the Lustrafjord," next). Route 55 continues to Sogndal, where you can choose to turn off for the Kaupanger and Mannheller ferries across the Sognefjord, or continue on Route 55 to Hella and the boat across to either Dragsvik (near Balestrand) or Vangsnes (across the Sognefjord, near Vik and Hopperstad Stave Church).

Route Timings: If you're approaching from Lom in the Gudbrandsdal Valley, figure about 1.5 hours over Sognefjell to the start of the Lustrafjord at Skjolden, then another 30 minutes to Gaupne (with the optional glacier detour: 2 hours to see it, 4 hours to hike on it). From Gaupne, figure 30 minutes to Solvorn or 40 minutes to Sogndal. Solvorn to Sogndal is about 30 minutes. Sogndal to Hella, and its boat to Balestrand, takes about 40 minutes. These estimated times are conservative, but they don't include photo stops.

Sights on the Lustrafjord

These attractions are listed as you'll reach them driving from north to south along the fjordside Route 55. If you're sleeping in this area, you could visit all four sights in a single day (but it'd be a busy, somewhat rushed day). If you're just passing through, Dale Church and Solvorn are easy, but the other two involve major detours—choose one or skip them both.

▲Dale Church (Dale Kyrkje) in Luster

The namesake town of Luster, on the west bank of the Lustrafjord, boasts a unique 13th-century Gothic church. In a land of wooden stave churches, this stone church, with its richly decorated interior, is worth a quick stop as you pass through town.

Cost and Hours: Free entry but donation requested, daily 10:00-20:00 but often closed for services and off-season, good posted English info inside, 5-kr English brochure, just off the main road—look for red steeple, WC in graveyard, fresh goodies at bakery across the street.

Visiting the Church: The soapstone core of the church dates from about 1250, but the wooden bell tower and entry porch were likely built around 1600. As you enter, on the left you'll see a tall, elevated platform with seating, surrounded by a wooden grill. Nicknamed a "birdcage" for the feathery fashions worn by the ladies of the time, this high-profile pew—three steps higher than the pulpit—was built in the late-17th century by a wealthy parishioner.

The beautifully painted pulpit, decorated with faded images of the four evangelists, dates from the 13th century. In the chancel (altar area), restorers have uncovered frescoes from three different time periods: the 14th, 16th, and 17th centuries. Most of the ones you see here were likely created around the year 1500. The crucifix high over the pews, carved around 1200, predates the church, as does the old bench (with lots of runic carvings)—making them more than eight centuries old.

▲▲Jostedal's Nigard Glacier

The Nigard Glacier (Nigardsbreen) is the most accessible branch of mainland Europe's largest glacier (the Jostedalsbreen, 185 square miles). Hiking to or on the Nigard

offers Norway's best easy opportunity for a hands-on glacier experience. It's a 45-minute detour from the Lustrafjord up Jostedal Valley. Visiting a glacier is a quintessential Norwegian experience, bringing you face-to-face with the majesty of nature. If you can spare the time, it's worth the detour (even if you don't do a guided hike). But if glaciers don't give you tingles and you're feeling pressed, skip it.

Getting There: It's straightforward for **drivers.** When the main Route 55 along the Lustrafjord reaches Gaupne, turn onto Route 604, which you'll follow for 25 miles up the Jostedal Valley to the Breheimsenteret Glacier Information Center. Access to the glacier itself is down the toll road past the information center (all described next).

From late June through August, a **Glacier Bus** connects the Nigard Glacier to various home-base towns around the region (leaves Sogndal at 8:45, passes through Solvorn en route, arrives at the glacier around 10:00; departs glacier at 17:00, arrives back in Sogndal around 18:35; buses or boats from other towns—including Flåm and Aurland—coordinate to meet this bus in Sogndal; combo-tickets include various glacier visits and hikes; no bus Sept-June; for complete timetable, see www.jostedal.com). While handy, the bus is designed for those spending the entire day at the glacier.

Visiting the Glacier: The architecturally striking Breheimsenteret Glacier Information Center services both Breheimen and

MORE SOGNEFJORD

Jostedalsbreen national parks. Drop by to confirm your glacier plans; you can also book excursions here. The center's highlights include a relaxing 15-minute film with highlights of the region, along with interactive glacier-related exhibits that explain these giant, slow-moving rivers of ice. The center also has a restaurant and gift shop (daily mid-June-mid-Aug 9:00-18:00, May-mid-June and mid-Aug-Sept 10:00-17:00, closed Oct-April, tel. 57 68 32 50, www.jostedal.com).

The best quick visit is to walk to, but not on, the glacier. (If you want to walk *on* it, see "Hikes on the Glacier," next.) From the information center, a 40-kr toll road continues two miles to a lake facing the actual tongue of the glacier. About 75 years ago, the glacier reached all the way to today's parking lot. (It's named for the ninth farm—*ni gard*—where it finally stopped, after crushing eight farms higher up the valley.) From the lot, you can hike all the way to the edge of today's glacier (about 45 minutes each way); or, to save about 20 minutes of walking, take a special boat to a spot that's a 20-minute hike from the glacier (30 kr one-way, 40 kr round-trip, 10-minute boat trip, 4/hour, mid-June-mid-Sept 10:00-17:00).

The walk is uneven but well-marked—follow the red *T*'s and take your time. You'll hike on stone polished smooth by the glacier, and scramble over and around boulders big and small that were deposited by it. The path takes you right up to the face of the Nigardsbreen. Respect the glacier. It's a powerful river of ice, and fatal accidents do happen. If you want to walk on the glacier, read the next listing first.

Hikes on the Glacier: Don't attempt to walk on top of the glacier by yourself. The Breheimsenteret Glacier Information

Center offers guided family-friendly walks that include about one hour on the ice (260 kr, 130 kr for kids, cash only, minimum age 6, I'd rate the walks PG-13 myself, about 4/day, generally between 11:30-15:00, no need to reserve—just call glacier center to find out time and show up). Leave the information center one hour before your tour, then meet the group on the ice, where you'll pay and receive your clamp-on crampons. One hour roped up with your group gives you the essential experience. You'll find yourself marveling at how well your crampons work on the 5,000-year-old-ice. Even if it's hot, wear long pants, a jacket, and your sturdiest shoes. (Think ahead. It's awkward to empty your bladder after you're roped up.)

Longer, more challenging, and much more expensive hikes get you higher views, more exercise, and real crampons (starting at 460 kr, includes boots, mid-May-mid-Sept daily at 11:45, also July-Aug daily at 13:00, 4 hours including 2 hours on the ice, book by phone the day before—tel. 57 68 32 50, arrive at the information center 45 minutes early to pay for tickets and pick up your gear). If you're adventurous, ask about even longer hikes and glacier kayaking. While it's legal to go on the glacier on your own, it's dangerous and crazy to do so without crampons.

▲▲Solvorn

On the west bank of the Lustrafjord, 10 miles northeast of Sogndal, idyllic Solvorn is a sleepy little Victorian town with colorful wood-

en sheds lining its waterfront. My favorite town on the Lustrafjord is tidy and quaint, well away from the bustle of the Nutshell action. Its tiny ferry crosses the fjord regularly to Urnes and its famous stave church (next). While not worth going far out of your way for, Solvorn is a mellow

and surprisingly appealing place to kill some time waiting for the ferry...or just munching a picnic while looking across the fjord. A pensive stroll or photo shoot through the village's back lanes is a joy (look for plaques that explain historic buildings in English). Best of all, Solvorn also has a pair of excellent accommodations: a splurge (Walaker Hotel) and a budget place (Eplet Bed & Apple), described later under "Sleeping on the Lustrafjord."

Getting There: Solvorn is a steep five-minute **drive** down a switchback road from the main Route 55. The main road into town leads right to the Urnes ferry (see next) and dead-ends into a handy parking lot (free, 2-hour posted—but unmonitored—limit). It's a 30-minute drive or bus trip into Sogndal, where you can transfer to other **buses** (2-4 buses/day between Solvorn and Sogndal, including the Glacier Bus to the Nigard Glacier—described earlier).

▲▲Urnes Stave Church

The hamlet of Urnes (sometimes spelled "Ornes") has Norway's oldest surviving stave church, dating from 1129. While not easy to reach (it's across the Lustrafjord from other attractions), it's worth the scenic ferry ride. The exterior is smaller and simpler than most stave churches, but its interior—modified in fits and starts over the centuries—is uniquely eclectic. If you want to

MORE SOGNEFJORD

pack along a bike (rentable in Solvorn), see "Bring a Bike?" at the end of this listing.

Cost and Hours: 80 kr, includes 20-minute English tour (departs at :40 past most hours, to coincide with ferry arrival—described below); May-Sept daily 10:30-17:45, closed off-season, tel. 57 68 39 45, www.stavechurch.com.

Services: A little café/restaurant is at the farm called Urnes Gard, across from the church (same hours as church, homemade apple cakes, tel. 57 68 39 44).

Getting There: Urnes is perched on the east bank of the Lustrafjord (across the fjord from Route 55 and Solvorn). Ferries running between Solvorn and Urnes depart Solvorn at the top of most hours and Urnes at the bottom of most hours (34 kr one-way passenger fare, 93 kr one-way for car and driver, no round-trip discount, 15-minute ride, mobile 91 79 42 11, www.lustrabaatane.no). You can either drive or walk onto the boat—but, since you can't drive all the way up to the church, you might as well leave your car in Solvorn. Once across, it's about a five-minute uphill walk to the main road and parking lot (where drivers must leave their cars; parking lot at the church only for disabled visitors). From here, it's a steep 15-minute walk up a switchback road to the church (follow signs for *Urnes*).

Planning Your Time: Don't dawdle on your way up to the church, as the tour is scheduled to depart at :40 past most hours, about 25 minutes after the ferry arrives (giving most visitors just enough time to make it up the hill to the church). The first boat of the day departs Solvorn at 10:00; the last boat departs Solvorn at 16:00 (last tour at 16:40); and the last boat back to Solvorn departs Urnes at 18:00. Confirm the "last boat" time, and keep an eye on your watch to avoid getting stranded in Urnes.

Visiting the Church: Most visitors to the church take the included 20-minute tour (scheduled to begin soon after the ferry arrives—described earlier). Here are some highlights:

Buy your ticket in the white house across from the church. Visit the little museum here after you see the church, so you don't miss the tour.

Many changes were made to the exterior to modernize the church after the Reformation (the colonnaded gallery was replaced, the bell tower was added, and mod-

ern square windows were cut into the walls). Go around t.
side of the church, toward the cemetery. This is the third ch
on this spot, but the carved doorway embedded in the wall h.
was inherited from the second church. Notice the two mysteriou.
beasts—a warm-blooded predator (standing) and a cold-blooded
dragon—weaving and twisting around each other, one entwining
the other. Yet, as they bite each other on the neck, it's impossible
to tell which one is "winning"...perhaps symbolizing the everlast-
ing struggle of human existence. The door you see in the middle,
however, has a very different message: the harmony of symmetrical
figure-eights, an appropriately calming theme for those entering
the church.

Now go around to the real entry door (with a wrought-iron
lock and handle probably dating from the first church) and head inside. While it feels ancient and creaky, a lot of what you see in here
is actually "new" compared to the 12th-century core of the church.
The exquisitely carved, voluptuous, column-topping capitals are re-
markably well-preserved originals. The interior was initially stark
(no pews) and dark—lit not by windows (which were added much
later), but by candles laid on the floor in the shape of a cross. Looking straight ahead, you see a cross with Mary on the left (where the
women stood) and John the Baptist on the right (with the men).
When they finally added seating, they kept things segregated: Notice the pews carved with hearts for women, crowns for men.

When a 17th-century wealthy family wanted to build a special
pew for themselves, they simply sawed off some of the pinecone-
topped columns to make way for it. When the church began to
lean, it was reinforced with the clumsy, off-center X-shaped sup-
ports. Churchgoers learned their lesson, and never cut anything
again.

The ceiling, added in the late 17th century, prevents visitors
from enjoying the Viking-ship roof beams. But all of these additions have stories to tell. Experts can read various cultural influences into the church decorations, including Irish (some of the
carvings) and Romanesque (the rounded arches).

Bring a Bike? To give your Lustrafjord excursion an added
dimension, take a bike on the ferry to Urnes (free passage, rentable
for 200 kr/day with helmets from Eplet Bed & Apple hostel in Solvorn, where you can park your car for free). From the stave church,
bike the super-scenic fjordside road (4.5 miles—with almost no
traffic—to big Feigumfossen waterfall and back).

Sleeping on the Lustrafjord

These accommodations are along the Lustrafjord, listed from north
to south.

N NES

$$ Nes Gard Farmhouse B&B rents 15 homey rooms, offering lots of comfort in a grand 19th-century farmhouse (S-760-820 kr, Db-980-1,080 kr, higher prices for July-Aug, rooms in main building more traditional, family apartment, bike rental-150 kr/day, tel. 57 68 39 43, mobile 95 23 26 94, www.nesgard.no, post@nesgard. no, Månum family). Mari and Asbjørn serve a three-course breakfast and dinner for 350 kr.

$ Viki Fjord Camping has great fjordside huts—many directly on the water, with fjord views and balconies—located directly across from the Feigumfossen waterfall (300-350 kr without a private bathroom, 400-900 kr with bathroom, price depends on size and season, no breakfast, sheets-70 kr, tel. 57 68 64 20, mobile 99 53 97 30, www.vikicamping.no, post@vikicamping.no, Berit and Svein).

IN SOLVORN

For more on this delightful little fjordside town—my favorite home base on the Lustrafjord—see the description earlier in this chapter. While it lacks the handy boat connections of Flåm, Aurland, or Balestrand, that's part of Solvorn's charm.

$$$ Walaker Hotel, a former inn and coach station, has been run by the Walaker family since 1690 (that's a lot of pressure on ninth-generation owner Ole Henrik). The hotel, set right on the Lustrafjord (with a garden perfect for relaxing and, if necessary, even convalescing), is open May through September. In the main house, the halls and living rooms are filled with tradition. Notice the patriotic hymns on the piano. The 22 rooms are divided into two types: nicely appointed standard rooms in the modern annex (big Sb-1,500 kr, Db-1,750 kr); or recently renovated "historic" rooms with all the modern conveniences in two different old buildings: rooms with Old World elegance in the main house, and brightly painted rooms with countryside charm in the Tingstova house next door (Sb-1,950 kr, Db-2,250 kr, 500 kr more for larger room #20 or room #23; non-smoking, Wi-Fi, sea kayak rental-350 kr/day, tel. 57 68 20 80, www.walaker.com, hotel@walaker.com). They serve excellent four-course dinners (575 kr plus drinks, nightly at 19:30, savor your dessert with fjordside setting on the balcony). Their impressive gallery of Norwegian art is in a restored, historic farmhouse out back (free for guests; Ole Henrik leads one-hour tours of the collection, peppered with some family history, nightly after dinner).

$-$$ Eplet Bed & Apple is my kind of hostel: innovative and friendly. It's creatively run by Trond and Agnethe, whose entrepreneurial spirit and positive attitude attract enjoyable guests. With welcoming public spaces and 22 beds in seven rooms (all with views, some with decks), this place is worth considering even if you don't normally sleep at hostels (open April-Sept only; camping space-100 kr, bunk in 7-bed dorm-200 kr, S-500 kr, D-600 kr, T-800 kr, S/D/T cost 50 kr less for 2 nights or more, no breakfast, no elevator, laundry-50 kr, kitchen, guest computer and Wi-Fi, free loaner bikes for guests, tel. 41 64 94 69, www.eplet.net, trondhenrik@eplet.net). It's about 300 yards uphill from the boat dock—look for the white house with a giant red apple painted on it. It's surrounded by a raspberry and apple farm (they make and sell tasty juices from both). The hostel rents bikes and helmets to non-guests for 200 kr/day. If you plan to bike along the fjord from Urnes, consider that if you stay at the hostel, the free bikes will save you 400 kr (for two people).

Eating in Solvorn: The **Linahagen Kafé,** next door to Walaker Hotel, serves good meals (150-kr salads and main dishes, June-Aug Mon-Fri 12:00-18:00, Sat 12:00-16:00, Sun 13:00-18:00, closed Sept-May, run by Tordis and her family).

IN SOGNDAL

Sogndal is the only sizeable town in this region. While it lacks the charm of Solvorn and Balestrand, it's big enough to have a busy shopping street and a helpful **TI** (daily 10:00-22:00, inside the MIX mini-mart at Parkvegen 5, mobile 99 23 15 00).

$$ Loftesnes Pensjonat, with 13 rooms, houses travelers mid-June through mid-August, and mostly students—reserving four rooms for travelers—during the school year (S-400 kr, Sb-420 kr, D-600 kr, Db-650 kr, no breakfast, kitchen, above a Chinese restaurant near the water, tel. 57 67 15 77, mobile 90 93 51 71, loftesnes.pensjonat@gmail.com).

$$ Sogndal Youth Hostel rents good, cheap beds (bunk in 4-bed room-310 kr, S-410 kr, D-620 kr, Db-755 kr, 10 percent less for members, sheets-70 kr, towel-40 kr, fully equipped members' kitchen, mid-June-mid-Aug only, closed 10:00-17:00, at fork in the road as you enter town, tel. 57 62 75 75, www.vandrerhjem.no, sogndal@hihostels.no).

MORE SOGNEFJORD

Lustrafjord Connections

Sogndal is the transit hub for the Lustrafjord region.

FROM SOGNDAL BY BUS

Buses go to **Lom** over the Sognefjell pass (2/day late June-Aug only, road closed off-season, 3.5 hours, 1/day off-season, goes around the pass, 4.75 hours, change in Skei), **Solvorn** (5/day, fewer Sat-Sun, 30 minutes), **Balestrand** (3/Mon-Fri, none Sat-Sun, 1.25 hours, includes ride on Hella-Dragsvik ferry), **Nigard Glacier** via the Glacier Bus (1/day, 3 hours, departs Sogndal daily at 8:45, returns to Sogndal in the afternoon, also stops at Solvorn in each direction, late June-Aug only). Most buses run less (or not at all) on weekends—check the latest at www.ruteinfo.net.

BY BOAT

Car ferries cost roughly $5 per hour for walk-ons and $20 per hour for a car and driver. Reservations are generally not necessary, and on many short rides, aren't even possible (for info and free and easy reservations for longer rides, call 55 90 70 70). Confirm schedules at www.ruteinfo.net. From near Sogndal, various boats fan out to towns around the Sognefjord. Most leave from two towns at the southern end of the Lustrafjord: **Kaupanger** (a 15-minute drive from Sogndal) and **Mannheller** (a 5-minute drive beyond Kaupanger, 20 minutes from Sogndal).

From Kaupanger: While Kaupanger is little more than a ferry landing, the small stave-type church at the edge of town merits a look. Boats go from Kaupanger all the way down the gorgeous Nærøyfjord to **Gudvangen,** which is on the Norway in a Nutshell route (where you catch the bus to Voss). Taking this boat allows you to see the best part of the Nutshell fjord scenery (the Nærøyfjord), but misses the other half of that cruise (Aurlandsfjord). From June through September, boats leave Kaupanger daily at 9:00 and 15:00 for the 2.75-hour trip (check in 15 minutes before departure); car and driver-700 kr, adult passenger-300 kr; reserve at least one day in advance—or longer in July-Aug; www.fjord2.no, post@fjord2.no). Prices are high because this route is mainly taken by tourists, not locals. The service was taken over by new owners in 2015 and may change; verify schedules and prices online. Boats also connect Kaupanger to **Lærdal,** but the crossing from Mannheller to Fodnes is easier (described next).

From Mannheller: Ferries frequently make the speedy 15-minute crossing to **Fodnes** (74 kr for a car and driver, 3/hour, no reservations possible). From Fodnes, drive through the five-mile-long tunnel to Lærdal and the main E-16 highway (near Borgund Stave Church, the long tunnel to Aurland, and the scenic overland road to the Stegastein fjord viewpoint—all described in the previous chapter).

To Balestrand: To reach Balestrand from the Lustrafjord, you'll take a short ferry trip (Hella-Dragsvik). For information on the car ferries to and from Balestrand, see "Balestrand Connections," earlier.

Scenic Drives from the Sognefjord

If you'll be doing a lot of driving, pick up a good local map. The 1:335,000-scale *Sør-Norge nord* map by Cappelens Kart is excellent (about 150 kr, available at local TIs and bookstores).

▲▲From the Lustrafjord to Aurland

The drive to the pleasant fjordside town of Aurland (see previous chapter) takes you either through the world's longest car tunnel, or

over an incredible mountain pass. If you aren't going as far as Lom and Jotunheimen, consider taking the pass, as the scenery here rivals the famous Sognefjell pass drive.

From Sogndal, drive 20 minutes to the Mannheller-Fodnes ferry (described under "Lustrafjord Connections," earlier), float across the Sognefjord, then drive from Fodnes to Lærdal. From Lærdal, you have two options to Aurland: The speedy route is on E-16 through the 15-mile-long **tunnel** from Lærdal, or the Aurlandsvegen **"Snow Road"** over the pass.

The tunnel is free, and impressively nonchalant—it's signed as if it were just another of Norway's countless tunnels. But driving it is a bizarre experience: A few miles in, as you find yourself trying not to be hypnotized by the monotony, it suddenly dawns on you what it means to be driving under a mountain for 15 miles. To keep people awake, three rest chambers, each illuminated by a differently colored light, break up the drive visually. Stop and get out—if no cars are coming, test the acoustics from the center.

The second, immeasurably more scenic, route is a breathtaking one-hour, 30-mile drive that winds over a pass into Aurland, cresting at over 4,000 feet and offering classic aerial fjord views (it's worth the messy pants). From the Mannheller-Fodnes ferry, take the first road to the right (to Erdal), then leave E-68 at Erdal (just west of Lærdal) for the Aurlandsvegen. This road, while well-

MORE SOGNEFJORD

maintained, is open only in summer, and narrow and dangerous during snowstorms (which can hit with a moment's notice, even in warm weather). Even in good weather, parts of the road can be a white-knuckle adventure, especially when meeting oncoming vehicles on the tiny, exposed hairpin turns. You'll enjoy vast and terrifying views of lakes, snowfields, and remote mountain huts and farmsteads on what feels like the top of Norway. As you begin the 12-hairpin zigzag descent to Aurland, you'll reach the "7"-shaped **Stegastein viewpoint**—well worth a stop.

▲From the Lustrafjord to Bergen, via Nærøyfjord and Gudvangen

Car ferries take tourists between Kaupanger and the Nutshell town of Gudvangen through an arm and elbow of the Sognefjord, including the staggering Nærøyfjord (for details on the ferry, see "Lustrafjord Connections," earlier). From Gudvangen, it's a 90-mile drive to Bergen via Voss (figure about one hour to Voss, then another two hours into Bergen). This follows essentially the same route as the Norway in a Nutshell (Gudvangen-Voss bus, Voss-Bergen train).

Get off the ferry in Gudvangen and drive up the Nærøy valley past a river. You'll see the two giant falls and then go uphill through a tunnel. After the tunnel, look for a sign marked *Stalheim* and turn right. Stop for a break at the touristy Stalheim Hotel. Then follow signs marked *Stalheimskleiva*. This incredible road doggedly worms its way downhill back into the depths of the valley. My brakes started overheating in a few minutes. Take it easy. As you wind down, you can view the falls from several turnouts.

The road rejoins E-16. You retrace your route through the tunnel and then continue into a mellower beauty, past lakes and farms, toward Voss. Just before you reach Voss itself, watch the right side of the road for Tvindefossen, a waterfall with a handy campground/WC/kiosk picnic area that's worth a stop. Highway E-16 takes you through Voss and into Bergen. If you plan to visit Edvard Grieg's Home and the nearby Fantoft Stave Church, now is the ideal time, since you'll be driving near them—and they're a headache to reach from downtown. Both are worth a detour if you're not rushed, and are open until 18:00 in summer.

▲▲From Balestrand to Bergen, via Vik

If you're based in Balestrand and driving to Bergen, you have two options: Take the Dragsvik-Hella ferry, drive an hour to Kaupanger (via Sogndal), and drive the route just described; or, take the following slower, twistier, more remote, and more scenic route, with a stop at the beautiful Hopperstad Stave Church. This route is slightly longer, with more time on mountain roads and less time on the boat. Figure 20 minutes from Vangsnes to Vik, then about 1.5 hours to Voss, then another 2 hours into Bergen.

From Vagsnes, head into Vik on the main Route 13. In Vik, follow signs from the main road to Hopperstad Stave Church (described earlier in this chapter). Then backtrack to Route 13 and follow it south, to Voss. You'll soon begin a series of switchbacks that wind you up and out of the valley. The best views are from the Storesvingen Fjellstove restaurant (on the left). Soon after, you'll

crest the ridge, go through a tunnel, and find yourself on top of the world, in a desolate and harshly scenic landscape of scrubby mountaintops, snow banks, lakes, and no trees, scattered with vacation cabins. After cruising atop the plateau for a while, the road twists its way down (next to a waterfall) into a very steep valley, which it meanders through the rest of the way to Voss. This is an hour-long, middle-of-nowhere journey, with few road signs—you might feel lost, but keep driving toward Voss. When Route 13 dead-ends into E-16, turn right (toward Voss and Bergen) and re-enter civilization. From here, the route follows the same roads as in the Lustrafjord-Bergen drive described earlier (including the Tvindefossen waterfall).

MORE SOGNEFJORD

GUDBRANDSDAL VALLEY AND JOTUNHEIMEN MOUNTAINS

Norway in a Nutshell is a great day trip, but with more time and a car, consider a scenic meander from Oslo to Bergen. You'll arc up the Gudbrandsdal Valley and over the Jotunheimen Mountains, then travel along the Lustrafjord (see previous chapter).

After an introductory stop in Lillehammer, with its fine folk museum, you might spend the night in a log-and-sod farmstead-turned-hotel, tucked in a quiet valley under Norway's highest peaks. Next, Norway's highest pass takes you on an exhilarating roller-coaster ride through the heart of the myth-inspiring Jotunheimen, bristling with Norway's biggest mountains. Then the road hairpins down into fjord country (see previous chapter).

PLANNING YOUR TIME

While you could spend five or six days in this area on a three-week Scandinavian rampage, this slice of the region is worth three days. By car, I'd spend them like this:

Day 1: Leave Oslo early, and spend midday at Lillehammer's Mai-haugen Open-Air Folk Museum for a tour and picnic. Drive up the Gudbrandsdal Valley, stopping at the stave church in Lom. Stay overnight in the Jotunheimen countryside.

Day 2: Drive the Sognefjell road over the mountains, then down along the Lustrafjord, stopping to visit the Dale Church and the Nigard Glacier (see previous chapter). Sleep in your choice of fjord towns,

Gudbrandsdal Valley &
Jotunheimen Mountains

1 Røisheim Hotel
2 Elvesæter Hotel
3 Bøverdalen Youth Hostel
4 Strind Gard
5 Spiterstulen Lodge
6 Juvasshytta Lodge
7 Leirvassbu Lodge

described in previous chapters (such as Solvorn, Balestrand, or Aurland).

Day 3: Cruise the Aurland and/or Nærøy fjords and try to visit another stave church or two (such as Urnes, Hopperstad, or Borgund) before carrying on to Bergen.

This plan can be condensed into two days if you skip the Nigard Glacier side-trip.

Lillehammer and the Gudbrandsdal Valley

The Gudbrandsdal Valley is the tradition-steeped country of Peer Gynt, the Norwegian Huck Finn. This romantic valley of time-worn hills, log cabins, and velvet farms has connected northern and southern Norway since ancient times. While not as striking as other parts of the Norwegian countryside, Gudbrandsdal offers a suitable first taste of the natural wonders that crescendo farther north and west (in Jotunheimen and the Sognefjord). Throughout this region, the government subsidizes small farms to keep the countryside populated and healthy. (These subsidies would not be permitted if Norway were a member of the European Union.)

Orientation to Lillehammer

The de facto capital of Gudbrandsdal, Lillehammer is a pleasant winter and summer resort town of 27,000. While famous for its brush with Olympic greatness (as host of the 1994 Winter Olympiad), Lillehammer is a bit disappointing—worthwhile only for its excellent Maihaugen Open-Air Folk Museum, or to break up the long drive between Oslo and the Jotunheimen region. If you do wind up here, Lillehammer has happy, old, woody pedestrian zones (Gågata and Storgata).

Tourist Information: Lillehammer's TI is inside the train station (mid-June-mid-Aug Mon-Fri 8:00-18:00, Sat-Sun 10:00-16:00; mid-Aug-mid-June Mon-Fri 8:00-16:00, Sat 10:00-14:00, closed Sun; Jernbanetorget 2, tel. 61 28 98 00, www.lillehammer.com).

Sights in Lillehammer

Lillehammer's two most worthwhile sights are up the hill behind the center of town. It's a fairly steep 15-minute walk from the train station to either sight and a 10-minute, mostly level walk between the two (follow the busy main road that connects them). Because the walk from the station is uphill (and not very well-signed), consider catching the bus from in front of the train station (bus #003 or #002 to Olympics Museum, 2/hour; bus #006 to Maihaugen, 1/hour; 35 kr one-way for either bus).

▲▲Maihaugen Open-Air Folk Museum (Maihaugen Friluftsmuseet)

This idyllic park, full of old farmhouses and pickled slices of folk culture, provides a good introduction to what you'll see as you drive

through the Gudbrandsdal Valley. Anders Sandvig, a "visionary dentist," started the collection in 1887. You'll divide your time between the fine indoor museum at the entrance and the sprawling exterior exhibits.

Upon arrival, ask about special events, crafts, or musical performances. A TV monitor shows what's going on in the park. Summer is busy with crafts in action and people re-enacting life in the past, à la Colonial Williamsburg. There are no tours, so it's up to you to initiate conversations with the "residents." Off-season it's pretty dead, with no live crafts and most buildings locked up.

Cost and Hours: 150 kr in summer, 110 kr off-season; 25 percent off when combined with Olympics Museum; June-Aug daily 10:00-17:00; Sept-May Tue-Sun 11:00-16:00, closed Mon; paid parking.

Information: Because English descriptions are scant, consider purchasing the English guidebook. Tel. 61 28 89 00, www.maihaugen.no.

Visiting the Museum: The outdoor section, with 200 buildings from the Gudbrandsdal region, is divided into three areas: the

"Rural Collection," with old sod-roof log houses and a stave church; the "Town Collection," with reconstructed bits of old-time Lillehammer; and the "Residential Area," with 20th-century houses that look like most homes in today's Norway. The time trip can be jarring: In the 1980s house, a bubble-gum-chewing girl enthuses about her new, "wireless" TV remote and plays ABBA tunes from a cassette-tape player.

The museum's excellent "We Won the Land" exhibit (at the entry) sweeps you through Norwegian history from the Ice Age to the Space Age. The Gudbrandsdal art section shows village life at its best. And you can walk through Dr. Sandvig's old dental office and the original shops of various crafts- and tradespeople.

Though the museum welcomes picnickers and has a simple

cafeteria, Lillehammer's town center (a 15-minute walk below the museum), with lots of fun eateries, is better for lunch (see "Eating in the Gudbrandsdal Valley," later).

Norwegian Olympics Museum
(Norges Olympiske Museum)

This cute museum is housed in the huge Olympic ice-hockey arena, Håkon Hall. With brief English explanations, an emphasis on Norwegians and Swedes, and an endearingly gung-ho Olympic spirit, it's worth a visit on a rainy day or for sports fans. The ground-floor exhibit traces the ancient history of the Olympics, then devotes one wall panel to each of the summer and winter Olympiads of the modern era (with special treatment for the 1952 Oslo games). Upstairs, walk the entire concourse, circling the arena seating while reviewing the highlights (and lowlights) of the 1994 games (remember Tonya Harding?). While you're up there, check out the gallery of great Norwegian athletes and the giant egg used in the Lillehammer opening ceremony.

Cost and Hours: 110 kr, 25 percent off when combined with Maihaugen Museum; June-Aug daily 10:00-17:00; Sept-May Tue-Sun 11:00-16:00, closed Mon; tel. 61 25 21 00, www.maihaugen. no.

Nearby: On the hillside above Håkon Hall (a 30-minute hike or quick drive) are two ski jumps that host more Olympics sights, including a ski lift, the ski jump tower, and a bobsled ride (www. olympiaparken.no). In the summer, ski jumpers practice on the jumps, which are sprayed with water.

IN THE GUDBRANDSDAL VALLEY

If you're driving from Oslo to the Gudbrandsdal Valley, you'll go right past the historic Eidsvoll Manor.

Scenic Drives

The main E-6 road north of Lillehammer (en route to Otta and Lom) passes through a bucolic valley with fine but unremarkable scenery. Along this road, a pair of toll-road side-trips (Gynt Veien and Peer Gynt Seterveien) loop off the E-6 road. While they sound romantic, they're basically windy, curvy dirt roads over high, desolate heath and scrub-brush plateaus with fine mountain views. They're scenic, but  pale in comparison with the Sogne-fjell road between Lom and the Lustrafjord (described later in this chapter).

Sleep Code

Abbreviations   **(6 kr = about $1, country code: 47)**
S = Single, **D** = Double/Twin, **T** = Triple, **Q** = Quad, **b** = bathroom
Price Rankings
  $$$ Higher Priced—Most rooms 1,000 kr or more.
   $$ Moderately Priced—Most rooms 600-1,000 kr.
    $ Lower Priced—Most rooms 600 kr or less.
Unless otherwise noted, credit cards are accepted, breakfast is included, and Wi-Fi is generally free. Everyone speaks English. Prices change; verify current rates online or by email. For the best prices, always book directly with the hotel.

Sleeping in the Gudbrandsdal Valley

I prefer sleeping in the more scenic and Norwegian-feeling Jotunheimen area (described later). But if you're sleeping here, Lillehammer and the surrounding valley offer several good options. My choices for Lillehammer are near the train station; the accommodations in Kvam provide a convenient stopping point in the valley.

IN LILLEHAMMER

$$$ Mølla Hotell, true to its name, is situated in an old mill along the little stream running through Lillehammer. The 58 rooms blend Old World charm with modern touches. It's more cutesy-cozy and less businesslike than other Lillehammer hotels in this price range (Db-1,000-1,450 kr depending on demand, elevator, guest computer and Wi-Fi, a block below Gågata at Elvegata 12, tel. 61 05 70 80, www.mollahotell.no, post@mollahotell.no).

$$$ First Hotel Breiseth is a business-class hotel with 89 rooms in a handy location directly across from the train station (Sb-820-1,200 kr, Db-1,000-1,320 kr, Wi-Fi, free parking, Jernbanegaten 1-5, tel. 61 24 77 77, www.firsthotels.no/breiseth, breiseth@firsthotels.no).

$ Vandrerhjem Stasjonen, Lillehammer's youth hostel, is actually upstairs inside the train station. With 100 beds in 33 institutional but new-feeling rooms—including 21 almost hotel-like doubles—it's a winner (340-kr bunk in a 3- to 4-bed dorm, Sb-745 kr, Db-990 kr, 15 percent cheaper for members, includes sheets and breakfast, elevator, Wi-Fi, Jernbanetorget 2, tel. 61 26 00 24, www.stasjonen.no, lillehammer@hihostels.no).

IN KVAM

This is a popular vacation valley for Norwegians, and you'll find loads of reasonable small hotels and campgrounds with huts for those who aren't quite campers (*hytter* means "cottages" or "cabins," *rom* is "private room," and *ledig* means "vacancy"). These huts normally cost about 400-600 kr, depending on size and amenities, and can hold from four to six people. Although they are simple, you'll have a kitchenette and access to a good WC and shower. When available, sheets rent for around 60 kr per person. Here are a couple of listings in the town of Kvam, located midway between Lillehammer and Lom.

$$$ Vertshuset Sinclair has a quirky Scottish-Norwegian ambience. The 15 fine rooms are in old-fashioned motel wings, while the main building houses an inexpensive cafeteria, described later (Sb-890 kr, Db-1,090 kr, family deals, free guest computer and Wi-Fi, tel. 61 29 54 50, www.vertshuset-sinclair.no, post@vertshuset-sinclair.no). The motel was named after a Scotsman who led a band of adventurers into this valley, attempting to set up their own Scottish kingdom. They failed. All were kilt.

$-$$ Kirketeigen Ungdomssenter ("Church Youth Center"), behind the town church, welcomes travelers year-round (camping spots-120 kr/tent; small cabins without water-400 kr; cabins with kitchen and bath-800 kr, sleeps up to 5 people; simple 4-bed rooms in the main building-450 kr for 2-4 people with sheets; sheets and blankets-100 kr, Wi-Fi, tel. 61 21 60 90, www.kirketeigen.no, post@kirketeigen.no).

Eating in the Gudbrandsdal Valley

In Lillehammer: Good restaurants are scattered around the city center, but for the widest selection, head to where the main pedestrian drag (Gågata) crosses the little stream running downhill through town. Poke a block or two up and down **Elvegata,** which stretches along the river and hosts a wide range of tempting eateries—from pubs (both rowdy and upscale) to pizza and cheap sandwich stands.

In the Valley: **Vertshuset Sinclair,** described earlier, has a cafeteria handy for a quick and filling bite on the road between Lillehammer and Lom (50-70-kr small dishes, 100-200-kr meals, daily 7:00-late).

Jotunheimen Mountains

Norway's Jotunheimen ("Giants' Home") Mountains feature the country's highest peaks and some of its best hikes and drives. This national park stretches from the fjords to the glaciers. You can play roller-coaster with mountain passes, take rugged hikes, wind up scenic toll roads, get up close to a giant stave church...and sleep in a time-passed rural valley. The gateway to the mountains is the unassuming town of Lom.

Lom

Pleasant Lom—the main town between Lillehammer and Sogndal—feels like a modern ski resort village. It's home to one of Norway's most impressive stave churches. While Lom has little else to offer, the church causes the closest thing to a tour-bus traffic jam this neck of the Norwegian woods will ever see.

Orientation to Lom

Park by the stave church—you'll see its dark spire just over the bridge. The church shares a parking lot with a gift shop/church museum and some public WCs. Across the street is the TI, in the sod-roofed building that also houses the Norwegian Mountain Museum. If you're heading over the mountains, Lom's bank (at the Kommune building) has the last ATM until Gaupne.

TOURIST INFORMATION

Lom's TI, a good source of information for hikes and drives in the Jotunheimen Mountains, may close for a couple of years starting in 2015; if it does, an alternate TI may open just across the river in Lom's Co-op Mega grocery store—ask around (if open, TI's hours likely July-mid-Aug Mon-Fri 9:00-17:00, Sat-Sun 9:00-15:00; shorter hours off-season and closed Sat-Sun Oct-April; tel. 61 21 29 90, www.visitjotunheimen.com).

GUDBRANDSDAL

Sights in Lom

▲▲Lom Stave Church (Lom Stavkyrkje)

Despite extensive renovations, Lom's church (from 1158) remains a striking example of a Nordic stave church.

Cost and Hours: Church—60 kr, daily mid-June-mid-Aug 9:00-19:00 (until 17:00 last half of Aug), mid-May-mid-June and Sept 10:00-16:00, closed in winter and during funerals; museum—10 kr, same hours as church, progressively shorter hours in shoulder season, in winter Mon-Sat 10:00-15:00, closed Sun; tel. 40 43 84 86.

Tours: Try to tag along with a guided tour of the church—or, if it's not too busy, a docent can give you a quick private tour (included in ticket). Even outside of opening times—including winter—small groups can arrange a tour (60 kr/person, 600-kr minimum, call 97 07 53 97 in summer or 61 21 73 00 in winter).

Visiting the Church: Buy your ticket and go inside to take in the humble **interior** (still used by locals for services—notice the posted hymnal numbers). Men sat on the right, women on the left, and prisoners sat with the sheriff in the caged area in the rear. Standing in the middle of the nave, look overhead to see the earliest surviving parts of the church, such as the circle of X-shaped St. Andrew crosses and the Romanesque arches above them. High above the door (impossible to see without a flashlight—ask a docent to show you) is an old painting of a dragon-

or lion-like creature—likely an old Viking symbol, possibly drawn here to smooth the forced conversion local pagans made to Christianity. When King Olav II (later to become St. Olav) swept through this valley in 1021, he gave locals an option: convert or be burned out of house and home.

On the white town flag, notice the spoon—a symbol of Lom. Because of its position nestled in the mountains, Lom gets less rainfall than other towns, so large spoons were traditionally used to spread water over the fields. The apse (behind the altar) was added in 1240, when trendy new Gothic cathedrals made an apse a must-have accessory for churches across Europe. Lepers came to the grilled window in the apse for a blessing. When the Reformation hit in 1536, the old paintings were whitewashed over. The church has changed over the years: Transepts, pews, and windows were added in the 17th century. And the circa-1720 paintings were done by a local priest's son.

Drop into the **gift shop/church museum** in the big black building in the parking lot. Its one-room exhibit celebrates 1,000 years of the stave church—interesting if you follow the loaner English descriptions. Inside you'll find a pair of beautiful model churches, headstones and other artifacts, and the only surviving stave-church dragon-head "steeple." In the display case near the early-1900s organ, find the little pencil-size stick carved with runes, dating from around 1350. It's actually a love letter from a would-be suitor. The woman rejected him, but she saved them both from embarrassment by hiding the stick under the church floor-boards beneath a pew...where it was found in 1973. (Docents inside the church like to show off a replica of this stick.)

Before or after your church visit, explore the tidy, thought-provoking **graveyard** surrounding the church. Also, check out the precarious-looking little footbridge over the waterfall (the best view is from the modern road bridge into town).

Norwegian Mountain Museum
(Norsk Fjellmuseum)

This worthwhile museum traces the history of the people who have lived off the land in the Jotunheimen Mountains from the Stone Age to today (and also serves as a national park office). It is one of the better museums in fjord country, with well-presented displays and plenty of actual artifacts. Beginning in 2015, a new exhibit, "Over the Ice: Discoveries from the Ice Show the Way," will explore prehistoric human and animal migrations in the surrounding mountains based on recent archaeological finds, including a 1,300-year-old ski.

Cost and Hours: 70 kr, mid-May-early-Oct daily 9:00-16:00, except until 19:00 daily July-mid-Aug, generally closed off-season, in the sod-roofed building across the road from the Lom Stave Church parking lot, tel. 61 21 16 00, http://fjell.museum.no.

Sleeping near Lom

Lom itself has a handful of hotels, but the most appealing way to overnight in this area is at a rural rest stop in the countryside. All of these are on Route 55 south of Lom, toward Sognefjord—first is Strind Gard, then Bøverdalen, Røisheim, and finally Elvesæter (all within 20 minutes of Lom).

$$$ Røisheim, in a marvelously remote mountain setting, is an extremely expensive storybook hotel composed of a cluster of centuries-old, sod-roofed log farmhouses. Its posh and generous living rooms are filled with antiques. Each of the 20 rooms (in 14 different buildings) is rustic but elegant, with fun "barrel bathtubs" and four-poster or canopy beds. Some rooms are in old, wooden farm buildings—*stabburs*—with low ceilings and heavy beams. The deluxe rooms are larger, with king beds and fireplaces. Call ahead so they'll be prepared for your arrival (open May-Sept; standard Db-3,000 kr, deluxe Db-3,600 kr; includes breakfast, packed lunch, and an over-the-top four-course traditional dinner served at 19:30; non-smoking, Wi-Fi, 10 miles south of Lom on Route 55, tel. 61 21 20 31, www.roisheim.no, booking@roisheim.no).

$$$ Elvesæter Hotel has its own share of Old World romance, but is bigger, cheaper, and more modest. Delightful public spaces bunny-hop through its traditional shell, while its 200 beds sprawl through nine buildings. The Elvesæter family has done a great job of retaining the historic character of their medieval farm, even though the place is big enough to handle large tour groups. The renovated "superior" rooms are new-feeling, but have sterile modern furniture; the older, cheaper "standard" rooms are well-worn but more characteristic (open May-Sept, standard Db-1,150 kr, superior Db-1,550 kr, extra bed-450 kr, family deals, includes breakfast, good 325-kr three-course dinners, Wi-Fi, swimming pool, farther up Route 55, just past Bøverdal, tel. 61 21 12 10, www.topofnorway.no, elveseter@topofnorway.no). Even if you're not staying here, stop by to wander through the public spaces and pick up a flier explaining the towering Sagasøyla (Saga Column). It was started in 1926 to celebrate the Norwegian constitution, and was to stand in front of Oslo's Parliament Building—but the project stalled after World War II (thanks to the artist's affinity for things German and membership in Norway's fascist party). It was eventually finished and erected here in 1992.

$ Bøverdalen Youth Hostel offers 32 cheap-but-comfortable beds and a far more rugged clientele—real hikers rather than car hikers. While a bit institutional, it's well-priced and well-run (open late May-Sept, bunk in 4- to 6-bed room-180 kr, D-550 kr, 4-person cabins-980 kr, sheets-65 kr, breakfast-85 kr, Wi-Fi, kitchen, hot meals, self-serve café, tel. 61 21 20 64, www.hihostels. no, boverdalen@hihostels.no, Anna Berit). It's in the center of the little community of Bøverdal (store, campground, and toll road up to Galdhøpiggen area).

$ Strind Gard is your very rustic option if you can't spring for Røisheim or Elvesæter, but still want the countryside-farm experience. This 150-year-old farmhouse, situated by a soothing waterfall, rents two rooms and one apartment, plus four sod-roofed log huts. The catch: Many of the buildings have no running water, so you'll use the shared facilities at the main building. While not everyone's cup of tea, this place will appeal to romantics who always wanted to sleep in a humble log cabin in the Norwegian mountains—it's downright idyllic for those who like to rough it (2-person huts: without bathroom-300-500 kr depending on size, beautiful private hut with bathroom-700 kr; rooms in main house: D-400-500 kr depending on size, apartment for 4-6 with private bath-700 kr; sheets and towels-70 kr, no breakfast, Wi-Fi, low ceilings, farm smells, valley views, 2 miles south of Lom on Route 55, tel. 61 21 12 37, www.strind-gard.no, post@strind-gard.no, Anne Jorunn and Trond Dalsegg).

Drives and Hikes in the Jotunheimen Mountains

Route 55, which runs between Lom and the Sognefjord to the south, is the sightseeing spine of this region. From this main (and already scenic) drag, other roads spin upward into the mountains—offering even better views and exciting drives and hikes. Many of these get you up close to Norway's highest mountain, Galdhøpiggen (8,100 feet). I've listed these attractions from north to south, as you'll reach them driving from Lom to the Sognefjord; except for the first, they all branch off from Route 55. Another great high-mountain experience is nearby—the hike to the Nigard Glacier near Lustrafjord.

Remember that the Norwegian Mountain Museum in Lom acts as a national park office, offering excellent maps and advice for drivers and hikers—a stop here is obligatory if you're planning a jaunt into the mountains (see "Orientation to Lom," earlier).

Besseggen

This trail offers an incredible opportunity to walk between two lakes separated by a narrow ridge and a 1,000-foot cliff. It's one of Norway's most beloved hikes, which can make it crowded in the summer. To get to the trailhead, drivers detour down Route 51 after Otta south to Maurvangen. Turn right to Gjendesheim to park your car. From Gjendesheim, catch the boat to Memurubu, where the path starts at the boat dock. Hike along the ridge—with a blue lake (Bessvatnet) on one side and a green lake (Gjende) on the other—and keep your balance. The six-hour trail loops back to Gjendesheim. Because the boat runs sporadically, time your visit to catch one (120 kr for 20-minute ride, 3 morning departures daily, latest schedules at www.gjende.no, mobile 91 30 67 44). This is a thrilling but potentially hazardous hike, and it's a major detour: Gjendesheim is about 1.5 hours and 50 miles from Lom.

Spiterstulen

From Røisheim, this 11-mile toll road (80 kr) takes you from Route 55 to the Spiterstulen mountain hotel/lodge in about 30 minutes (3,600 feet). This is the best destination for serious all-day hikes to Norway's two mightiest mountains, Glittertinden and Galdhøpiggen (a 5-hour hike up and a 3-hour hike down, doable without a guide). Or consider a guided, two-hour glacier walk (tel. 61 21 94 00, www.spiterstulen.no).

Juvasshytta

This toll road takes you (in about 40 minutes) to the highest you can drive and the closest you can get to Galdhøpiggen (6,050 feet) by car. The road starts in Bøverdal, and costs 85 kr; at the end of it, daily, guided, six-hour hikes go across the glacier to the summit and back (200 kr, late June-late Sept daily at 10:00, July-mid-Aug also daily at 11:30, check in 30 minutes before, strict age limit—no kids under age 7, 4 miles each way, easy ascent but can be dangerous without a guide, hiking boots required—possible to rent from nearby ski resort). You can sleep in the newly updated **$$$ Juvasshytta lodge** (Db-1,140 kr with sheets, D without sheets-860 kr, sheets-100 kr, includes breakfast, dinner-330 kr, open June-Sept, tel. 61 21 15 50, www.juvasshytta.no).

Leirvassbu

This 11-mile, 50-kr toll road (about 30 minutes one-way from Bøverkinnhalsen, south of Elvesæter) is most scenic for car hikers. It takes you to a lodge at 4,600 feet with great views and easy walks. A serious (5-hour round-trip) hike goes to the lone peak, Kyrkja—"The Cathedral," which looms like a sanded-down mini-Matterhorn on the horizon (6,660 feet).

▲▲Sognefjell Drive to the Sognefjord

Norway's highest pass (at 4,600 feet, the highest road in northern Europe) is a thrilling drive through a cancan line of mountains, from Jotunheimen's Bøverdal Valley to the Lustrafjord (an arm of the Sognefjord—see previous chapter). Centuries ago, the farmers of Gudbrandsdal took their horse caravans over this difficult mountain pass on treks to Bergen. Today, the road (Route 55) is still narrow, windy, and otherworldly (and usually closed mid-Oct-May).

As you begin to ascend just beyond Elvesæter, notice the viewpoint on the left for the Leirdalen Valley—capped at the end with the Kyrkja peak (described earlier). Next you'll twist up into a lake-filled valley, then through a mild canyon with grand waterfalls. Before long, as you corkscrew up more switchbacks, you're above the tree line, enjoying a "top of the world" feeling. The best views (to the south) are of the cut-glass range called Hurrungane ("Noisy Children"). The 10 hairpin turns between Turtagrø and Fortun are exciting. Be sure to stop, get out, look around, and enjoy the lavish views. Treat each turn as if it were your last.

Just before you descend to the fjord, the terrain changes, and you reach a pullout on the right, next to a hilltop viewpoint—offering your first glimpse of the fjord. The Lustrafjord village of Skjolden is just around the bend (and down several more switchbacks). Entering Skjolden, continue following Route 55, which now traces the west bank of the Lustrafjord.

Gudbrandsdal and Jotunheimen Connections

Cars are better, but if you're without wheels: **Oslo to Lillehammer** (trains almost hourly, 2.5 hours, just 2 hours from Oslo airport), **Lillehammer to Otta** (6 trains/day, 1.5 hours); a bus meets some trains (confirm schedule at the train station in Oslo) for travelers heading on to **Lom** (2 buses/day, 1 hour) and onward from **Lom to Sogndal** (2 buses/day late June-Aug only, road closed off-season, 3.5 hours).

ROUTE TIPS FOR DRIVERS

Use low gears and lots of patience both up (to keep the engine cool) and down (to save your brakes). Uphill traffic gets the right-of-way, but drivers, up or down, dive for the nearest fat part of the road whenever they meet. Ask backseat drivers not to scream until you've actually been hit or have left the road.

From Oslo to Jotunheimen: It's 2.5 hours from Oslo to Lille-hammer and 3 hours after that to Lom. Wind out of Oslo following signs for *E-6* (not to *Drammen*, but for *Stockholm* and then to *Trondheim*). In a few minutes, you're in the wide-open pastoral countryside of eastern Norway. Norway's Constitution Hall—Eidsvoll Manor—is a five-minute detour off E-6, several miles south of Eidsvoll in Eidsvoll Verk (follow the signs to *Eidsvoll Bygningen*). Then E-6 takes you along Norway's largest lake (Mjøsa), through the town of Hamar, and past more lake scenery into Lille-hammer. Signs direct you uphill from downtown Lillehammer to the Maihaugen Open-Air Folk Museum. From Lillehammer, signs to *E-6/Trondheim* take you up the valley of Gudbrandsdal. At Otta, exit for Lom. Halfway to Lom, on the left, look for the long suspension bridge spanning the milky-blue river—a good opportunity to stretch your legs, and a scenic spot to enjoy a picnic.

BERGEN

Bergen is permanently salted with robust cobbles and a rich sea-trading heritage. Norway's capital in the 13th century, Bergen's wealth and importance came thanks to its membership in the heavyweight medieval trading club of merchant cities called the Hanseatic League. Bergen still wears her rich maritime heritage proudly—nowhere more scenically than the colorful wooden warehouses that make up the picture-perfect Bryggen district along the harbor.

Protected from the open sea by a lone sheltering island, Bergen is a place of refuge from heavy winds for the giant working boats that serve the North Sea oil rigs. (Much of Norway's current affluence is funded by the oil it drills just offshore.) Bergen is also one of the most popular cruise-ship ports in northern Europe, hosting about 300 ships a year and up to five ships a day in peak season. Each morning is rush hour, as cruisers hike past the fortress and into town.

Bergen gets an average of 80 inches of rain annually (compared to 30 inches in Oslo). A good year has 60 days of sunshine. The natives aren't apologetic about their famously lousy weather. In fact, they seem to wear it as a badge of pride. "Well, that's Bergen," they'll say matter-of-factly as they wring out their raincoats. When I complained about an all-day downpour, one resident cheerfully informed me, "There's no such thing as bad weather—just inappropriate clothing"...a local mantra that rhymes in Norwegian.

With about 240,000 people, Bergen has big-city parking problems and high prices, but visitors sticking to the old center find it charming. Enjoy Bergen's salty market, then stroll the easy-on-foot old quarter, with cute lanes of delicate old wooden houses.

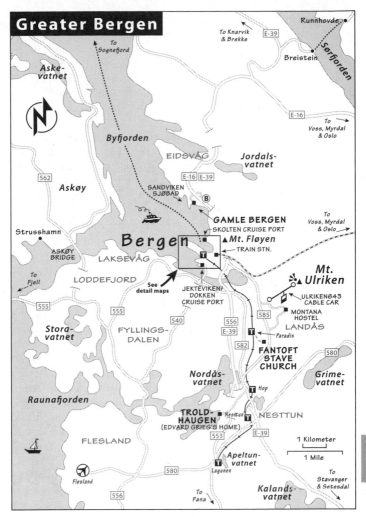

From downtown Bergen, a funicular zips you up a little mountain for a bird's-eye view of this sailors' town. A short foray into the countryside takes you to a variety of nearby experiences: a dramatic cable-car ride to a mountaintop perch (Ulriken643); a scenic stave church (Fantoft); and the home of Norway's most beloved composer, Edvard Grieg, at Troldhaugen.

PLANNING YOUR TIME

Bergen can be enjoyed even on the tail end of a day's scenic train ride from Oslo before returning on the overnight train. But that teasing taste will make you wish you had more time. On a three-week tour of Scandinavia, Bergen is worth a whole day.

While Bergen's sights are visually underwhelming and pricey, nearly all come with thoughtful tours in English. If you dedicate the time to take advantage of these tours, otherwise barren attractions (such as Håkon's Hall and Rosenkrantz Tower, the Bryggen quarter, the Leprosy Museum, and Gamle Bergen) become surprisingly interesting.

For a busy day, you could do this (enjoying tours at all but the last): 9:00—Stroll through the Fish Market; 10:00—Visit Håkon's Hall and Rosenkrantz Tower (joining a guided tour); 12:00—Take the Bryggen Walking Tour (June-Aug only); 14:00—Check out the Leprosy Museum and cathedral; 16:00—Enjoy some free time in town (consider returning to the Bryggens Museum using your tour ticket), or catch the bus out to Gamle Bergen; 18:00—Ride up the Fløibanen funicular. If you visit off-season, some sights have shorter hours (Håkon's Hall and Rosenkrantz Tower) or are closed altogether (Leprosy Museum).

Although Bergen has plenty of attractions and charms of its own, it's most famous as the "Gateway to the Fjords." If you plan to use Bergen as a springboard for fjord country, you have three options: Pick up a rental car here (fjord wonder is a three-hour drive away); take the express boat down the Sognefjord (about four hours to Balestrand and Flåm/Aurland); or do the "Norway in a Nutshell" as a scenic loop from Bergen. The "Nutshell" option also works well as a detour midway between Bergen and Oslo (hop the train from either city to Voss or Myrdal, then take a bus or spur train into the best of the Sognefjord; scenic ferry rides depart from there). While there are a million ways to enjoy the fjords, first-timers should start with this region (covered thoroughly in the Norway in a Nutshell and More on the Sognefjord chapters).

Also note that Bergen, a geographic dead-end, is actually an efficient place to begin or end your Scandinavian tour. Consider flying into Bergen and out of another city, such as Helsinki (or vice versa).

Orientation to Bergen

Bergen clusters around its harbor—nearly everything listed in this chapter is within a few minutes' walk. The busy Torget (the square with the Fish Market) is at the head of the harbor. As you face the sea from here, Bergen's TI is at the left end of the Fish Market. The town's historic Hanse-

atic Quarter, Bryggen (BREW-gun), lines the harbor on the right. Express boats to the Sognefjord (Balestrand and Flåm) dock at the harbor on the left.

Charming cobbled streets surround the harbor and climb the encircling hills. Bergen's popular Fløibanen funicular climbs high above the city to the top of Mount Fløyen for the best view of the town. Surveying the surrounding islands and inlets, it's clear why this city is known as the "Gateway to the Fjords."

TOURIST INFORMATION

The centrally located TI is upstairs in the long, skinny, modern, Torghallen market building, next to the Fish Market (June-Aug daily 8:30-22:00; May and Sept daily 9:00-20:00; Oct-April Mon-Sat 9:00-16:00, closed Sun; handy budget eateries downstairs and in Fish Market; tel. 55 55 20 00, www.visitbergen.com).

The TI covers Bergen and western Norway, provides information and tickets for tours, has a fjord information desk, books rooms, and maintains a very handy events board listing today's and tomorrow's slate of tours, concerts, and other events. Pick up this year's edition of the free *Bergen Guide* (also likely at your hotel), which has a fine map and lists all sights, hours, and special events. This booklet can answer most of your questions. If you need assistance and there's a line, take a number. They also have free Wi-Fi (password posted on wall).

Bergen Card: You have to work hard to make this greedy little card pay off (200 kr/24 hours, 260 kr/48 hours, sold at TI and Montana Family & Youth Hostel). It gives you free use of the city's tram and buses, half off the Mount Fløyen funicular, free admission to most museums (but not the Hanseatic Museum; aquarium included only in winter), and discounts on some events and sights such as Edvard Grieg's Home.

ARRIVAL IN BERGEN

By Train or Bus: Bergen's train and bus stations are on Strømgaten, facing a park-rimmed lake. The small, manageable train station has an office open long hours for booking all your travel in Norway— you can get your Nutshell reservations here (Mon-Fri 6:35-19:00, Sat 7:30-16:00, Sun 7:30-16:00). There are luggage lockers (50 kr/day, daily 6:00-23:30), pay toilets, a newsstand, sandwich shop, and coffee shop. (To get to the bus station, follow the covered walkway behind the Narvesen newsstand via the Storcenter shopping mall.) Taxis wait to the right (with the tracks at your back); a tram stop is to your left, just around the corner. From the train station, it's a 10-minute walk to the TI: Cross the street (Strømgaten) in front of the station and take Marken, a cobbled street that eventually turns into a modern retail street. Continue walking in the same direction until you reach the water.

By Plane: Bergen's cute little Flesland Airport is 12 miles south of the city center (airport code: BGO, tel. 67 03 15 55, www. avinor.no/bergen). The airport bus runs between the airport and downtown Bergen, stopping at the Radisson Blu Royal Hotel in Bryggen, the harborfront area near the TI (if you ask), the Radisson Blu Hotel Norge (in the modern part of town at Ole Bulls Plass), and the bus station (about 95 kr, pay driver, 4/hour at peak times, less in slow times, 30-minute ride). Two different companies run this bus, but the cost and frequency is about the same—just take the first one that shows up. Taxis take up to four people and cost about 400 kr for the 20-minute ride (depending on the time of day).

By Car: Driving is a headache in Bergen; avoid it if you can. Approaching town on E-16 (from Voss and the Sognefjord area), follow signs for *Sentrum,* which spits you out near the big, modern bus station and parking garage. Parking is difficult and costly—ask your hotelier for tips. Note that all drivers entering Bergen must pay a 25-kr toll, but there are no toll-collection gates (since the system is automated). Assuming they bill you, it'll just show up on your credit card (which they access through your rental-car company). For details, ask your rental company or see www.autopass. no.

By Cruise Ship: Bergen is easy for cruise passengers, regardless of which of the city's two ports your ship uses.

The **Skolten** cruise port is just past the fortress on the main harborfront road. Arriving here, simply walk into town (stroll with the harbor on your right, figure about 10 minutes to Bryggen, plus five more minutes to the Fish Market and TI). After about five minutes, you'll pass the fortress—the starting point for my self-guided walk. A taxi into downtown costs about 70-80 kr, and hop-on, hop-off buses pick up passengers at the port (though in this compact town, I'd just walk).

The **Jekteviken/Dokken** cruise port is in an industrial zone to the south, a bit farther out (about a 20-minute walk). To discourage passengers from walking through all the containers, the port operates a convenient and free **shuttle bus** that zips you into town. It drops you off along Rasmus Meyers Allé right in front of the Kode Art Museums, facing the cute manmade lake called Lille Lungegårdsvann. From here, it's an easy 10-minute walk to the TI and Fish Market: Walk with the lake on your right, pass through the park (with the pavilion) and head up the pedestrian mall called Ole Bulls Plass, and turn right (at the bluish slab) up the broad square called Torgallmenningen. Note that my self-guided Bergen walk conveniently ends near the shuttle-bus stop. A taxi from the cruise port into downtown runs about 110 kr.

For more in-depth cruising information, pick up my *Rick Steves Northern European Cruise Ports* guidebook.

HELPFUL HINTS

Museum Tours: Many of Bergen's sights are hard to appreciate without a guide. Fortunately, several include a wonderful and intimate guided tour with admission. Make the most of the following sights by taking advantage of their included tours: Håkon's Hall and Rosenkrantz Tower, Bryggens Museum, Hanseatic Museum, Leprosy Museum, Gamle Bergen, and Edvard Grieg's Home.

Crowd Control: In high season, cruise-ship passengers mob the waterfront between 10:00 and 15:00; to avoid the crush, consider visiting an outlying sight during this time, such as Gamle Bergen or Edvard Grieg's Home.

Internet Access: The **TI** offers free, fast Wi-Fi (look for the password posted on the wall), but no terminals. The **Bergen Public Library,** next door to the train station, has free terminals in their downstairs café (30-minute limit, Mon-Thu 10:00-18:00, Fri 10:00-16:00, Sat 10:00-15:00, closed Sun, Strømgaten 6, tel. 55 56 85 60). The church-run **Kafe Magdalena,** just off the harbor at Kong Oscars Gate 5, has two free terminals.

Laundry: If you drop your laundry off at **Hygienisk Vask & Rens,** you can pick it up clean the next day (70 kr/kilo, no self-service, Sun-Fri 8:30-16:30, closed Sat, Halfdan Kjerulfsgate 8, tel. 55 31 77 41).

Updates to This Book: For updates to this book, check www.ricksteves.com/update.

GETTING AROUND BERGEN

Most in-town sights can easily be reached by foot; only the aquarium and Gamle Bergen (and farther-flung sights such as the Fantoft Stave Church, Edvard Grieg's Home at Troldhaugen, and the Ulriken643 cable car) are more than a 10-minute walk from the TI.

By Bus: City buses cost 41 kr per ride (pay driver in cash), or 31 kr per ride if you buy a single-ride ticket from a machine or convenience stores such as Narvesen, 7-Eleven, Rimi, and Deli de Luca. The best buses for a Bergen joyride are #6 (north along the coast) and #11 (into the hills).

By Tram: Bergen's recently built light-rail line (Bybanen) is a convenient way to visit Edvard Grieg's Home or the Fantoft Stave Church. The tram begins next to Byparken (on Kaigaten, between Bergen's little lake and Ole Bulls Plass), then heads to the train station and continues south. Buy your 31-kr ticket from the machine prior to boarding (to use a US credit card, you'll need to know your PIN code). You can also buy single-ride tickets at Narvesen, 7-Eleven, Rimi, and Deli de Luca stores. You'll get a gray *minikort* pass. Validate the pass when you board by holding it next to the card reader (watch how other passengers do it). Ride it about 20 minutes to the Paradis stop for Fantoft Stave Church (don't get off at the "Fantoft" stop, which is farther from the church); or continue to the next stop, Hop, to hike to Troldhaugen.

By Ferry: The *Beffen*, a little orange ferry, chugs across the harbor every half-hour, from the dock a block south of the Bryggens Museum to the dock—directly opposite the fortress—a block from the Nykirken church (20 kr, Mon-Fri 7:30-16:00, plus Sat May-Aug 11:00-16:00, never on Sun, 3-minute ride). The *Vågen* ferry runs from the Fish Market every half-hour to a dock near the aquarium (50 kr one-way, daily June-Aug 10:00-17:30, off-season 10:00-16:00, 10-minute ride). These short "poor man's cruises" have good harbor views.

By Taxi: For a taxi, call 07000 or 08000 (they're not as expensive as you might expect).

Tours in Bergen

▲▲▲Bryggen Walking Tour

This tour of the historic Hanseatic district is one of Bergen's best activities. Local guides take visitors on an excellent 1.5-hour walk

in English through 900 years of Bergen history via the old Hanseatic town (20 minutes in Bryggens Museum, 20-minute visit to the medieval Hanseatic Assembly Rooms, 20-minute walk through Bryggen, and 20 minutes in Hanseatic Museum). Tours leave from the Bryggens Museum (next to the Radisson Blu Royal Hotel). When you consider that the price includes entry tickets to all three sights, the tour more than pays for itself (120 kr, June-Aug daily at 11:00 and 12:00, maximum 30 in group, no tours Sept-May, tel. 55 58 80 10, bryggens. museum@bymuseet.no). While the museum visits are a bit rushed, your tour ticket allows you to re-enter the museums for the rest of the day. The 11:00 tour can sell out, especially in July; to be safe, you can call, email, or drop by ahead of time to reserve a spot.

Local Guide
Sue Lindelid is a British expat who has spent more than 25 years showing visitors around Bergen (800 kr/2-hour tour, 900 kr/3 or more people; 1,000 kr/3-hour tour, 1,200 kr/3 or more people; mobile 90 78 59 52, suelin@hotmail.no).

▲Bus Tours
The TI sells tickets for various bus tours, including a 2.5-hour Grieg Lunch Concert tour that goes to Edvard Grieg's Home at Troldhaugen—a handy way to reach that distant sight (250 kr, discount with Bergen Card, includes 30-minute concert but not lunch, June-mid-Sept daily at 11:30, departs from TI). Buses are comfy, with big views and a fine recorded commentary. There are also several full-day tour options from Bergen, including bus/boat tours to nearby Hardanger and Sogne fjords. The TI is packed with brochures describing all the excursions.

Hop-On, Hop-Off Buses
City Sightseeing links most of Bergen's major sights and also stops at the Skolten cruise port, but doesn't go to the Fantoft Stave Church, Troldhaugen, or Ulriken643 cable car. If your sightseeing plans don't extend beyond the walkable core of Bergen, skip the bus and save some kroner (150 kr/24 hours, late May-Aug 9:00-16:30, 2/hour, also stops right in front of Fish Market, mobile 97 78 18 88, www.citysightseeing-bergen.net).

▲Harbor Tour
The *White Lady* leaves once daily at 11:00 (summer only) from the Fish Market for a 1.5-hour cruise. The ride is both scenic and informative, with a relaxing sun deck and good—if scant—recorded narration (150 kr, June-Aug). A daily four-hour afternoon fjord trip is also available (500 kr, June-Aug, tel. 55 25 90 00, www.whitelady.no).

Tourist Train
The tacky little "Bergen Express" train departs from in front of the Hanseatic Museum for a 55-minute loop around town (150 kr, 2/hour in peak season, otherwise hourly; runs daily May 10:00-16:00, June-Aug 10:00-19:00, Sept 10:00-15:00; headphone English commentary).

Bergen Walk

For a quick self-guided orientation stroll through Bergen, follow this walk from the city's fortress, through its old wooden Hanseatic Quarter and Fish Market, to the modern center of town. This walk is also a handy sightseeing spine, passing most of Bergen's best museums; ideally, you'll get sidetracked and take advantage

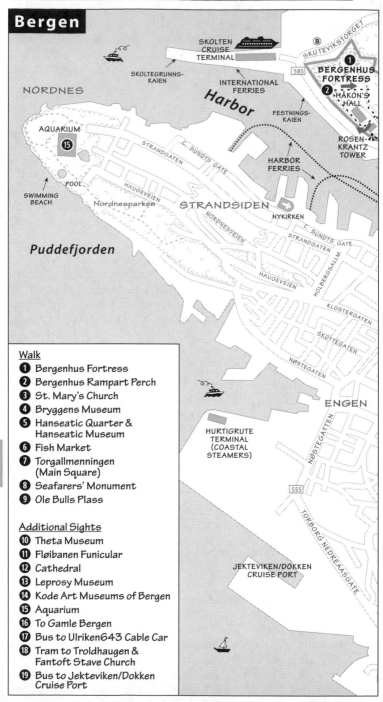

Bergen

NORDNES

AQUARIUM
15

SWIMMING
BEACH

POOL

Puddefjorden

Nordnesparken

HAUGEVEIEN

STRANDGATEN

C. SUNDTS GATE

Harbor

SKOLTEN
CRUISE
TERMINAL

SKOLTEGRUNNS-
KAIEN

INTERNATIONAL
FERRIES

FESTNINGS-
KAIEN

HARBOR
FERRIES

B

SKUTEVIKSTORGET

585

1
BERGENHUS
FORTRESS

2
HÅKON'S
HALL

ROSEN-
KRANTZ
TOWER

STRANDSIDEN

NORDNESVEIEN

NYKIRKEN

C. SUNDTS GATE

STRANDGATEN

HAUGEVEIEN

HOLBERGSALLM.

KLOSTERGATEN

SKOTTEGATEN

NØSTEGATEN

ENGEN

HURTIGRUTE
TERMINAL
(COASTAL
STEAMERS)

555

NØSTEGATTEN

TORBORG NEDREAASGATE

JEKTEVIKEN/DOKKEN
CRUISE PORT

Walk
1 Bergenhus Fortress
2 Bergenhus Rampart Perch
3 St. Mary's Church
4 Bryggens Museum
5 Hanseatic Quarter &
    Hanseatic Museum
6 Fish Market
7 Torgallmenningen
    (Main Square)
8 Seafarers' Monument
9 Ole Bulls Plass

Additional Sights
10 Theta Museum
11 Fløibanen Funicular
12 Cathedral
13 Leprosy Museum
14 Kode Art Museums of Bergen
15 Aquarium
16 To Gamle Bergen
17 Bus to Ulriken643 Cable Car
18 Tram to Troldhaugen &
    Fantoft Stave Church
19 Bus to Jekteviken/Dokken
    Cruise Port

BERGEN

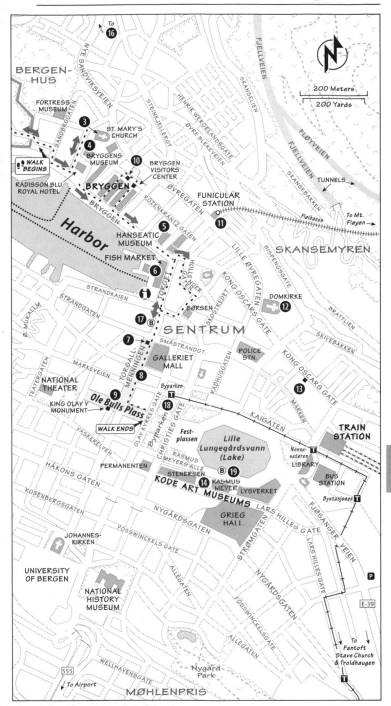

Bergen at a Glance

▲▲▲Bryggen Walking Tour Wonderful 1.5-hour tour of the historic Hanseatic district that covers 900 years of history and includes short visits to the Bryggens Museum, Hanseatic Assembly Rooms, and Hanseatic Museum, plus a walk through Bryggen. **Hours:** June-Aug daily at 11:00 and 12:00. See page 162.

▲▲Bryggens Museum Featuring early bits of Bergen (1050-1500), found in a 1950s archaeological dig. **Hours:** Mid-May-Aug daily 10:00-16:00; Sept-mid-May Mon-Fri 11:00-15:00, Sat 12:00-15:00, Sun 12:00-16:00. See page 179.

▲▲Hanseatic Museum Small museum highlighting Bryggen's glory days, located in an old merchant house furnished with artifacts from the time German merchants were tops in trading—most interesting with included tour. **Hours:** Daily May-Sept 9:00-17:00; Oct-April Tue-Sat 11:00-14:00, Sun 11:00-16:00, closed Mon. See page 179.

▲▲Fløibanen Funicular Zippy lift to top of Mount Fløyen for super views of Bergen, islands, and fjords, with picnic ops, an eatery, playground, and hiking trails. **Hours:** Mon-Fri 7:30-23:00, Sat-Sun 8:00-23:00. See page 180.

▲Harbor Tour Scenic 1.5-hour cruise, with recorded narration, leaving from the Fish Market. **Hours:** June-Aug at 11:00. See page 166.

▲Fish Market Lively market with cheap seafood eateries and free samples. **Hours:** Daily 7:00-19:00; Sept-May Mon-Sat 7:00-16:00, closed Sun. See page 174.

▲Bergenhus Fortress: Håkon's Hall and Rosenkrantz Tower Fortress with a 13th-century medieval banquet hall, a climbable tower offering a history exhibit and views, and a worthwhile, included tour. **Hours:** Mid-May-Aug—hall open daily 10:00-16:00, tower open daily 9:00-16:00; Sept-mid-May—hall open daily 12:00-15:00, tower open Sun only 12:00-15:00. See page 178.

of their excellent tours (included with admission) along the way. I've pointed out the museums you'll pass en route—all of them are described in greater detail later, under "Sights in Bergen."

• *Begin where Bergen did, at its historic fortress. From the harborfront road, 50 yards before the stone tower with the water on your left, veer up the ramp behind the low stone wall on the right, through a gate, and into the fortress complex. Stand before the stony skyscraper.*

▲**Kode Art Museums of Bergen** Collection spread among four neighboring lakeside buildings: Lysverket (international and Norwegian artists), Rasmus Meyer (Norwegian artists, including Munch), Stenersen (contemporary art), and Permanenten (decorative arts). **Hours:** Daily 11:00-17:00, closed Mon mid-Sept-mid-May. See page 182.

▲**Aquarium** Well-presented sea life, with a walk-through "shark tunnel" and feeding times at the top of most hours in summer. **Hours:** Daily May-Aug 10:00-18:00, Sept-mid-Oct daily 10:00-16:00, mid-Oct-April Tue-Sun 10:00-16:00, closed Mon. See page 182.

▲**Gamle Bergen (Old Bergen)** Quaint gathering of 50 homes and shops dating from 18th-20th century, with guided tours of museum interiors at the top of the hour. **Hours:** Mid-May-Aug daily 9:00-16:00, closed Sept-mid-May. See page 183.

Leprosy Museum Former hospital for lepers, with small exhibit and worthwhile free tour offered on the top of every hour. **Hours:** Mid-May-Aug daily 11:00-15:00, closed Sept-mid-May. See page 181.

Near Bergen
▲▲**Edvard Grieg's Home, Troldhaugen** Home of Norway's greatest composer, with artifacts, tours, and concerts. **Hours:** Daily May-Sept 9:00-18:00, Oct-April 10:00-16:00. See page 185.

▲**Ulriken643 Cable Car** A quick ride up to the summit of Ulriken, Bergen's tallest mountain, with nonstop views, a restaurant, and hiking trails. **Hours:** Daily 9:00-21:00, off-season 9:00-17:00. See page 184.

Fantoft Stave Church Replica of a 12th-century wooden church in atmospheric wooded setting. **Hours:** Mid-May-mid-Sept daily 10:30-18:00, interior closed off-season. See page 186.

BERGEN

❶ Bergenhus Fortress
In the 13th century, Bergen became the Kingdom of Norway's first real capital. (Until then, kings would circulate, staying on royal farms.) This fortress—built in the 1240s, and worth ▲—was a garrison, with a tower for the king's residence (Rosenkrantz Tower) and a large hall for his banquets (Håkon's Hall).

Rosenkrantz Tower, the keep of the 13th-century castle, was expanded in the 16th century by the Danish-Norwegian king, who wanted to exercise a little control over the German merchants who dominated his town. He was tired of the Germans making all the money without paying taxes. This tower—with its cannon trained not on external threats but toward Bryggen—while expensive, paid for itself many times over as Germans got the message and paid their taxes.

• *Step through the gate (20 yards to the right of the tower) marked 1728 and into the courtyard of the Bergenhus Fortress. In front of you stands Håkon's Hall with its stepped gable. Tours for both the hall and the tower leave from the building to the right of Håkon's Hall.*

Pop into the museum lobby to enjoy a free exhibit about the massive 1944 explosion of the German ammunition ship in the harbor. For the best view of Håkon's Hall, walk through the gate and around the building to the left. Stand on the rampart between the hall and the harbor.

Håkon's Hall is the largest secular medieval building in Norway. When the pope sent a cardinal to perform Håkon's coronation there was no suitable building in Norway for such a VIP. King Håkon fixed that by having this impressive banqueting hall built in the mid-1200s. When Norway's capital moved to Oslo in 1299, the hall was abandoned and eventually used for grain storage. For a century it had no roof. In the Romantic 19th century, it was appreciated and restored. It's essentially a giant, grand reception hall used today as it was eight centuries ago, for banquets.

• *Continue walking along the rampart (climbing some steps and going about 100 yards past Håkon's Hall) to the far end of Bergenhus Fortress where you find a statue of a king and a fine harbor view.*

❼ Bergenhus Rampart Perch and Statue of King Håkon VII

The cannon on the ramparts here illustrates how the fort protected this strategic harbor. The port is busy with both cruise ships and support ships for the nearby North Sea oil rigs. Long before this modern commerce, this is where the cod fishermen of the north met the traders of Europe. Travelers in the 12th century described how there were so many trading vessels here "you could cross the harbor without getting your feet wet." Beyond the ships is an island protecting Bergen from the open sea.

Look left and right at the dangerous edge with no railing. If someone were to fall and get hurt here and then try to sue, the Norwegian judge's verdict would be: stupidity—case dismissed. Around you are Bergen's "seven mountains." One day each summer locals race to climb each of these in rapid succession, accomplishing the feat in less than 12 hours.

The statue is of the beloved King Håkon VII (1872-1957), grandfather of today's king. While exiled in London during World

War II, King Håkon kept up Norwegian spirits through radio broadcasts. The first king of modern Norway (after the country won its independence from Sweden in 1905), he was a Danish prince married to Queen Victoria's granddaughter—a savvy monarch who knew how to play the royalty game.

A few steps behind the statue (just right of tree-lined lane) is the site of Bergen's first cathedral, built in 1070. A hedge grows where its walls once stood. The statue of Mary marks the place of the altar, its pedestal etched with a list of 13th-century kings of Norway crowned and buried here.

These castle grounds (notice the natural amphitheater on the left) host cultural events and music festivals; Bruce Springsteen, the Stones, and Rihanna have all packed this outdoor venue in recent years.

Continuing around Håkon's Hall, follow the linden tree-lined lane. On the left, a massive concrete structure disguised by ivy looms as if evil. It was a German bunker built during the Nazi occupation—easier now to ignore than dismantle.

Twenty yards ahead on the right is a rare set of free public toilets. Notice they come with blue lights to discourage heroin junkies from using these WCs as a place to shoot up. The blue lights make it hard to see veins.

• *You've now returned to the tower and circled the castle grounds. Before leaving, consider taking one of the guided tours of the hall and tower that leave at the top of each hour (described in "Sights in Bergen," later). Head back down the ramp, out to the main road, and continue with the harbor on your right. (After a block, history buffs could follow* Bergenhus *signs, up the street to the left, to the free and fascinating* **Fortress Museum**—*with its collection of Norwegian military history and Nazi occupation exhibits.) Proceed one more block along the harbor until you reach the open, park-like space on your left. Walk 100 yards (just past the handy Rema 1000 supermarket) to the top of this park where you'll see...*

❸ St. Mary's Church (Mariakirken)

Dating from the 12th century, this is Bergen's oldest building in continuous use. It's closed for a couple of years while a 100-million-kroner renovation is under way. This stately church of the Hanseatic merchants has a dour stone interior, enlivened by a colorful, highly decorated pulpit.

In the park below the church, find the statue of Snorri Sturluson.

In the 1200s, this Icelandic scribe and scholar wrote down the Viking sagas. Thanks to him, we have a better understanding of this Nordic era. A few steps to the right, look through the window of the big modern building at an archaeological site showing the oldest remains of Bergen—stubs of the 12th-century trading town's streets tumbling to the harbor before land reclamation pushed the harbor farther out.

• *The window is just a sneak peek at the excellent* ❹ *Bryggens Museum, which provides helpful historical context for the Hanseatic Quarter we're about to visit (see listing later, under "Sights in Bergen.") The museum's outstanding* **Bryggen Walking Tour** *is your best bet for seeing this area (June-Aug daily at 11:00 and 12:00, see "Tours in Bergen," earlier). Continue down to the busy harborfront. On the left is the most photographed sight in town, the Bryggen quarter. To get your bearings, first read the "Bryggen's History" sidebar; if it's nice out, cross the street to the wharf and look back for a fine overview of this area. (Or, in the rain, huddle under an awning.)*

❺ Bergen's Hanseatic Quarter (Bryggen)

Bergen's fragile wooden old town is its iconic front door. The long "tenements" (rows of warehouses) hide atmospheric lanes that creak and groan with history.

Remember that while we think of Bergen as "Norwegian," Bryggen was German—the territory of *Deutsch*-speaking merchants and traders. (The most popular surname in Bergen is the German name Hanson—"son of Hans.") From the front of Bryggen, look back at the Rosenkrantz Tower. The little red holes at its top mark where cannons once pointed at the German quarter, installed by Norwegian royalty who wanted a slice of all that taxable trade revenue. Their threat was countered by German grain—without which the Norwegians would've starved.

Notice that the first six houses are perfectly straight; they were built in the 1980s to block the view of a modern hotel behind. The more ramshackle stretch of 11 houses beyond date from the early 1700s. Each front hides a long line of five to ten businesses.

• *To wander into the heart of this woody medieval quarter, head down Bredsgården, the lane a couple of doors before the shop sign featuring the anatomically correct unicorn. We'll make a loop to the right: down this lane nearly all the way, under a passage into a square (with a well, a vibrant outdoor restaurant, and a big wooden cod), and then back to the harbor down a parallel lane. Read the information below, then explore, stopping at the big wooden cod.*

Bit by bit, Bryggen is being restored using medieval techniques and materials. As you explore, you may stumble upon a rebuilding project in action.

Strolling through Bryggen, you feel swallowed up by history. Long rows of planky buildings (medieval-style double tenements) lean haphazardly across narrow al-leys. The last Hanseatic merchant moved out centuries ago, but this is still a place of (touristy) commerce. You'll find artists' galleries, T-shirt boutiques, leather workshops, at-mospheric restaurants, fishing tack-le shops, sweaters, sweaters, sweat-ers...and trolls.

Look up at the winch and pul-ley systems on the buildings. These connected ground-floor workrooms with top-floor storerooms. Notice that the overhanging storerooms upstairs were supported by timbers with an elbow created by a tree trunk and its root—considered the strongest way to make a right angle in construction back then. Turning right at the top of the lane, you enter a lively cobbled square. On the far side is that big wooden fish.

The wooden cod (next to a well) is a reminder that the eco-nomic foundation of Bergen—the biggest city in Scandinavia until 1650 and the biggest city in Norway until 1830—was this fish. The stone building behind the carved cod was one of the fireproof cookhouses serving a line of buildings that stretched to the harbor. Today it's the Hetland Gallery, filled with the entertaining work of a popular local artist famous for fun caricatures of the city. Facing the same square is the Bryggen visitors center, worth peeking into.

• *Enjoy the center and the shops. Then return downhill to the harbor-front, turn left, and continue the walk.*

Half of Bryggen (the brick-and-stone stretch to your left be-tween the old wooden facades and the head of the bay) was torn down around 1900. Today the stately buildings that replaced it—far less atmospheric than Bryggen's original wooden core—are filled with tacky trinket shops and touristy splurge restaurants. They do make a nice architectural cancan of pointy gables, each with its date of construction indicated near the top.

Head to the lone wooden red house at the end of the row,

Bryggen's History

Pretty as Bryggen is today, it has a rough-and-tumble history. A horrific plague decimated the population and economy of Norway in 1350, killing about half of its people. A decade later, German merchants arrived and established a Hanseatic trading post, bringing order to that rustic society. For the next four centuries, the port of Bergen was essentially German territory.

Bergen's old German trading center was called "the German wharf" until World War II (and is now just called "the wharf," or "Bryggen"). From 1370 to 1754, German merchants controlled Bergen's trade. In 1550, it was a Germanic city of 1,000 workaholic merchants—surrounded and supported by some 5,000 Norwegians.

The German merchants were very strict and lived in a harsh, all-male world (except for Norwegian prostitutes). This wasn't a military occupation, but a mutually beneficial economic partnership. The Norwegian cod fishermen of the far north shipped their dried cod to Bergen, where the Hanseatic merchants marketed it to Europe. Norwegian cod provided much of Europe with food (a source of easy-to-preserve protein) and cod oil (which lit the lamps until about 1850).

While the city dates from 1070, little survives from before the last big fire in 1702. In its earlier heyday, Bergen was one of the largest wooden cities in Europe. Congested wooden buildings, combined with lots of small fires (to provide heat and light in this cold and dark corner of Europe), spelled disaster for Bergen. Over the centuries, the city suffered countless fires, including 10 devastating ones. Back then, it wasn't a question of *if* there would be a fire, but *when* there would be a fire—with major blazes every 20 or so years. Each time the warehouses burned, the merchants would toss the refuse into the bay and rebuild. Gradually, the land crept out,

BERGEN

which houses the **Hanseatic Museum.** The man who owned this building recognized the value of the city's heritage and kept its 18th-century interior intact. Once considered a nutcase, today he's celebrated as a visionary, as his decision has left visitors with a fine example of an old merchant house that they can tour. This highly recommended museum is your best chance to get a peek inside one of those old wooden tenements.

• *The Fish Market is just across the street. Before enjoying that, we'll circle a few blocks inland and around to the right.*

The red-brick building (with frilly white trim, stepped gable, and a Starbucks) is the old meat market. It was built in 1877, after the importance of hygiene was recognized and the meat was moved and so did the buildings. (Looking at the Hanseatic Quarter from the harborfront, you can see how the buildings have settled. The foundations, composed of debris from the many fires, settle as they rot.)

After 1702, the city rebuilt using more stone and brick, and suffered fewer fires. But this one small wooden quarter was built after the fire, in the early 1700s. To prevent future blazes, the Germans forbade all fires and candles for light or warmth except in isolated and carefully guarded communal houses behind each tenement. It was in these communal houses that apprentices studied, people dried out their soggy clothes, hot food was cooked, and the men drank and partied. When there was a big banquet, one man always stayed sober—a kind of designated fire watchman.

Flash forward to the 20th century. One of the biggest explosions of World War II occurred in Bergen's harbor on April 20, 1944. An ammunition ship loaded with 120 tons of dynamite blew up just in front of the fortress. The blast leveled entire neighborhoods on either side of the harbor (notice the ugly 1950s construction opposite the fortress) and did serious damage to Håkon's Hall and Rosenkrantz Tower. How big was the blast? There's a hut called "the anchor cabin" a couple of miles away in the mountains. That's where the ship's anchor landed. The blast is considered to be accidental, despite the fact that April 20 happened to be Hitler's 55th birthday and the ship blew up about 100 yards away from the Nazi commander's headquarters (in the fortress).

After World War II, Bryggen was again slated for destruction. Most of the locals wanted it gone—it reminded them of the Germans who had occupied Norway for the miserable war years. Then excavators discovered rune stones indicating that the area predated the Germans. This boosted Bryggen's approval rating, and the quarter was saved. Today this picturesque and historic zone is the undisputed tourist highlight of Bergen.

BERGEN

inside from today's Fish Market. At the intersection just beyond, look left (uphill past the meat market) to see the Fløibanen station. Ahead, on the right, is an unusually classy McDonald's in a 1710 building that was originally a bakery.

But let's look at Norwegian fast food: Across the street, Söstrene Hagelin is a celebration of white and fishy cuisine—very Norwegian. A few steps uphill, the tiny red shack flying the Norwegian flags is the popular 3-Kroneren hot-dog stand (described in "Eating in Bergen," later). Review the many sausage options.

At the McDonald's, wander the length of the cute lane of 200-year-old buildings. Called Hollendergaten, its name comes from a time when the king organized foreign communities of traders into various neighborhoods; this was where the Dutch lived. The curving street marks the former harborfront—these buildings were originally right on the water.

Hooking left, you reach the end of Hollendergaten. Turn right back toward the harborfront. Ahead is the grand stone Børsen building (now Matbørsen, a collection of trendy restaurants), once the stock exchange. Step inside to enjoy its 1920s Art Deco-style murals celebrating Bergen's fishing heritage.

• *Now, cross the street and immerse yourself in Bergen's beloved Fish Market.*

❻ Fish Market (Fisketorget)

A fish market has thrived here since the 1500s, when fishermen rowed in with their catch and haggled with hungry residents. While it's now become a food circus of eateries selling fishy treats to tourists—no local would come here to actually buy fish—this famous market is still worth ▲, offering lots of smelly photo fun and free morsels to taste (June-Aug daily 7:00-19:00, less lively on Sun; Sept-May Mon-Sat 7:00-16:00, closed Sun). Many stands sell premade smoked-salmon

(laks) sandwiches, fish soup, and other snacks ideal for a light lunch (confirm prices before ordering). To try Norwegian jerky, pick up a bag of dried cod snacks *(torsk)*. The red meat is minke (pronounced mink-ee) whale, caught off the coast of northern Norway. Norwegians, notorious for their whaling, defend it as a traditional livelihood for many of their people. They remind us that they only harvest the minke whale, which is not on an endangered list. In recent years, Norway has assigned itself a quota of nearly 1,300 minke whales a year, with the actual catch coming to a bit over half of that.

• *Watch your wallet: If you're going to get pickpocketed in Bergen, it'll likely be here. When done exploring, with your back to the market, hike a block to the right (note the pointy church spire in the distance and the big blocky stone monument dead ahead) into the modern part of town and a huge, wide square. Pause at the intersection just before crossing into the square, about 20 yards before the blocky monument. Look left to see Mount Ulriken with its TV tower. A cable car called Ulriken643 takes you to its 2,110-foot summit. (Shuttle buses leave from this corner, at the top and bottom of the hour, to its station.) Now, walk up to that big square monument and meet some Vikings.*

❼ Seafarers' Monument

Nicknamed "the cube of goat cheese" for its shape, this 1950 monument celebrates Bergen's contact with the sea and remembers those who worked on it and died in it.
Study the faces: All social classes are represented. The statues relate to the scenes depicted in the reliefs above. Each side represents a century (start with the Vikings and work clockwise): 10th century—Vikings, with a totem pole in the panel above recalling the pre-Columbian

Norwegian discovery of America; 18th century—equipping Europe's ships; 19th century—whaling; 20th century—shipping and war. For the 21st century, see the real people—a cross-section of today's Norway—sitting at the statue's base. Major department stores (Galleriet, Xhibition, and Telegrafen) are all nearby.

• *The monument marks the start of Bergen's main square...*

❽ Torgallmenningen

Allmenningen means "for all the people." Torg means "square." And, while this is the city's main gathering place, it was actually created as a firebreak. The residents of this wood-built city knew fires were inevitable. The street plan was designed with breaks, or open spaces like this square, to help contain the destruction. In 1916, it succeeded in stopping a fire, which is why it has a more modern feel today.

Walk the length of the square to the angled slab of blue stone (quarried in Brazil) at the far end. This is a monument to King Olav V, who died in 1991, and a popular meeting point: Locals like to say, "Meet you at the Blue Stone." It marks the center of a park-like swath known as...

BERGEN

❾ Ole Bulls Plass

This drag leads from the National Theater (above on right) to a little lake (below on left).

Detour a few steps up for a better look at the **National The-**

ater, built in Art Nouveau style in 1909. Founded by violinist Ole Bull in 1850, this was the first theater to host plays in the Norwegian language. After 450 years of Danish and Swedish rule, 19th-century Norway enjoyed a cultural awakening, and Bergen became an artistic power. Ole

The Hanseatic League, Blessed by Cod

Middlemen in trade, the clever German merchants of the Hanseatic League ruled the waves of northern Europe for 500 years (c. 1250-1750). These sea-traders first banded together in a Hanse, or merchant guild, to defend themselves against pirates. As they spread out from Germany, they established trading posts in foreign lands, cut deals with local leaders for trading rights, built boats and wharves, and organized armies to protect ships and ports.

By the 15th century, these merchants had organized more than a hundred cities into the Hanseatic League, a free-trade zone that stretched from London to Russia. The League ran a profitable triangle of trade: Fish from Scandinavia was exchanged for grain from the eastern Baltic and luxury goods from England and Flanders. Everyone benefited, and the German merchants—the middlemen—reaped the profits.

At its peak, in the 15th century, the Hanseatic League was the dominant force—economic, military, and political—in northern Europe. This was an age when much of Europe was fragmented into petty kingdoms and dukedoms. Revenue-hungry kings and robber-baron lords levied chaotic and extortionist tolls and duties. Pirates plagued shipments. It was the Hanseatic League, rather than national governments, that brought the stability that allowed trade to flourish.

Bergen's place in this Baltic economy was all about cod—a

BERGEN

Bull collaborated with the playwright Henrik Ibsen. Ibsen commissioned Edvard Grieg to compose the music for his play *Peer Gynt*. These three lions of Norwegian culture all lived and worked right here in Bergen.

Head downhill on the square to a delightful fountain featuring a **statue of Ole Bull** in the shadow of trees. Ole Bull was an 1800s version of Elvis. A pop idol and heartthrob in his day, Ole Bull's bath water was bottled and sold by hotels, and women fainted when they heard him play violin. Living up to his name, he fathered over 40 children. Speaking of children, I love to hang out here watching families frolic in the pond, oblivious to the waterfall troll (see the statue with the harp below Ole Bull). According to legend, the troll bestows musical talent on anyone—like old Ole—who gives him a gift (he likes meat).

From here, the park spills farther downhill to a cast-iron pavilion given to the city by Germans in 1889, and on to the little manmade lake (Lille Lungegårdsvann), which is circled by an en-form of protein that could be dried, preserved, and shipped anywhere. Though cursed by a lack of natural resources, the city was blessed with a good harbor conveniently located between the rich fishing spots of northern Norway and the markets of Europe. Bergen's port shipped dried cod and fish oil southward and imported grain, cloth, beer, wine, and ceramics.

Bryggen was one of four principal Hanseatic trading posts (Kontors), along with London, Bruges, and Novgorod. It was the last Kontor opened (c. 1360), the least profitable, and the final one to close. Bryggen had warehouses, offices, and living quarters. Ships docked here were unloaded by counterpoise cranes. At its peak, as many as a thousand merchants, journeymen, and apprentices lived and worked here.

Bryggen was a self-contained German enclave within the city. The merchants came from Germany, worked a few years here, and retired back in the home country. They spoke German, wore German clothes, and attended their own churches. By law, they were forbidden to intermarry or fraternize with the Bergeners, except on business.

The Hanseatic League peaked around 1500, then slowly declined. Rising nation-states were jealous of the Germans merchants' power and wealth. The Reformation tore apart old alliances. Dutch and English traders broke the Hanseatic monopoly. Cities withdrew from the League and Kontors closed. In 1754, Bergen's Kontor was taken over by the Norwegians. When it closed its doors on December 31, 1899, a sea-trading era was over, but the city of Bergen had become rich...by the grace of cod.

joyable path. This green zone is considered a park and is cared for by the local parks department.

• *If you're up for a lakeside stroll, now's your chance. Also notice that alongside the lake (to the right as you face it from here) is a row of buildings housing the enjoyable* **Kode Art Museums**. *And to the left of the lake are some fine residential streets (including the picturesque, cobbled Marken); within a few minutes' walk are the* **Leprosy Museum** *and the* **cathedral.**

Sights in Bergen

Several museums listed here—including the Bryggens Museum, Håkon's Hall, Rosenkrantz Tower, Leprosy Museum, and Gamle Bergen—are part of the Bergen City Museum (Bymuseet) organization. If you buy a ticket to any of them, you can pay half-price at any of the others simply by showing your ticket.

▲Bergenhus Fortress: Håkon's Hall and Rosenkrantz Tower

The tower and hall, sitting boldly out of place on the harbor just beyond Bryggen, are reminders of Bergen's importance as the first permanent capital of Norway. Both sights feel vacant and don't really speak for themselves; the included guided tours, which provide a serious introduction to Bergen's history, are essential for grasping their significance.

Cost and Hours: Hall and tower—90 kr for both (or 60 kr each), includes a guided tour; mid-May-Aug—hall open daily 10:00-16:00, tower open daily 9:00-16:00; Sept-mid-May—hall open daily 12:00-15:00, tower open Sun only 12:00-15:00; tel. 55 31 60 67, free WC.

Visiting the Hall and Tower: The hall and the tower are described in my "Bergen Walk," earlier. Consider them as one sight and start with Håkon's Hall (mid-May-Aug tours leave daily from the building to the right of Håkon's Hall at the top of the hour, last one departs at 15:00; few tours off-season). Tours include both buildings.

Håkon's Hall, dating from the 13th century, is the largest secular medieval building in Norway. Built as a banqueting hall, that's essentially what it is today. While it's been rebuilt, the ceiling's design is modeled after grand wooden roofs of that era. Beneath the hall is a whitewashed cellar.

Rosenkrantz Tower, the keep of a 13th-century castle, is today a stack of barren rooms connected by tight spiral staircases, with a good history exhibit on the top two floors and a commanding view from its rooftop. In the 16th century, the ruling Danish-Norwegian king enlarged the tower and trained its cannon on the German-merchant district, Bryggen, to remind the merchants of the importance of paying their taxes.

Fortress Museum (Bergenhus Festningmuseum)

This humble museum (which functioned as a prison during the Nazi occupation), set back a couple of blocks from the fortress, will interest historians with its thoughtful exhibits about military history, especially Bergen's WWII experience (look for the Norwegian

Nazi flag). You'll learn about the resistance movement in Bergen (including its underground newspapers), the role of women in the Norwegian military, and Norwegian troops who have served with UN forces in overseas conflicts.

Cost and Hours: Free, daily 11:00-17:00, ask to borrow a translation of the descriptions at the entrance, just behind Thon Hotel Bergen Brygge at Koengen, tel. 55 54 63 87.

▲▲Bryggens Museum

This modern museum explains the 1950s archaeological dig to uncover the earliest bits of Bergen (1050-1500). Brief English explanations are posted. From September through May, when there is no tour, consider buying the good museum guidebook (25 kr).

Cost and Hours: 70 kr; in summer, entry included with Bryggen Walking Tour described earlier; mid-May-Aug daily 10:00-16:00; Sept-mid-May Mon-Fri 11:00-15:00, Sat 12:00-15:00, Sun 12:00-16:00; inexpensive cafeteria; in big, modern building just beyond the end of Bryggen and the Radisson Blu Royal Hotel, tel. 55 58 80 10, www.bymuseet.no.

Visiting the Museum: The manageable, well-presented permanent exhibit occupies the ground floor. First up are the foundations from original wooden tenements dating back to the 12th century (displayed right where they were excavated) and a giant chunk of the hull of a 100-foot-long, 13th-century ship that was found here. Next, an exhibit (roughly shaped like the long, wooden double-tenements outside) shows off artifacts and explains lifestyles from medieval Bryggen. Behind that is a display of items you might have bought at the medieval market. You'll finish with exhibits about the church in Bergen, the town's role as a royal capital, and its status as a cultural capital. Upstairs are two floors of temporary exhibits.

▲▲Hanseatic Museum (Hanseatiske Museum)

This little museum offers the best possible look inside the wooden houses that are Bergen's trademark. Its creaky old rooms—with hundred-year-old cod hanging from the ceiling—offer a time-tunnel experience back to Bryggen's glory days. It's located in an atmospheric old merchant house furnished with dried fish, antique ropes, an old oxtail (used for wringing spilled cod-liver oil back into the bucket), sagging steps, and cupboard beds from the early 1700s—one with a

medieval pinup girl. You'll explore two upstairs levels, fully furnished and with funhouse floors. The place still feels eerily lived-in; neatly sorted desks with tidy ledgers seem to be waiting for the next workday to begin.

Cost and Hours: 70 kr; entry included with Bryggen Walking Tour; daily May-Sept 9:00-17:00; Oct-April Tue-Sat 11:00-14:00, Sun 11:00-16:00, closed Mon; Finnegården 7a, tel. 55 54 46 96 or 55 54 46 90, www.museumvest.no.

Tours: There are scant English explanations, but it's much better if you take the good, included 45-minute guided tour (3/day in English—call to confirm, mid-May-mid-Sept only, times displayed just inside door). Even if you tour the museum with the Bryggen Walking Tour, you're welcome to revisit (using the same ticket) and take this longer tour.

Theta Museum

This small museum highlights Norway's resistance movement. You'll peek into the hidden world of a 10-person cell of courageous students, whose group—called Theta—housed other fighters and communicated with London during the Nazi occupation in World War II. It's housed in Theta's former headquarters—a small upstairs room in a wooden Bryggen building.

Cost and Hours: 30 kr, June-Aug Tue, Sat, and Sun 14:00-16:00, closed Mon, Wed-Fri, and Sept-May, Enhjørningsgården.

▲▲Fløibanen Funicular

Bergen's popular funicular climbs 1,000 feet in seven minutes to the top of Mount Fløyen for the best view of the town, surrounding islands, and fjords all the way to the west coast. The top is a popular picnic or pizza-to-go dinner spot, perfect for enjoying the sunset (Peppes Pizza is tucked behind the Hanseatic Museum, a block away from the base of the lift). The Fløien Folkerestaurant, at the top of the funicular, offers affordable self-service food all day in season. Behind the station, you'll find a playground and a fun giant troll photo op. The top is also the starting point for many peaceful hikes.

You'll buy your funicular ticket at the base of the Fløibanen (notice the photos in the entry hall of the construction of the funicular and its 1918 grand opening).

If you'll want to hike down from the top, ask for the *Fløyen Hiking Map* when you buy your ticket; you'll save 50 percent by purchasing only a one-way ticket up. From the top, walk behind

the station and follow the signs to the city center. The top half of the 30-minute hike is a gravelly lane through a forest with fine views. The bottom is a paved lane through charming old wooden homes. It's a steep descent. To save your knees, you could ride the lift most of the way down and get off at the Promsgate stop to wander through the delightful cobbled and shiplap lanes (note that only the :00 and :30 departures stop at Promsgate).

Cost and Hours: 85 kr round-trip, 43 kr one-way, Mon-Fri 7:30-23:00, Sat-Sun 8:00-23:00, departures 4/hour—on the quarter-hour most of the day, runs continuously if busy, tel. 55 33 68 00, www.floibanen.no.

Cathedral (Domkirke)

Bergen's main church, dedicated to St. Olav (the patron saint of Norway), dates from 1301. Drop in to enjoy its stoic, plain interior with stuccoed stone walls and a giant wooden pulpit. Sit in a hard, straight-backed pew and just try to doze off. Like so many old Norwegian structures, its roof makes you feel like you're huddled under an overturned Viking ship. The church is oddly lopsided, with just one side aisle. Before leaving, look up to see the gorgeous wood-carved organ over the main entrance. In the entryway, you'll see portraits of each bishop dating all the way back to the Reformation.

Cost and Hours: Free; mid-June-mid-Aug Mon-Fri 10:00-16:00, Sun 9:30-13:00, closed Sat; shorter hours off-season.

Leprosy Museum (Lepramuseet)

Leprosy is also known as "Hansen's Disease" because in the 1870s a Bergen man named Armauer Hansen did groundbreaking work in understanding the ailment. This unique museum is in St. Jørgens Hospital, a leprosarium that dates back to about 1700. Up until the 19th century, as much as 3 percent of Norway's population had leprosy. This hospital—once called "a grave-yard for the living" (its last patient died in 1946)—has a meager exhibit in a thought-provoking dorm for the dying. It's most worthwhile if you read the translation of the exhibit (borrow a copy at the entry) or take the free tour (at the top of each hour). As you leave, if you're interested, ask if you can see the medicinal herb garden out back.

Cost and Hours: 70 kr, mid-May-Aug daily 11:00-15:00, closed Sept-mid-May, between train station and Bryggen at Kong Oscars Gate 59, tel. 55 96 11 55, www.bymuseet.no.

▲Kode Art Museums of Bergen (Kunstmuseene i Bergen)

If you need to get out of the rain (and you enjoyed the National Gallery in Oslo), check out this collection, filling four neighboring buildings facing the lake along Rasmus Meyers Allé. The Lysverket building has an eclectic cross-section of both international and Norwegian artists. The Rasmus Meyer branch specializes in Norwegian artists and has an especially good Munch exhibit. The Stenersen building has installations of contemporary art, while the Permanenten building has decorative arts. Small description sheets in English are in each room.

Cost and Hours: 100 kr, daily 11:00-17:00, closed Mon mid-Sept-mid-May, Rasmus Meyers Allé 3, tel. 55 56 80 00, www.kunstmuseene.no.

Visiting the Museums: Many visitors focus on the **Lysverket** ("Lighthouse"; from outside, enter through Door 4), featuring

an easily digestible collection. Here are some of its highlights: The ground floor includes an extensive display of works by Nikolai Astrup (1880-1928), who depicts Norway's fjords with bright colors and Expressionistic flair. One flight up is a great collection of J. C. Dahl and his students, who captured the majesty of Norway's natural wonders (look for Adelsteen Normann's impressive, photorealistic view of Romsdalfjord). "Norwegian Art 1840-1900" includes works by Christian Krohg, as well as some portraits by Harriet Backer. Also on this floor are icons and various European Old Masters.

Up on the third floor, things get modern. The Tower Hall (Tårnsalen) features Norwegian modernism and a large exhibit of Bergen's avant-garde art (1966-1985), kicked off by "Group 66." The International Modernism section has four stars: Pablo Picasso (sketches, etchings, collages, and a few Cubist paintings), Paul Klee (the Swiss childlike painter), and the dynamic Norwegian duo of Edvard Munch and Ludvig Karisten. Rounding it out are a smattering of Surrealist, Abstract Expressionist, and Op Art pieces.

▲Aquarium (Akvariet)

Small but fun, this aquarium claims to be the second-most-visited sight in Bergen. It's wonderfully laid out and explained in English.

Check out the view from inside the "shark tunnel" in the tropical shark exhibit.

Cost and Hours: 250 kr, kids-150 kr, daily May-Aug 10:00-18:00, Sept-mid-Oct daily 10:00-16:00, mid-Oct-April Tue-Sun 10:00-16:00, closed Mon, feeding times at the top of most hours in summer, cheery cafeteria with light sandwiches, Nordnesbakken 4, tel. 40 10 24 20, www.akvariet.no.

Getting There: It's at the tip of the peninsula on the south end of the harbor—about a 20-minute walk or short ride on bus #11 from the city center. Or hop on the handy little *Vågen* "Akvariet" ferry that sails from the Fish Market to near the aquarium (50 kr one-way, 80 kr round-trip, 2/hour, June-Aug 10:00-17:30, off-season until 16:00).

Nearby: The lovely park behind the aquarium has views of the sea and a popular swimming beach (described later, under "Activities in Bergen"). The totem pole erected here was a gift from Bergen's sister city in the US—Seattle.

▲Gamle Bergen (Old Bergen)

This Disney-cute gathering of 50-some 18th- through 20th-century homes and shops was founded in 1934 to save old buildings from destruction as Bergen modernized. Each of the buildings was moved from elsewhere in Bergen and reconstructed here. Together, they create a virtual town that offers a cobbled look at the old life. It's free to wander through the town and park to enjoy the facades of the historic buildings, but to get into the 20 or so museum buildings, you'll have to join a tour (departing on the hour 10:00-16:00).

Cost and Hours: Free entry, 80-kr tour (in English) required for access to buildings, mid-May-Aug daily 9:00-16:00, closed Sept-mid-May, tel. 55 39 43 04, www.bymuseet.no.

Getting There: Take any bus heading west from Bryggen (such as #6, direction: Lønborglien) to Gamle Bergen (stop: Nyhavnsveien). You'll get off after the tunnel at a freeway pullout and walk 200 yards, following signs to the museum. Any bus heading back into town takes you to the center (buses come by every few minutes). With the easy bus connection, there's no reason to taxi.

ACTIVITIES IN BERGEN
▲Strolling

Bergen is a great town for wandering. Enjoy a little Norwegian paseo. On a balmy Norwegian summer evening, I'd stroll from the castle, along the harborfront, up the main square to Ole Bulls Plass, and around the lake.

Shopping

Most shops are open Mon-Fri 9:00-17:00, Thu until 19:00, Sat 9:00-15:00, and closed Sunday. Many of the tourist shops at the harborfront strip along Bryggen are open daily—even during holidays—until 20:00 or 21:00.

Ting (Things) offers a fun alternative to troll shopping, with contemporary housewares and quirky gift ideas (daily 10:00-22:30, at Bryggen 13, a block past the Hanseatic Museum, tel. 55 21 54 80).

Husfliden is a shop popular for its handmade goodies and reliably Norwegian sweaters (fine variety and quality but expensive, just off Torget, the market square, at Vågsallmenninge 3, tel. 55 54 47 40).

The Galleriet Mall, a shopping center on Torgallmenningen, holds six floors of shops, cafés, and restaurants. You'll find a pharmacy, photo shops, clothing, sporting goods, bookstores, mobile-phone shops, and a basement grocery store (Mon-Fri 9:00-21:00, Sat 9:00-18:00, closed Sun).

Swimming

Bergen has two seaside public swimming areas: one at the aquarium and the other in Gamle Bergen. Each is a great local scene on a hot sunny day. **Nordnes Sjøbad,** near the aquarium, offers swimmers an outdoor heated pool and a protected area of the sea (65 kr, kids-30 kr, mid-May-Aug Mon-Fri 7:00-19:00, Sat 7:00-14:00, Sun 10:00-14:00, Sat-Sun until 19:00 in good weather, closed off-season, Nordnesparken 30, tel. 53 03 91 90). **Sandviken Sjobad,** at Gamle Bergen, is free and open all summer. It comes with changing rooms, a roped-off bit of the bay (no pool), a high dive, and lots of sunbathing space.

SIGHTS NEAR BERGEN
▲Ulriken643 Cable Car

It's amazingly easy and quick to zip up six minutes to the 643-meter-high (that's 2,110 feet) summit of Ulriken, the tallest mountain near Bergen. Stepping out of the cable car, you enter a different

world, with views stretching to the ocean. A chart clearly shows the many well-marked and easy hikes that fan out over the vast, rocky, grassy plateau above the tree line (circular walks of various lengths, a 40-minute hike down, and a 4-hour hike to the top of the Fløibanen funicular). For less exercise, you can simply sunbathe, crack open a picnic, or enjoy the Ulriken restaurant.

Cost and Hours: 150 kr round-trip, 90 kr one-way, 8/hour, daily 9:00-21:00, off-season 9:00-17:00, tel. 53 64 36 43, www. ulriken643.no.

Getting There: It's about three miles southeast of Bergen. From the Fish Market, you can take a blue double-decker shuttle bus that includes the cost of the cable-car ride (250 kr, ticket valid 24 hours, May-Sept daily 9:00-17:00, 2/hour, departs from the corner of Torgallmenningen and Strandgaten, buy ticket as you board or at TI). Alternatively, the public bus stops 200 yards from the lift station.

▲▲Edvard Grieg's Home, Troldhaugen

Norway's greatest composer spent his last 22 summers here (1885-1907), soaking up inspirational fjord beauty and composing many

of his greatest works. Grieg fused simple Norwegian folk tunes with the bombast of Europe's Romantic style. In a dreamy Victorian setting, Grieg's "Hill of the Trolls" is pleasant for anyone and essential for diehard fans. You can visit his house on your own, but it's more enjoyable if you take the included 20-minute tour. The house and adjacent museum are full of memories and artifacts, including the composer's Steinway. The walls are festooned with photos of the musical and literary superstars of his generation. When the hugely popular Grieg died in 1907, 40,000 mourners attended his funeral. His little studio hut near the water makes you want to sit down and modulate.

Cost and Hours: 90 kr, includes guided tour in English, daily May-Sept 9:00-18:00, Oct-April 10:00-16:00, café, tel. 55 92 29 92, www.troldhaugen.com.

Grieg Lunch Concert: Troldhaugen offers a great guided tour/concert package that includes a shuttle bus from the Bergen TI to the doorstep of Grieg's home on the fjord (departs 11:30), an hour-long tour of the home, a half-hour concert (Grieg's greatest piano hits, at 13:00), and the ride back into town (you're back in the center by 14:00). Your guide will narrate the ride out of town as well as take you around Grieg's house (250 kr, daily June-mid-Sept). Lunch isn't included, but there is a café on site, or you could bring a sandwich along. You can skip the return bus ride and spend more time in Troldhaugen. While the tour rarely sells out, it's wise to drop by the TI earlier that day to reserve your spot.

Evening Concerts: Ask at the TI about piano performances in the concert hall at Grieg's home—a gorgeous venue with the fjord stretching out behind the big black grand piano (220 kr, 150

kr with Bergen Card, concerts roughly mid-June-late Aug Sun at 18:00, free round-trip shuttle bus leaves TI at 17:00, show your concert ticket).

To avoid the long walk from the tram stop, consider the Grieg Lunch Concert package (described earlier). If you're driving into Bergen from

the east (such as from the Sognefjord), you'll drive right by Troldhaugen on your way into town.

Fantoft Stave Church

This huge, preserved-in-tar stave church burned down in 1992. It was rebuilt and reopened in 1997, but it will never be the same. Situated in a quiet forest next to a mysterious stone cross, this replica of a 12th-century wooden church is bigger, though no better, than

others covered in this book. But it's worth a look if you're in the neighborhood, even after-hours, for its atmospheric setting.

Cost and Hours: 50 kr, mid-May-mid-Sept daily 10:30-18:00, interior closed off-season, no English information, tel. 55 28 07 10, www.fantoftstavkirke.com.

Getting There: It's three miles south of Bergen on E-39 in Paradis. Take the tram (from Byparken, between the lake and Ole Bulls Plass) or bus #83 (from Torget, by the Fish Market) to the Paradis stop (not the "Fantoft" stop). From Paradis, walk uphill to the parking lot on the

left, and find the steep footpath to the church.

BERGEN NIGHTSPOTS

With the high latitude, Bergen stays light until 23:00 in the summer. On warm evenings, people are out enjoying the soft light and the mellow scene.

For a selection of cool nightspots, visit the **Pingvinen Pub** and **Café Opera** (both described in "Eating in Bergen," later) and explore the neighboring streets.

For something a little funkier, **Skostredet** ("Shoe Street," recalling the days when cobblers set up shop here) is emerging as the hip, bohemian-chic area. You'll sort through cafés, pubs, and retro shops. There's an American-style Rock and Roll '59er Diner. And **Folk og Røvere** ("People and Robbers") is an unpretentious bar with cheap beer (nightly until late, Skostredet 12).

For candlelit elegance, enjoy a drink at the historic **Dyvekes Wine Cellar.** Named for the mistress of King Christian II of Denmark (her portrait is on the signboard hanging above the door), the atmosphere of the ground-floor bar and the cellar downstairs is hard to beat (daily from 15:00, 80-90 kr for wine by glass, beer on tap, Hollendergaten 7).

For live blues, try **Madam Felle Nightclub** (on the Bryggen strip), which has live music many evenings (often without a cover).

And if you're really drunk at 3:00 in the morning and need a spicy hotdog, the **3-Kroneren** *pølse* stand is open (described in "Eating in Bergen," later).

Sleeping in Bergen

Busy with business travelers and popular with tourists, Bergen can be jammed any time of year. Even with this crush, proud and pricey hotels may be willing to make deals. You might save a bundle by checking the websites of the bigger hotels for their best prices. Otherwise, Bergen has some fine budget alternatives to normal hotels that can save you money.

HOTELS

$$$ Hotel Havnekontoret, with 116 rooms and the best location in town, fills a grand old shipping headquarters dating from the 1920s. It's an especially fine value on weekends and in the summer, for those who eat the included dinner. While part of a chain, it has a friendly spirit. Guests are welcome to climb its historic tower (with a magnificent view) or enjoy its free sauna and exercise room downstairs. If you aren't interested in fancy dining, the room price includes virtually all your food—a fine breakfast, self-service waffles and pancakes in the afternoon, fruit and coffee all day, and a light dinner buffet each evening. If you take advantage of them (and the free loaner bikes for guests), these edible extras are easily worth 600 kr per day per couple, making the cost of this fancy hotel little more than a hostel (Db 1,700-2,300 kr, extra bed-300 kr, book online to save, Wi-Fi, facing the harbor across the street from the Radisson Blu Royal Hotel at Slottsgaten 1, tel. 55 60 11 00, www.choicehotels.no, cc.havnekontoret@choice.no).

$$$ Hotel Park Bergen is classy, comfortable, and in a fine residential neighborhood a 15-minute uphill walk from the town center (10 minutes from the train station). It's tinseled in Old World, lived-in charm, yet comes with all of today's amenities. The

Sleep Code

Abbreviations   **(6 kr = about $1, country code: 47)**
S = Single, **D** = Double/Twin, **T** = Triple, **Q** = Quad, **b** = bathroom
Price Rankings
 $$$ Higher Priced—Most rooms 1,400 kr or more.
  $$ Moderately Priced—Most rooms 900-1,400 kr.
   $ Lower Priced—Most rooms 900 kr or less.
Hotel staff speak English, breakfast is included, Wi-Fi is gen-
erally free, and credit cards are accepted unless otherwise
noted. Prices change; verify current rates online or by email.
For the best prices, always book directly with the hotel.

35 rooms are split between two buildings, with 22 in the classy
old-fashioned hotel and 13 in the modern annex across the street
(Sb-1,110 kr, Db-1,500 kr, extra bed-350 kr, winter weekend discounts, Wi-Fi, Harald Hårfagres Gate 35, tel. 55 54 44 00, www.
hotelpark.no, booking@hotelpark.no).

$$$ Thon Hotel Rosenkrantz, with 129 rooms, is one block
behind Bryggen, between the Bryggens Museum and the Fløibanen
funicular station—right in the heart of Bergen's appealing old
quarter. However, the next-door nightclub is noisy on Friday and
Saturday nights—be sure to request a quiet room (average rates:
Sb-1,295-2,095 kr, Db-1,095-2,295 kr, elevator, guest computer,
Wi-Fi, Rosenkrantzgaten 7, tel. 55 30 14 00, www.thonhotels.no/
rosenkrantz, rosenkrantz@thonhotels.no).

$$ P-Hotel has 43 basic rooms just up from Ole Bulls Plass.
While it's not particularly charming and some rooms come with
street noise, it's got a prime location. Ask for a room facing the
courtyard in the renovated wing (Sb-975 kr, Db-1,350 kr, prices
vary—check online for best deal, credit card only—no cash, box
breakfast in your room, elevator, Wi-Fi, Vestre Torggate 9, tel. 80
04 68 35, www.p-hotels.no, bergen@p-hotels.no).

$$ Thon Hotel Bergen Brygge, beyond Bryggen near
Håkon's Hall, is part of Thon's cheaper "Budget" chain. However,
the 229 spartan rooms can be just about as nice as those in its sister
hotels. Because of its relatively good prices and great location, it
fills up quickly—book ahead. Light sleepers, beware: Many rooms
face the fortress grounds, which sometimes host summer evening
concerts. Ask for a room on the quiet side, bring earplugs, or go
elsewhere (Db-925-1,500 kr, you save if you book online, eleva-
tor, guest computer, Wi-Fi, Bradbenken 3, tel. 55 30 87 00, www.
thonhotels.com/bergenbrygge, bergen.brygge@thonhotels.no).

$$ Basic Hotel Victoria is an old hotel turned into a college dorm that becomes a utilitarian, minimalist budget hotel each

summer. There are no public spaces, the tiny reception is open only 9:00-23:00, and you won't get your towels changed. But its 43 modern, bright, simple rooms are plenty comfortable for the price (open June-Aug only, Sb-995 kr, Db-1,095 kr, Tb-1,395 kr, Wi-Fi, Kong Oscars Gate 29, tel. 55 31 44 04, www.basichotels.no, victoria@basichotels.no).

$ **Citybox** is a unique, no-nonsense hotel concept: plain, white, clean, and practical. It rents 55 rooms online and provides you with a confirmation number. Check-in is automated—just punch in your number and get your ticket. The call-in reception is staffed daily 9:00-17:00, except May-Oct until 23:00 (S-600 kr, Sb-700 kr, D-950 kr, Db-1,050 kr, extra bed-150 kr, family room for up to four-1,450 kr, prices fluctuate—check online for best deals, no breakfast, elevator, just away from the bustle in a mostly residential part of town at Nygårdsgaten 31, tel. 55 31 25 00, www.citybox.no, post@citybox.no).

PRIVATE HOMES AND PENSIONS

If you're looking for local character and don't mind sharing a shower, these accommodations—far more quiet, homey, and convenient than hostel beds—might just be the best values in town. Both require guests to climb outdoor stairways, which may be tough for those not packing light.

$ **Guest House Skiven** is a humble little place beautifully situated on a steep, traffic-free cobbled lane called "the most painted street in Bergen." Alf and Elizabeth Heskja (who live upstairs) rent four bright, non-smoking doubles that share a shower, two WCs, and a kitchen (D-650 kr for Rick Steves readers, no breakfast, Wi-Fi, 4 blocks from train station, at Skivebakken 17, mobile 90 05 30 30, www.skiven.no, rs@skiven.no). From the train station, go down Kong Oscars Gate, uphill on D. Krohns Gate, and up the stairs at the end of the block on the left.

$ **Skansen Pensjonat** (not to be confused with the nearby Skansen Apartments) is situated 100 yards directly behind the entrance to the Fløibanen funicular. Jannicke Alvær rents seven tastefully decorated rooms with views over town (small non-view S-500 kr, larger S-550 kr, D-900 kr, fancy D on corner with view and balcony-1,000 kr, apartment-1,100 kr, includes breakfast, 2 showers on ground floor, 2 WCs, sinks in rooms, family room with TV; all non-smoking, Wi-Fi, Vetrlidsalmenning 29, tel. 55 31 90 80, www.skansen-pensjonat.no, post@skansen-pensjonat.no). Follow the switchback road behind the Fløibanen funicular station to the paved plateau with benches, and look for the sign.

BERGEN

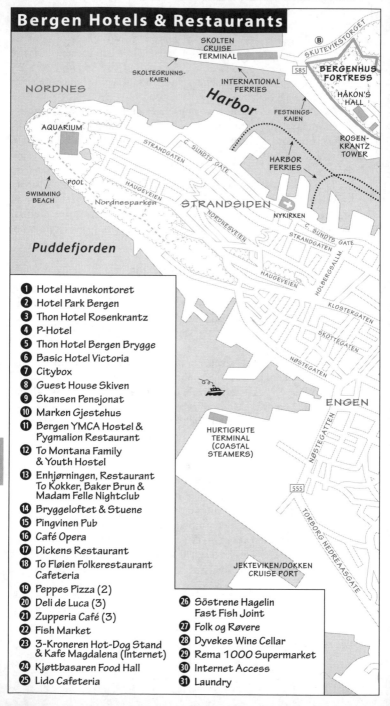

Bergen Hotels & Restaurants

SKOLTEN CRUISE TERMINAL

SKUTEVIKSTORGET

B

585

BERGENHUS FORTRESS

HÅKON'S HALL

SKOLTEGRUNNS-KAIEN

INTERNATIONAL FERRIES

Harbor

FESTNINGS-KAIEN

ROSEN-KRANTZ TOWER

NORDNES

AQUARIUM

STRANDGATEN

C. SUNDTS GATE

HARBOR FERRIES

POOL

SWIMMING BEACH

HAUGEVEIEN

Nordnesparken

STRANDSIDEN

NYKIRKEN

NORDNESVEIEN

C. SUNDTS GATE

STRANDGATEN

Puddefjorden

HAUGEVEIEN

HOLBERGSALLM

KLOSTERGATEN

KLOSTERGATEN

SKOTTEGATEN

NØSTEGATEN

ENGEN

HURTIGRUTE TERMINAL (COASTAL STEAMERS)

NØSTEGATEN

555

TORBORG NEDREAASGATE

JEKTEVIKEN/DOKKEN CRUISE PORT

1 Hotel Havnekontoret
2 Hotel Park Bergen
3 Thon Hotel Rosenkrantz
4 P-Hotel
5 Thon Hotel Bergen Brygge
6 Basic Hotel Victoria
7 Citybox
8 Guest House Skiven
9 Skansen Pensjonat
10 Marken Gjestehus
11 Bergen YMCA Hostel & Pygmalion Restaurant
12 To Montana Family & Youth Hostel
13 Enhjørningen, Restaurant To Kokker, Baker Brun & Madam Felle Nightclub
14 Bryggeloftet & Stuene
15 Pingvinen Pub
16 Café Opera
17 Dickens Restaurant
18 To Fløien Folkerestaurant Cafeteria
19 Peppes Pizza (2)
20 Deli de Luca (3)
21 Zupperia Café (3)
22 Fish Market
23 3-Kroneren Hot-Dog Stand & Kafe Magdalena (Internet)
24 Kjøttbasaren Food Hall
25 Lido Cafeteria
26 Söstrene Hagelin Fast Fish Joint
27 Folk og Røvere
28 Dyvekes Wine Cellar
29 Rema 1000 Supermarket
30 Internet Access
31 Laundry

BERGEN

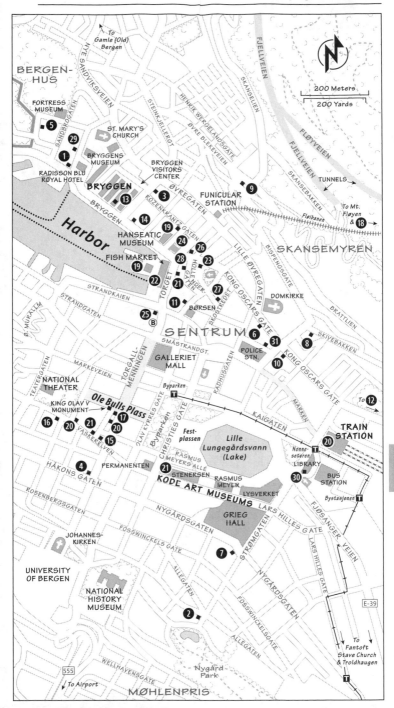

BERGEN

DORMS AND HOSTELS

$ Marken Gjestehus is a quiet, tidy, and conveniently positioned 100-bed place between the station and the harborfront. Its rooms, while spartan, are modern and cheery. Prices can rise with demand, especially in summer (dorm bed in 8-bed room-270 kr, in 10-bed room-280 kr, in 4-bed room-320 kr, S-600 kr, D-750 kr, Db-920 kr, lower prices off-season, includes sheets, extra bed-135 kr, towels-15 kr, breakfast voucher-130 kr, Wi-Fi, elevator, kitchen, laundry, open all year but with limited reception hours, fourth floor at Kong Oscars Gate 45, tel. 55 31 44 04, www.marken-gjestehus. com, post@marken-gjestehus.com).

$ Bergen YMCA Hostel, located two blocks from the Fish Market, is the best location for the price, and its rooms are nicely maintained (bunk in 12- to 32-bed dorm with shared shower and kitchen-195 kr, bunk in 4-6-bed family room with private bathroom and kitchen-280-320 kr, Db with kitchen-950 kr, includes sheets, breakfast-65 kr, Wi-Fi, roof terrace, fully open June-Aug, few dorm beds off-season, Nedre Korskirkeallmenningen 4, tel. 55 60 60 55, www.bergenhostel.com, booking@bergenhostel.com).

Away from the Center: **$ Montana Family & Youth Hostel (IYHF),** while one of Europe's best, is high-priced for a hostel and way out of town. Still, the bus connections (#12, 20 minutes from the center) and the facilities—modern rooms, classy living room, no curfew, huge free parking lot, and members' kitchen—are excellent (dorm bed in 20-bed room-225 kr—cheaper off-season, bed in Q-295 kr, Sb-670 kr, Db-850 kr, 10 percent cheaper for members, sheets-70 kr, includes breakfast, 30 Johan Blytts Vei, tel. 55 20 80 70, www.montana.no, bergen.montana@hihostels.no).

Eating in Bergen

Bergen has numerous choices: restaurants with rustic, woody atmosphere, candlelight, and steep prices (main dishes around 300 kr); trendy pubs and cafés that offer good-value meals (100-190 kr); cafeterias, chain restaurants, and ethnic eateries with less ambience where you can get quality food at lower prices (100-150 kr); and takeaway sandwich shops, bakeries, and cafés for a light bite (50-100 kr).

You can always get a glass or pitcher of water at no charge, and fancy places give you free seconds on potatoes—just ask. Remember, if you get your food to go, it's taxed at a lower rate and you'll save 12 percent.

SPLURGES IN BRYGGEN

You'll pay a premium to eat at these restaurants, but you'll have a memorable meal in a pleasant setting. If they appear to be beyond your budget, remember that you can fill up on potatoes and drink tap water to dine for exactly the price of the dinner plate.

Enhjørningen Restaurant ("The Unicorn") is *the* place in Bergen for fish. With thickly painted walls and no right angles, this dressy-yet-old-time wooden interior wins my "Bryggen Atmosphere" award. The dishes, while not hearty, are close to gourmet and beautifully presented (320-350-kr main dishes, 580-620-kr multicourse meals, nightly 16:00-22:30, reservations smart, #29 on Bryggen harborfront—look for anatomically correct unicorn on the old wharf facade and dip into the alley and up the stairs, tel. 55 30 69 50, www.enhjorningen.no).

Restaurant To Kokker, down the alley from Enhjørningen (and with the same owners), serves more meat and game. The

prices and quality are equivalent, but even though it's also in an elegant old wooden building, I like The Unicorn's atmosphere much better (350-kr mains, 625-750-kr multicourse meals, Mon-Sat 17:00-23:00, closed Sun, tel. 55 30 69 55).

Bryggeloftet & Stuene Restaurant, in a brick building just before the wooden stretch of Bryggen, is a vast eatery serving seafood, vegetarian, and traditional meals. To dine memorably yet affordably, this is your best Bryggen bet. Upstairs feels more elegant and less touristy than the main floor—if there's a line downstairs, just head on up (150-180-kr lunches, 200-350-kr dinners, Mon-Sat 11:00-23:30, Sun 13:00-23:30, try reserving a view window upstairs—no reservations for outside seating, #11 on Bryggen harborfront, tel. 55 30 20 70).

NEAR THE FISH MARKET

Pygmalion Restaurant has a happy salsa vibe, with local art on the walls and a fun, healthy international menu. It's run with creativity and passion by Sissel. Her burgers are a hit, and there are always good vegetarian options, hearty salads, and pancakes (80-kr wraps, 180-kr burgers, 150-200-kr main plates, daily 11:00-22:00, two blocks inland from the Fish Market at Nedre Korskirkealmenning 4, tel. 55 31 32 60).

CHARACTERISTIC PLACES NEAR OLE BULLS PLASS

Bergen's "in" cafés are stylish, cozy, small, and open very late—a great opportunity to experience its yuppie scene. Around the cinema on Neumannsgate, there are numerous ethnic restaurants, including Italian, Middle Eastern, and Chinese.

Pingvinen Pub ("The Penguin") is a homey place in a charming neighborhood, serving traditional Norwegian home cooking to an enthusiastic local clientele. The pub has only indoor seating, with a long row of stools at the bar and five charming, living-room-cozy tables—a great setup for solo diners. After the kitchen closes, the place stays open very late as a pub. For Norwegian fare in a completely untouristy atmosphere, this is a good, affordable option. Their seasonal menu (reindeer in the fall, whale in the spring) is listed on the board (160-220-kr main dishes, nightly until 22:00, Vaskerelven 14 near the National Theater, tel. 55 60 46 46).

Café Opera, with a playful-slacker vibe and chessboards for the regulars, is the hip budget choice for its loyal, youthful following. With two floors of seating and tables out front across from the theater, it's a winner (light 60-80-kr sandwiches until 16:00, 100-200-kr dinners, daily 10:00-24:00, Engen 18, tel. 55 23 03 15).

Dickens is a lively, checkerboard-tiled, turn-of-the-century-feeling place. The window tables in the atrium are great for people-watching, as is the fine outdoor terrace, but you'll pay higher prices for the view (200-kr lunches, 250-300-kr dinners, daily 11:00-23:00, Kong Olav V's Plass 4, tel. 55 36 31 30).

ATOP MOUNT FLØYEN, AT THE TOP OF THE FUNICULAR

Fløien Folkerestaurant Cafeteria offers meals indoors and out with a panoramic view. It's self-service, with sandwiches for around 60 kr and a 139-kr soup buffet (May-Aug daily 10:00-22:00, Sept-April Sat-Sun only 12:00-17:00, tel. 55 33 69 99).

GOOD CHAIN RESTAURANTS

You'll find these chain restaurants in Bergen and throughout Norway. All are open long hours daily. In good weather, enjoy a takeout meal with sun-worshipping locals in Bergen's parks.

Peppes Pizza has cold beer and good pizzas (medium size for 1-2 people-200-220 kr, large for 2-3 people-220-300 kr, takeout possible; consider the Thai Chicken, with satay-marinated chicken, pineapple, peanuts, and coriander). There are six Peppes in Bergen, including one behind the Hanseatic Museum near the Fløibanen funicular station and another inside the Zachariasbryggen harborfront complex, next to the Fish Market (with views over the harbor).

BERGEN

Baker Brun makes 50-70-kr sandwiches, including wonderful shrimp baguettes and pastries such as *skillingsbolle*—cinnamon rolls—warm out of the oven. Their branch in the Bryggen quarter is a prime spot for a simple, inexpensive bite (open from 7:00, seating inside or takeaway).

Deli de Luca is a cut above other takeaway joints, adding sushi, noodle dishes, and calzones to the normal lineup of sandwiches. While a bit more expensive than the others, the variety and quality are appealing (open 24/7, 60-kr sandwiches and calzones, branches in train station and near Ole Bulls Plass at Torggaten 5, branch with indoor seating on corner of Engen and Vaskerelven, tel. 55 23 11 47).

Zupperia is a lively, popular chain that offers burgers, salads, Norwegian fare, and Asian dishes for 75 to 150 kr; their Thai soup is a local favorite. For a lighter meal, order off the lunch menu (120-150 kr) any time of day (daily 12:00-22:00, but Nordahl Bruns location closed Mon). Branches are across from the Fish Market at Market 13, near the National Theater at Vaskerelven 12, and between Ole Bulls Plass and the lake (Nordahl Bruns Gate 9).

BUDGET BETS NEAR THE FISH MARKET

The Fish Market has lots of stalls bursting with salmon sandwiches, fresh shrimp, fish-and-chips, and fish cakes. For a tasty, memorable, and inexpensive Bergen meal, assemble a seafood picnic here (ask for prices first; June-Aug daily 7:00-19:00; Sept-May Mon-Sat 7:00-16:00, closed Sun). Also be sure to peruse the places next door in the ground floor of the TI building, Torghallen.

3-Kroneren, your classic hot-dog stand, sells a wide variety of sausages (various sizes and flavors—including reindeer). The well-described English menu makes it easy to order your choice of artery-clogging guilty pleasures (20-kr tiny weenie, 55-kr medium-size weenie, 75-kr jumbo, open daily from 11:00 until 5:00 in the morning, you'll see the little hot-dog shack a block up Kong Oscars Gate from the harbor, Kenneht is the boss). Each dog comes with a free little glass of fruit punch.

Kjøttbasaren, upstairs in the restored meat market of 1887, is a genteel-feeling food hall with stalls selling groceries such as meat, cheese, bread, and olives, plus *lefse*, reindeer sausage, and goat cheese—a great opportunity to assemble a bang-up picnic (Mon-Fri 10:00-17:00, Thu until 18:00, Sat 9:00-16:00, closed Sun). You can picnic at the top or bottom of the Fløibanen funicular, just up the street.

Lido Cafeteria offers basic, affordable food with great harbor and market views, better ambience than most self-service places, and a museum's worth of old-town photos on the walls. For cold items (such as 50-100-kr open-face sandwiches and desserts), grab what you want, pay the cashier, and find a table. For hot dishes (120-170-kr Norwegian standards, including one daily special discounted to 110 kr), get a table, order and pay at the cashier, and they'll bring your food to you (120-kr salad bar, Mon-Fri 10:00-19:00, Sat and Sun 10:00-18:00; second floor at Torgallmenningen 1a, tel. 55 32 59 12).

Söstrene Hagelin Fast Fish Joint is an easygoing eatery that's cheerier than its offerings—a dreary extravaganza of Norway's white cuisine. It's all fish here: fish soup, fish burgers, fish balls, fish cakes, and even fish pudding (meals for around 60 kr, Mon-Sat 10:00-22:00, Sun 12:00-18:00, Kong Oscars Gate 2).

Kafe Magdalena, a humble little community center just two blocks off the Fish Market, is run by the church and staffed by volunteers. While it's designed to give Bergen's poor citizens an inviting place to enjoy, everyone's welcome (it's a favorite of local guides). There's little choice here; the menu is driven by what's available to the mission cheap (40-kr daily plate, 70 kr for bigger meal served after 13:30, nice cheap open-face sandwiches, waffles, coffee, Mon-Fri 11:00-16:00, closed Sat-Sun, Kong Oscars Gate 5). They have two computer terminals with Internet access and free Wi-Fi.

PICNICS AND GROCERIES

While you'll be tempted to drop into 7-Eleven-type stores, you'll pay for the convenience. Pick up your groceries for half the price at a real supermarket. The **Rema 1000 supermarket,** just across from the Bryggens Museum and St. Mary's Church, is particularly handy (Mon-Fri 7:00-23:00, Sat 8:00-21:00, closed Sun).

Bergen Connections

Bergen is conveniently connected to **Oslo** by plane and train (trains depart Bergen daily at 7:57, 11:59, 15:59, and 22:59—but no night train on Sat, arrive at Oslo seven scenic hours later, additional departures in summer and fall, confirm times at station, 50-kr seat reservation required—but free with first-class rail pass, book well in advance if traveling mid-July-Aug). From Bergen, you can take the Norway in a Nutshell train/bus/ferry route; for information, see the Norway in a Nutshell chapter. Train info: tel. 81 50 08 88, and then 9 for English, www.nsb.no.

To get to **Stockholm** or **Copenhagen,** you'll go via Oslo. Before buying a ticket for a long train trip from Bergen, look into cheap flights.

By Express Boat to Balestrand and Flåm (on Sognefjord): A handy express boat links Bergen with Balestrand (4 hours) and Flåm (5.5 hours).

By Bus to Kristiansand: If you're heading to Denmark on the ferry from Kristiansand, catch the Haukeli express bus (departing Bergen daily at 8:25). After a nearly two-hour layover in Haukeli, take the bus at 14:55, arriving at 19:00 in Kristiansand in time for the evening ferry to Denmark.

By Boat to Denmark: Fjordline runs a boat from Bergen to Hirtshals, Denmark (18 hours; departs daily at 13:30; boat from Hirtshals departs daily at 20:00; seat in reclining chair around 1,750 kr, tel. 81 53 35 00, www.fjordline.com).

By Boat to the Arctic: Hurtigruten coastal steamers depart nearly daily (June-Oct at 20:00, Nov-May at 22:30) for the seven-day trip north up the scenic west coast to Kirkenes on the Russian border.

This route was started in 1893 as a postal and cargo delivery service along the west coast of Norway. Although no longer delivering mail, their ships still fly the Norwegian postal flag by special permission and deliver people, cars, and cargo from Bergen to Kirkenes. A lifeline for remote areas, the ships call at 34 fishing villages and cities.

For the seven-day trip to Kirkenes, allow from $1,600 and up per person based on double occupancy (includes three meals per day, taxes, and port charges). Prices vary greatly depending on the season (highest June-July), cabin, and type of ship. Their fleet includes those with a bit of brass built in the 1960s, but the majority of the ships were built in the mid-1990s and later. Shorter voyages are possible (including even just a day trip to one of the villages along the route). Cabins should be booked well in advance. Ship services include a 24-hour cafeteria, a launderette on newer boats, and optional port excursions. Check online for senior and off-season (Oct-March) specials at www.hurtigruten.com.

Call Hurtigruten in New York (US tel. 866-552-0371) or in Norway (tel. 81 00 30 30). For most travelers, the ride makes a great one-way trip, but a flight back south is a logical last leg (rather than returning to Bergen by boat—a 12-day round-trip).

BERGEN

SOUTH NORWAY

Stavanger • Setesdal Valley • Kristiansand

South Norway is not about must-see sights or jaw-dropping scenery—it's simply pleasant and pretty. Spend a day in the harborside town of Stavanger. Delve into the oil industry at the surprisingly interesting Norwegian Petroleum Museum. Peruse the Stavanger Cathedral, window-shop in the old town, cruise the harbor, or hoof it up Pulpit Rock for a fine view.

A series of time-forgotten towns stretch across the Setesdal Valley, with sod-roofed cottages and locals who practice fiddles and harmonicas, rose painting, whittling, and gold- and silver-work. The famous Setesdal filigree echoes the rhythmical designs of the Viking era and Middle Ages. Each town has a weekly rotating series of hikes and activities for the regular, stay-put-for-a-week visitor. The upper valley is dead in the summer but enjoys a bustling winter.

In Kristiansand, Norway's answer to a seaside resort, you can promenade along the strand, sample a Scandinavian zoo, or set sail to Denmark.

PLANNING YOUR TIME

Even on a busy itinerary, Stavanger warrants a day. The port town is connected by boat to Bergen (and Hirtshals, Denmark) and by train to Kristiansand.

Frankly, without a car, the Setesdal Valley is not worth the trouble. There are no trains in the valley, bus schedules are as sparse as the population, and the sights are best for joyriding. If you're in Bergen with a car, and want to get to Denmark, this route is more interesting than repeating Oslo. On a three-week Scandinavian trip, I'd do it in one long day, as follows: 7:00—Leave Bergen;

9:00—Catch Kvanndal ferry to Utne; 10:00—Say good-bye to the last fjord at Odda; 13:00—Lunch in Hovden at the top of Setesdal Valley; 14:00—Frolic south with a few short stops in the valley; 16:30—Arrive in Kristiansand for dinner. Spend the night and catch the 9:00 boat to Denmark the next morning.

Kristiansand is not a destination town, but rather a place to pass through, conveniently connecting Norway to Denmark by ferry.

Stavanger

This burg of about 125,000 is a mildly charming (if unspectacular) waterfront city whose streets are lined with unpretentious shiplap cottages that echo its perennial ties to the sea. Stavanger feels more cosmopolitan than most small Norwegian cities, thanks in part to its oil industry—which brings multinational workers (and their money) into the city. Known as Norway's festival city, Stavanger hosts several lively events, including jazz in May (www.maijazz. no), Scandinavia's biggest food festival in July (www.gladmat.no), and chamber music in August (www.icmf.no). With all of this culture, it's no surprise that Stavanger was named a European Capital of Culture for 2008.

From a sightseeing perspective, Stavanger barely has enough to fill a day: The Norwegian Petroleum Museum is the only big-time sight in town, and Gamle Stavanger (the "old town") offers pleasant wandering on cobbled lanes. The city's fine cathedral is worth a peek, but beyond those options, the chief activity is dodging the thousands of cruise passengers routinely dumped here throughout the summer season. For most visitors, the main reason  to come to Stavanger is to use it as a launch pad for side-tripping to Lysefjord and/or the famous, iconic Pulpit Rock: an eerily flat-topped peak thrusting up from the fjord, offering perfect, eagle's-eye views deep into the Lysefjord.

Orientation to Stavanger

The most scenic and interesting parts of Stavanger surround its harbor. Here you'll find the Maritime Museum, lots of shops and restaurants (particularly around the market plaza and along Kirkegata, which connects the cathedral to the Petroleum Museum), the

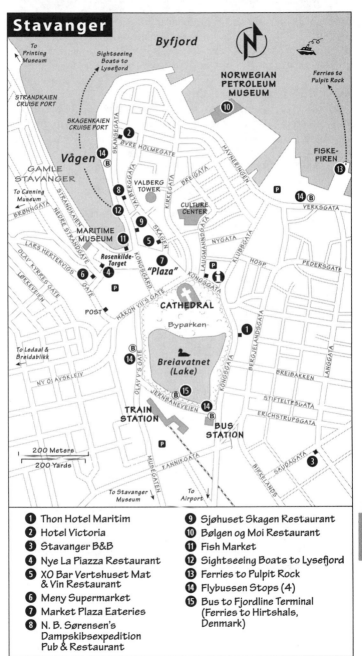

Stavanger

Byfjord

To Printing Museum

Sightseeing Boats to Lysefjord

STRANDKAIEN CRUISE PORT

SKAGENKAIEN CRUISE PORT

NORWEGIAN PETROLEUM MUSEUM

Ferries to Pulpit Rock

Vågen

GAMLE STAVANGER

To Canning Museum

BRØNNGATA

STRANDKAIEN

NEDRE STRANDGATE

LARS HERTERVIGS

OLAV KYRRES GATE

LØKKEVEIEN

MARITIME MUSEUM

SKANSEGATA

ØVRE HOLMEGATE

VALBERGGATA

VALBERG TOWER

KIRKEGATA

BREIGATA

HAVNERINGEN

FISKE-PIREN

CULTURE CENTER

HAUGMANNSGATA

NYGATA

KLUBBGATA

VERKSGATA

Rosenkilde-Torget

KONGSGARD

SKAGEN

"Plaza"

HOSP

PEDERSGATE

KONGSGATA

HAKON VII'S GATE

POST

CATHEDRAL

Byparken

Breiavatnet (Lake)

OLAV V'S GATE

JERNBANEVEIEN

BERGJELANDSGATA

KONGSGATA

LANGGATA

PREIBAKKEN

STIFTELTPSGATA

ERICHSTRUPSGATA

TRAIN STATION

BUS STATION

NY OLAVSKLEIV

200 Meters
200 Yards

MUSÉGATEN

VANNIKGATA

BIRKELANDS

SAUDAGATA

To Ledaal & Breidablikk

To Stavanger Museum

To Airport

1 Thon Hotel Maritim
2 Hotel Victoria
3 Stavanger B&B
4 Nye La Piazza Restaurant
5 XO Bar Vertshuset Mat & Vin Restaurant
6 Meny Supermarket
7 Market Plaza Eateries
8 N. B. Sørensen's Dampskibsexpedition Pub & Restaurant

9 Sjøhuset Skagen Restaurant
10 Bølgen og Moi Restaurant
11 Fish Market
12 Sightseeing Boats to Lysefjord
13 Ferries to Pulpit Rock
14 Flybussen Stops (4)
15 Bus to Fjordline Terminal (Ferries to Hirtshals, Denmark)

indoor fish market, and a produce market (Mon-Fri 9:00-18:00, Sat 9:00-16:00, closed Sun). The artificial Lake Breiavatnet—bordered by Kongsgaten on the east and Olav V's Gate on the west—separates the train and bus stations from the harbor.

TOURIST INFORMATION
The helpful staff at the TI can help you plan your time in Stavanger, and can also give you hiking tips and day trip information. Pick up a free city guide and map (June-Aug daily 9:00-20:00; Sept-May Mon-Fri 9:00-16:00, Sat 9:00-14:00, closed Sun; Domkirkeplassen 3, tel. 51 85 92 00, www.regionstavanger.com).

ARRIVAL IN STAVANGER
By Cruise Ship: Conveniently, cruise liners dock right at the Vågen harbor in the very center of town. Some tie up on the west side

of the harbor (called **Strandkaien**), and others put in along the east side (called **Skagenkaien**)—but both are an easy five- to fifteen-minute walk to the central market plaza (depending on how far out the ship is docked).

By Train and Bus: Stavanger's train and bus stations are a five-minute walk around Lake Breiavatnet to the inner harbor, cathedral, and TI (train ticket and reservation office Mon-Fri 7:00-17:30, Sat 9:00-16:30, Sun 10:00-16:30). Luggage lockers and Norway-wide train timetables are available at the train station.

By Plane: Stavanger's Sola Airport is about nine miles outside the city (airport code: SVG, tel. 67 03 10 00, www.avinor.no). It's connected to downtown by the Flybussen (110 kr, buy ticket on bus, Mon-Fri 7:45-24:30, 2/hour, less Sat-Sun, 20-30 minutes, tel. 51 59 90 60, www.flybussen.no). This airport bus shuttles travelers to the bus station (Byterminalen) and train station (next to each other), the Atlantic Hotel near the city center, and the Pulpit Rock ferry terminal (Fiskepiren). To get to the airport from the city center, catch the shuttle at any of these stops.

Sights in Stavanger

▲Stavanger Cathedral (Domkirke)

While it's hardly the most impressive cathedral in Scandinavia, Stavanger's top church—which overlooks the town center on a small ridge—has a harmonious interior and a few intriguing details worth lingering over. Good English information throughout the church brings meaning to the place.

Cost and Hours: 30-kr until 15:30, free after 15:30, open June-Aug daily 11:00-19:00, free and open shorter hours off-season, tel. 51 84 04 00, www.kirken.stavanger.no.

Visiting the Church: St. Swithun's Cathedral (its official name) was originally built in 1125 in a Norman style, with basket-

handle Romanesque arches. After a fire badly damaged the church in the 13th century, a new chancel was added in the pointy-arched Gothic style. You can't miss where the architecture changes about three-quarters of the way up the aisle. On the left, behind the baptismal font, notice the ivy-lined railing on the stone staircase; this pattern is part of the city's coat of arms. And nearby, appreciate the colorful, richly detailed "gristle Baroque"-style pulpit (from 1658). Notice that the whole thing is resting on Samson's stoic shoulders—even as he faces down a lion.

Stroll the church, perusing its several fine "epitaphs" (tomb markers), which are paintings in ornately decorated frames. Go on a scavenger hunt for two unique features; both are on the second columns from the back of the church. On the right, at the top facing away from the nave, notice the stone carvings of Norse mythological figures: Odin on the left, and a wolf-like beast on the right. Although the medieval Norwegians were Christians, they weren't ready to entirely abandon all of their pagan traditions. On the opposite column, circle around the base and look at ankle level, facing away from the altar. Here you see a grotesque sculpture that looks like a fish head with human hands. Notice that its head has been worn down. One interpretation is that early worshippers would ritualistically put their foot on top of it, as if to push the evil back to the underworld. Mysteriously, both of these features are one-offs—you won't find anything like them on any other column in the church.

▲▲Norwegian Petroleum Museum (Norsk Oljemuseum)

This entertaining, informative museum—dedicated to the discovery of oil in Norway's North Sea in 1969 and the industry built up around it—offers an unapologetic look at the country's biggest moneymaker. With half of Western Europe's oil reserves, the formerly poor agricultural nation of Norway is the Arabia of the North, and a world-class player. It's ranked third among the world's top oil exporters, producing 1.6 million barrels a day.

Cost and Hours: 100 kr; June-Aug daily 10:00-19:00; Sept-May Mon-Sat 10:00-16:00, Sun 10:00-18:00; tel. 51 93 93 00, www.norskolje.museum.no. The small museum shop sells various petroleum-based products. The museum's Bølgen og Moi restaurant, which has an inviting terrace over the water, serves lunch and dinner (see listing under "Eating in Stavanger," later).

Visiting the Museum: The exhibit describes how oil was formed, how it's found and produced, and what it's used for. You'll see models of oil rigs, actual drill bits, see-through cylinders that you can rotate to investigate different types of crude, and lots of explanations (in English) about various aspects of oil. Interactive exhibits cover everything from the "History of the Earth" (4.5 billion years displayed on a large overhead globe, showing how our planet has changed—stay for the blast that killed the dinosaurs), to day-to-day life on an offshore platform, to petroleum products in our lives (though the peanut-butter-and-petroleum-jelly sandwich is a bit much). Kids enjoy climbing on the model drilling platform, trying out the emergency escape chute at the platform outside, and playing with many other hands-on exhibits.

Several included movies delve into specific aspects of oil: The kid-oriented "Petropolis" 3-D film is primitive but entertaining and informative, tracing the story of oil from creation to extraction. Other movies (in the cylindrical structures outside) highlight intrepid North Sea divers and the construction of an oil platform. Each film is 12 minutes long, and runs in English at least twice hourly.

Even the museum's architecture was designed to echo the foundations of the oil industry—bedrock (the stone building), slate and chalk deposits in the sea (slate floor of the main hall), and the rigs (cylindrical platforms). While the museum has its fair share of propaganda, it also has several good exhibits on the environmental toll of drilling and consuming oil.

Gamle Stavanger

Stavanger's "old town" centers on Øvre Strandgate, on the west side of the harbor. Wander the narrow, winding, cobbled back lanes, with tidy wooden houses, oasis gardens, and flower-bedecked en-

tranceways. Peek into a workshop or gallery to find ceramics, glass, jewelry, and more. Many shops are open roughly daily 10:00-17:00, coinciding with the arrival of cruise ships (which loom ominously right next to this otherwise tranquil zone).

Museum Stavanger (M.U.S.T.)

This "museum" is actually 10 different museums scattered around town. The various branches include the **Stavanger Museum,** featuring the history of the city and a zoological exhibit (Muségate 16); the **Maritime Museum** (Sjøfartsmuseum), near the bottom end of Vågen harbor (Nedre Strandgate 17-19); the **Norwegian Canning Museum** (Norsk Hermetikkmuseum—the *brisling,* or herring, is smoked the first Sunday of every month and mid-June–mid-Aug Tue and Thu—Øvre Strandgate 88A); **Ledaal,** a royal residence and manor house (Eiganesveien 45); and **Breidablikk,** a wooden villa from the late 1800s (Eiganesveien 40A). The **Printing Museum** is closed but is slated to reopen by 2016.

Cost: You can buy one 100-kr ticket to cover all of them, or you can pay 70 kr for any individual museum (if doing at least two, the combo-ticket is obviously the better value). Note that a single 70-kr ticket gets you into the Maritime Museum, Canning Museum, and Printing Museum (when open), which are a three-for-one sight. You can get details and buy tickets at any of the museums; handiest is the Maritime Museum right along the harbor.

Hours: Museum hours vary but generally open mid-June–mid-Aug daily 10:00 or 11:00-16:00; off-season Tue-Sun 11:00-16:00, closed Mon, except Ledaal and Breidablikk—these are open Sun only in winter; www.museumstavanger.no.

DAY TRIPS TO LYSEFJORD AND PULPIT ROCK

The nearby Lysefjord is an easy day trip. Those with more time (and strong legs) can hike to the top of the 1,800-foot-high Pulpit Rock (Preikestolen). The dramatic 270-square-foot plateau atop the rock gives you a fantastic view of the fjord and surrounding mountains. The TI has brochures for several boat tour companies and sells tickets.

Boat Tour of Lysefjord

Rødne Clipper Fjord Sightseeing offers three-hour round-trip excursions from Stavanger to Lysefjord (including a view of Pulpit Rock—but no stops). Conveniently, their boats depart from the main Vågen harbor in the heart of town (east side of the harbor, in front of Skansegata, along Skagenkaien; 450 kr; mid-May–mid-

Sept daily at 10:00 and 14:00, also Thu-Sat at 12:00 July-Aug; early May and late Sept daily at 12:00 Oct-April Wed-Sun only at 11:00; tel. 51 89 52 70, www.rodne.no). A different company, **Norled,** also runs similar trips, as well as slower journeys up the Lysefjord on a "tourist car ferry" (www.norled.no).

Ferry and Bus to Pulpit Rock

Hiking up to the top of Pulpit Rock is a popular outing that will take the better part of a day; plan on at least four hours of hiking (two hours up, two hours down), plus time to linger at the top for photos, plus round-trip travel from Stavanger (about an hour each way by a ferry-and-bus combination)—eight hours minimum should do it. The trailhead is easily reached in summer by public transit or tour package. Then comes the hard part: the hike to the top. The total distance is 4.5 miles and the elevation gain is roughly 1,000 feet. Pack a lunch and plenty of water, and wear good shoes.

Two different companies sell ferry-and-bus packages to the trailhead from Stavanger. Ferries leave from the Fiskepiren boat terminal to Tau; buses meet the incoming ferries and head to Pulpit Rock cabin or to Preikestolen Fjellstue, the local youth hostel. Be sure to time your hike so that you can catch the last bus leaving Pulpit Rock cabin for the ferry (confirm time when booking your ticket). These trips generally go daily from mid-May through mid-September; weekends only in April, early May, and late September; and not at all from October to March (when the ferry stops running). As the details tend to change from year to year, confirm schedules with the TI or the individual companies: **Tide Reiser** (240 kr, best options for an all-day round-trip are departures at 8:40 or 9:20, return bus from trailhead corresponds with ferry to Stavanger, tel. 55 23 88 87, www.tidereiser.com) and **Boreal** (150 kr for the bus plus 92 kr for the ferry—you'll buy the ferry ticket separately, best options depart at 8:40 or 9:20, last return bus from trailhead to ferry leaves at 19:55, tel. 51 56 41 00, www.pulpitrock. no).

Rødne Clipper Fjord Sightseeing (listed earlier) may run a handy trip in July and August that begins with a scenic Lysefjord cruise, then drops you off at Oanes to catch the bus to the Pulpit Rock hut trailhead; afterwards, you can catch the bus to Tau for the ferry return to Stavanger. It's similar to the options described above, but adds a scenic fjord cruise at the start. To confirm this is still going and get details, contact Rødne (750 kr plus 46 kr for return ferry to Stavanger, tel. 51 89 52 70, www.rodne.no).

Sleep Code

Abbreviations   **(6 kr = about $1, country code: 47)**
S = Single, **D** = Double/Twin, **T** = Triple, **Q** = Quad, **b** = bathroom
Price Rankings
  $$$ Higher Priced—Most rooms 1,000 kr or more.
   $$ Moderately Priced—Most rooms 600-1,000 kr.
Unless otherwise noted, credit cards are accepted, breakfast
is included, and Wi-Fi is generally free. Everyone speaks Eng-
lish. Prices change; verify current rates online or by email. For
the best prices, always book directly with the hotel.

Sleeping in Stavanger

$$$ Thon Hotel Maritim, with 223 rooms, is two blocks from the
train station near the artificial Lake Breiavatnet. It can be a good
deal for a big business-class hotel (flexible rates: Db-1,750-2,245 kr
on weekdays, likely 1,150 on weekends, almost as cheap in July, Sb
is always 200 kr less, elevator, Wi-Fi, Kongsgaten 32, tel. 51 85 05
00, www.thonhotels.no/maritim, mailto:maritim@thonhotels.no).

$$$ Hotel Victoria has 107 business-class rooms over a state-
ly, high-ceilinged lobby facing the Skagenkaien embankment right
on the harbor (in summer and weekends: Sb-890 kr, Db-1,140 kr;
weekdays outside of summer: Sb-1,940 kr, Db-2,440 kr; elevator, Wi-Fi, Skansegata 1, tel. 51 86 70 00, www.victoria-hotel.no,
victoria@victoria-hotel.no).

$$ Stavanger B&B is Stavanger's best budget option. This
large red house among a sea of white houses has tidy, tiny rooms. The
lodgings are basic, verging on institutional—not cozy or doily—but
they're affordable and friendly. The shared toilet is down the hall;
14 rooms have their own showers, while eight share showers on the
hall. Waffles, coffee, and friendly chatter are served up every eve-
ning at 21:00 (S-790 kr, D-890 kr, 100 kr less per room for shared
shower, extra bed-150 kr, guest computer and Wi-Fi, 10-minute
uphill walk behind train station in residential neighborhood, Vike-
dalsgate 1A, tel. 51 56 25 00, www.stavangerbedandbreakfast.no,
post@sbb.no). If you let them know in advance, they may be able to
pick you up or drop you off at the boat dock or train station.

Eating in Stavanger

CASUAL DINING
Nye La Piazza, just off the harbor, has an assortment of pasta and
other Italian dishes, including pizza, for 150-200 kr (100-kr lunch

SOUTH NORWAY

special, 300-320-kr meat options, Mon-Sat 13:00-23:00, Sun 13:00-22:00, Rosenkildettorget 1, tel. 51 52 02 52).

XO Bar Vertshuset Mat & Vin, in an elegant setting, serves up big portions of traditional Norwegian food and pricier contemporary fare (300-400 kr, light meals-150-190 kr, open Mon-Wed 11:00-23:30, Thu-Sat 11:00-1:30, a block behind main drag along harbor at Skagen 10 ved Prostebakken, mobile 91 00 03 07).

Meny is a large supermarket with a good selection and a fine deli for super-picnic shopping (Mon-Fri 9:00-20:00, Sat until 18:00, closed Sun, in Straen Senteret shopping mall, Lars Hertervigs Gate 6, tel. 51 50 50 10).

Market Plaza Eateries: The busy square between the cathedral and the harbor is packed with reliable Norwegian chain restaurants. If you're a fan of **Deli de Luca, Peppes Pizza,** or **Dickens Pub,** you'll find all of them within a few steps of here.

DINING ALONG THE HARBOR WITH A VIEW

The harborside street of Skansegata is lined with lively restaurants and pubs, and most serve food. Here are a couple options:

N. B. Sørensen's Dampskibsexpedition consists of a lively pub on the first floor (225-340 kr for pasta, fish, meat, and vegetarian dishes; Mon-Wed 11:00-24:00, Sat 11:00-late, Sun 13:00-23:00) and a fine-dining restaurant on the second floor, with tablecloths, view tables overlooking the harbor, and entrées from 300 kr (Mon-Sat 18:00-23:00, closed Sun, Skagenkaien 26, tel. 51 84 38 20). The restaurant is named after an 1800s company that shipped from this building, among other things, Norwegians heading to the US. Passengers and cargo waited on the first floor, and the manager's office was upstairs. The place is filled with emigrant-era memorabilia.

Sjøhuset Skagen, with a woodsy interior, invites diners to its historic building for lunch or dinner. The building, from the late 1700s, housed a trading company. Today, you can choose from local seafood specialties with an ethnic flair, as well as plenty of meat options (180-195-kr lunches, 230-400-kr dinners, Mon-Sat 11:30-23:00, Sun 13:00-21:30, Skagenkaien 16, tel. 51 89 51 80).

Bølgen og Moi, the restaurant at the Petroleum Museum, has fantastic views over the harbor (lunch: 190-kr lunch special, 190-250-kr main dishes, served Mon 11:00-16:00; dinner: 250-kr main dishes, 500 kr three-course meal, served Tue-Sat 18:00-20:00—reservations recommended; Kjeringholmen 748, tel. 51 93 93 53).

Stavanger Connections

From Stavanger by Train to: Kristiansand (4-7/day, 3-3.5 hours), **Oslo** (4/day, 8-8.5 hours, overnight possible).

By Bus to Bergen: Kystbussen operates buses between Stavanger and Bergen (hourly, 5.5 hours, 440 kr one-way, 800 kr round-trip, tel. 52 70 35 26, http://kystbussen.no).

By Boat to Hirtshals, Denmark: For details on this boat, see the "Sailing Between Norway and Denmark" sidebar.

The Setesdal Valley

Welcome to the remote, and therefore very traditional, Setesdal Valley. Probably Norway's most authentic cranny, the valley is a

mellow montage of sod-roofed water mills, ancient churches, derelict farmhouses, yellowed recipes, and gentle scenery.

The Setesdal Valley joined the modern age with the construction of the valley highway in the 1950s. All along the valley you'll see the unique two-story storage sheds called *stab-burs* (the top floor was used for storing clothes; the bottom, food) and many sod roofs. Even the bus stops have rooftops the local goats love to munch.

In the high country, just over the Sessvatn summit (3,000 feet), you'll see herds of goats and summer farms. If you see an *ekte geitost* sign, that means genuine, homemade goat cheese is for sale. (It's sold cheaper and in more manageable sizes in grocery stores.) To some, it looks like a decade's accumulation of earwax. I think it's delicious. Remember, *ekte* means all-goat—really strong. The more popular and easier-to-eat version is a mix of cow and goat cheese.

For more information on the Setesdal Valley, see www.setesdal.com.

FROM ODDA TO HOVDEN

Attractions from here to Kristiansand are listed roughly from north to south.

Odda

At the end of the Hardanger Fjord, just past the huge zinc and copper industrial plant, you'll hit the industrial town of Odda (well-stocked **TI** for whole region and beyond; in summer daily 9:00-19:00; off-season Mon-Fri 9:00-15:00, closed Sat-Sun; on market square at Torget 2-4, tel. 53 65 40 05, www.visitodda.com). Odda brags that Kaiser Wilhelm came here a lot, but he's dead and I'd drive right through. If you want to visit the tongue of a glacier, drive to Buar and hike an hour to Buarbreen. From Odda, drive

into the land of boulders. The many mighty waterfalls that line the road seem to have hurled huge rocks (with rooted trees) into the rivers and fields. Stop at the giant double waterfall (on the left, pullout on the right, drive slowly through it if you need a car wash).

Røldal

Continue over Røldalsfjellet and into the valley below, where the old town of Røldal is trying to develop some tourism. Drive on by. Its old church isn't worth the time or money. Lakes are like frosted mirrors, making desolate huts come in pairs. Haukeliseter, a group of sod-roofed buildings filled with cultural clichés and tour groups, offers pastries, sandwiches, and reasonable hot meals (from 100 kr) in a lakeside setting. Try the traditional *rømmegrøt* porridge.

Haukeli

This highway and transportation junction has daily bus service to/from Bergen and to/from Kristiansand (Haukeli Motell café open Mon-Fri 11:00-17:00, Sun 11:00-18:00, closed Sat, tel. 35 07 02 14). Turn right over the river onto Route 9, toward Hovden.

Hovden

A ski resort at the top of the Setesdal Valley (2,500 feet), Hovden is barren in the summer and painfully in need of charm. Still, it makes a good home base if you want to explore the area for a couple of days. Locals come here to walk and relax for a week.

Tourist Information: The TI is open all year (Mon-Fri 9:00-16:00, summer Sat 10:00-15:00, July also Sun 10:00-15:00, otherwise closed Sat-Sun, tel. 37 93 93 70, www.hovden.com, post@hovden.com).

Sights and Activities in Hovden

Boat Rental
Hegni Center, on the lake at the south edge of town, rents rowboats, canoes, and kayaks (250-350 kr/day, 195-200 kr/half-day, hourly rentals also possible, cash only, mid-June-mid-Aug daily 11:00-18:00, mid-Aug-mid-Sept Sat-Sun 11:00-15:00, mid-Sept-mid-Oct Sat-Sun only 11:00-16:00, closed mid-Oct-mid-June, tel. 37 93 93 70).

Hikes and Mountain Biking near Hovden
Good walks offer you a chance to see reindeer, moose, arctic fox, and wabbits—so they say. The TI and most hotels stock brochures, maps, and other information about moderate to strenuous hikes in the area as well as biking options. Berry picking is popular in late August, when small, sweet blueberries are in season. A chairlift sometimes takes sightseers to the top of a nearby peak, with great views in clear weather. Bikers can ride the trails downhill (100 kr, 110 kr to bring a bike, June-July daily 11:00-14:00, Aug-mid-Oct Wed and Sat-Sun only). Hunting season starts in late August for reindeer (only in higher elevations) and later in the fall for grouse and moose.

Moose Safari
The TI offers a 2.5-hour *Elg Safari* (*elg* is Norwegian for "moose"). Learn more about this "king of the forest" during a late-night drive through Setesdal's back roads with a stop for moose-meat soup (340 kr, June-Aug only; generally Tue, Fri, and Sun at 22:00—other days on request; 50 percent money-back guarantee if you don't see a moose, tel. 37 93 93 70, post@hovden.com).

Museum of Iron Production (Jernvinnemuseum)
Learn about iron production from the late Iron Age (about 1,000 years ago) with the aid of drawings, exhibits, and recorded narration from a "Viking" (available in English). The museum is about

SOUTH NORWAY

Sailing Between Norway and Denmark

Two companies sail between the tips of Norway and Denmark. **Color Line** and **Fjordline** sail fast boats between Kristiansand, Norway, and Hirtshals, Denmark (2.25-3.25 hours). In addition, Fjordline boats connect Stavanger, Norway, and Hirtshals (11 hours, covered next). They also link Bergen with Hirtshals, though at 18.5 hours, it's a long haul. (For information on an Oslo-Copenhagen cruise—run by a different company—see page 83.)

Both Color Line and Fjordline offer car packages (covering up to 5 people and the car) and have various on-board amenities such as restaurants, coffee bars, duty-free shops, and several classes of travel. I've listed prices in euros, as they appear on the companies' websites.

Sailing Between Kristiansand and Hirtshals, Denmark: Color Line ships generally sail twice daily, all year, with a few more sailings added during summer, but mysteriously they sail only once a day in mid-April. Sailing from Norway to Denmark, Color Line boats usually leave Kristiansand at 8:00 and 16:30, arriving in Hirtshals at 11:15 and 19:45. Going from Denmark to Norway, the boats leave Hirtshals at 12:15 and 20:45, arriving in Kristiansand at 15:30 and midnight. Fares vary with day of week and season (cheaper weekdays and off-season). During the summer, one-way passenger fares start at €20/person mid-week, €40/person on weekends; car packages start at €70 mid-week and €102 on weekends.

Fjordline's seasonal ferry makes the crossing two times a day from late June to mid-August in a speedy 2.25 hours. The schedule is cut back in late spring and early fall, with no ferries

100 yards behind the Hegni Center (look for the sign from the road to *Jernvinnemuseum*).

Cost and Hours: Free, late-June-mid-Aug daily 11:00-19:00, otherwise ask for the key at the TI or Hegni Center.

Swimming Pool

A super indoor spa/pool complex, the Hovden Badeland provides a much-needed way to spend an otherwise dreary and drizzly early evening here.

Cost and Hours: 135-150 kr for 3 hours or more, cheaper for shorter visits, daily 10:00-19:00 in summer, shorter hours off-season, tel. 37 93 93 93, www.badeland.com.

from September to mid-May. In high season, sailing from Norway to Denmark, Fjordline boats leave Kristiansand at 8:30 and 15:00, arriving in Hirtshals at 10:45 and 17:15. Going from Denmark to Norway, the boats leave Hirtshals at 11:45 and 18:00, arriving in Kristiansand at 14:00 and 20:15. One-way passenger fares start at €21/person mid-week; car packages start at €55 mid-week.

Sailing Between Stavanger and Hirtshals, Denmark: Fjordline ships sailing from Norway to Denmark travel overnight, which can save you the cost of a hotel. Enjoy an evening in Stavanger, then sleep (or vomit) as you sail to Denmark. The boat generally sails daily, departing Stavanger at 21:00 and arriving in Hirtshals at 8:00 the next day. Ships also sail daily from Denmark to Norway, departing Hirtshals at 21:00 and arriving in Stavanger at 7:00 in the morning.

Fares vary, depending on how far in advance you book, the time of year, the day of the week, and the type of accommodation you want. Basic one-way fares range from €13 to €102, plus the cost of meals (€17 breakfast, €43 dinner) and accommodations (an airline-type seat or cabin). A seat, referred to as a "sleeperette," starts at €21. But if you're efficient enough to spend a night traveling, you owe yourself the comfort of a private room. Cabins start at around €115 for a basic, two-berth, inside cabin, and go up to €300 or more for a "Fjord Class" cabin with a double bed and ocean view. Car packages range from €100 and up.

Reservations: To get the best fare, book online and early—as soon as you can commit to a firm date (http://fjordline.no and www.colorline.com). This is especially true for Fjordline. Many cheaper fares are nonrefundable and nonchangeable, so be sure to check the details carefully when you book. Days of the week and departure/arrival times can vary—confirm specific schedules when you make your reservations.

Sleeping and Eating in Hovden

$$ Hovden Fjellstoge is a big, old ski chalet renting Hovden's only cheap beds. Even if you're just passing through, their café is a good choice for lunch or an early dinner. Check out the mural in the balcony overlooking the lobby—an artistic rendition of this area's history. Behind the mural is a frightening taxidermy collection (hotel: Sb-from 750 kr, bunk-bed Db-from 990 kr, includes breakfast; cabins: from 890 kr for 2-4 people with bathroom and kitchen; breakfast-110 kr, sheets-100 kr, towel-20 kr; tel. 37 93 95 43, www.hovdenfjellstoge.no, post@hovdenfjellstoge.no).

SOUTH NORWAY

FROM HOVDEN TO KRISTIANSAND

▲Dammar Vatnedalsvatn

Nine miles south of Hovden is a two-mile side-trip to a 400-foot-high rock-pile dam (look for the *Dammar* signs). Enjoy the great view and impressive rockery. This is one of the highest dams in northern Europe. Read the chart. Sit out of the wind a few rows down the rock pile and ponder the vastness of Norwegian wood.

▲Bykle

The most interesting folk museum and church in Setesdal are in the teeny town of Bykle. The 17th-century church has two balconies—one for men and one for women (free, late June-mid-Aug daily 11:00-17:00, closed off-season, tel. 37 93 63 03, www.setesdalsmuseet.no).

Grasbrokke

On the east side of the main road (at the *Grasbrokke* sign) is an old water mill (1630). A few minutes farther south, at the sign for *Sanden Såre Camping*, exit onto a little road to stretch your legs at another old water mill with a fragile, rotten-log sluice.

Flateland

The **Setesdal Museum** (Rygnestadtunet) offers more of what you saw at Bykle (about 30 kr, two buildings; late June-Aug daily 11:00-17:00; closed off-season; 1 mile east of the road, tel. 37 93 63 03, www.setesdalsmuseet.no). Unless you're a glutton for culture, I wouldn't do both.

Honnevje

Past Flateland is a nice picnic and WC stop, with a dock along the water for swimming...for hot-weather days or polar bears.

▲Valle

This is Setesdal's prettiest village (but don't tell Bykle). In the center, you'll find fine silver- and gold-work, homemade crafts next to the TI, and old-fashioned *lefse* cooking demonstrations (in the small log house by the Valle Motell). The fine suspension bridge attracts kids of any age (b-b-b-b-bounce), and anyone interested in a great view over the river to strange mountains that look like polished, petrified mudslides. European rock climbers, tired of the over-climbed Alps, often entertain spectators with their sport. Is anyone climbing? (TI tel. 37 93 75 29.)

Sleeping in Valle: **$$ Valle Motell** rents basic rooms (Sb-625 kr, Db-790 kr, includes breakfast, cabins with kitchen and bath but no breakfast-725-1195 kr, tel. 37 93 77 00, www.valle-motell.no, post@valle-motell.no).

Nomeland

The Sylvartun silversmith shop, whose owner Hallvard Bjørgum is also a renowned Hardanger fiddle player, sells Setesdal silver in a 17th-century, grass-roofed log cabin next to the main road.

Grendi

The Ardal Church (1827) has a rune stone in its yard. Three hundred yards south of the church is a 900-year-old oak tree.

Evje

A huge town by Setesdal standards (3,500 people), Evje is famous for its gems and mines. Fancy stones fill the shops here. Rock hounds find the nearby mines fun; for a small fee, you can hunt for gems. The TI is by Route 9 in the center of Evje (mid-June–mid-Aug Mon-Fri 10:00-17:00, Sat 10:00-14:00, closed Sun; tel. 37 93 14 00). The **Setesdal Mineral Park** is on the main road, two miles south of town (140 kr, late-June–mid-Aug daily 10:00-18:00, shorter hours off-season, closed mid-Oct–April, tel. 37 93 13 10, www.mineralparken.no).

Kristiansand

This "capital of the south" has 85,000 inhabitants, a pleasant Renaissance grid-plan layout (Posebyen), a famous zoo with Norway's biggest amusement park (6 miles toward Oslo on the main road), a daily bus to Bergen, and lots of big boats going to Denmark. It's the closest thing to a beach resort in Norway. Markensgate is the bustling pedestrian market street—an enjoyable place for good browsing, shopping, eating, and people-watching. Stroll along the Strand Promenaden (marina) to Christiansholm Fortress.

Orientation to Kristiansand

The TI is at Rådhusgata 18, a few blocks from the boat, bus, and train station (mid-June–mid-Aug Mon-Fri 8:00-18:00, Sat 10:00-18:00, Sun 12:00-18:00; mid-Aug–mid-June Mon-Fri 8:00-15:30, Sat 10:00-15:00, closed Sun; tel. 38 12 13 14, www.visitkrs.no). The bank at the Color Line terminal opens for each arrival and departure (even the midnight ones). The Fønix Kino cinema complex is within two blocks of the ferry and TI (110-140 kr, seven screens, movies shown in English, schedules at the entrance, tel. 38 10 42 00).

SOUTH NORWAY

Sleeping and Eating in Kristiansand

Kristiansand hotels are expensive and nondescript. The otherwise uninteresting harbor area has a cluster of wooden buildings called **Fiskebasaren** ("Fish Bazaar"). The indoor fish market is only open during the day, but numerous restaurants (serving fish, among other dishes) provide a nice atmosphere for dinner. Follow Vester Strandgate past the Fønix movie theater to Østre Strandgate, take a right, and follow the signs to Fiskebrygga.

$$$ Rica Hotel Norge is a modern option (Sb-1,700 kr, Db-1,900 kr, prices are averaged—rates vary with demand, Dronningensgate 5, tel. 38 17 40 00, www.hotel-norge.no, firmapost@hotel-norge.no).

$$$ Thon Hotel Wergeland is inviting for a large chain hotel. It's within earshot of the church bells and busy Kirkegate—ask for a quieter room away from the street (Sb-1,395 kr, Db-1,695 kr, prices are averaged—rates vary with demand, includes breakfast, non-smoking rooms, no elevator, guest computer and Wi-Fi, Kirkegate 15, tel. 38 17 20 40, www.thonhotels.no/wergeland, wergeland@thonhotels.no).

Kristiansand Connections

From Kristiansand by Train to: Stavanger (4-7/day, 3-3.5 hours), **Oslo** (5/day, 4.5 hours).

By Boat to Hirtshals, Denmark: For details on this boat, see the "Sailing Between Norway and Denmark" sidebar.

ROUTE TIPS FOR DRIVERS

Bergen to Kristiansand via the Setesdal Valley (10 hours): Your first key connection is the Kvanndal-Utne ferry (departures hourly 6:00-22:30, fewer on weekends, reservations not possible or even necessary if you get there 20 minutes early, breakfast in cafeteria, www.norled.no). If you make the 9:00, your day will be more relaxed. Driving comfortably, with no mistakes or traffic, it's two hours from your Bergen hotel to the ferry dock. Leaving Bergen is a bit confusing. Pretend you're going to Oslo on the road to Voss (Route E-16, signs for *Nestune, Landås, Nattland*). About a half-hour out of town, after a long tunnel, leave the Voss road and take Route 7 heading for Norheimsund, and then Kvanndal. This road, treacherous for the famed beauty of the Hardanger Fjord it hugs as well as for its skinniness, is faster and safer if you beat the traffic (which you will with this plan).

The ferry drops you in Utne, where a lovely road takes you to Odda and up into the mountains. From Haukeli, turn south on Route 9 and wind up to Sessvatn at 3,000 feet. Enter the

Setesdal Valley. Follow the Otra River downhill for 140 miles south to the major port town of Kristiansand. Skip the secondary routes. The most scenic stretch is between Hovden and Valle. South of Valle, there is a lot more logging (and therefore less scenic). As you enter Kristiansand, pay a 21-kr toll and follow signs for Denmark.

PRACTICALITIES

This section covers just the basics on traveling in this region (for much more information, see *Rick Steves Scandinavia*). You'll find free advice on specific topics at www.ricksteves.com/tips.

Money

Norway uses the Norwegian kroner: 1 krone equals about $0.17. To roughly convert prices in kroner to dollars, multiply by two, then drop a zero (e.g., 15 kr = about $3, 100 kr = about $20). Check www.oanda.com for the latest exchange rates.

The standard way for travelers to get kroner is to withdraw money from ATMs using a debit or credit card, ideally with a Visa or MasterCard logo. Before departing, call your bank or credit-card company: Confirm that your card(s) will work overseas, ask about international transaction fees, and alert them that you'll be making withdrawals in Europe. Also ask for the PIN number for your credit card in case it'll help you use Europe's "chip-and-PIN" payment machines (see below); allow time for your bank to mail your PIN to you. To keep your valuables safe while traveling, wear a money belt.

Dealing with "Chip and PIN": Much of Europe (including Norway) is adopting a chip-and-PIN system for credit cards, and some merchants rely on it exclusively. European chip-and-PIN cards are embedded with an electronic chip, in addition to the magnetic stripe used on our American-style cards. This means that your credit (and debit) card might not work at payment machines, such as those at train and subway stations, toll roads, parking garages, luggage lockers, and self-serve gas pumps. Memorizing your credit card's PIN lets you use it at some chip-and-PIN machines—just enter the PIN when the machine asks for the "kode." If a machine won't take your card, look for a machine that takes cash or see if there's a cashier nearby who can process your transaction. Often the easiest solution is to pay for your purchases with cash you've withdrawn from an ATM using your debit card (Europe's ATMs still accept magnetic-stripe cards).

Phoning

Smart travelers use the telephone to reserve or reconfirm rooms, reserve restaurants, get directions, research transportation connections, confirm tour times, phone home, and lots more.

To call Norway from the US or Canada: Dial 011-47 and then the local number. (The 011 is our international access code, and 47 is Norway's country code.)

To call Norway from a European country: Dial 00-47 followed by the local number. (The 00 is Europe's international access code.)

To call within Norway: Dial the local number.

Tips on Phoning: A mobile phone—whether an American one that works in Norway, or a European one you buy when you arrive—is handy, but can be pricey. If traveling with a smartphone, consider getting an international plan from your provider and try to switch off data-roaming until you have free Wi-Fi. With Wi-Fi, you can use your smartphone to make free or inexpensive domestic and international calls by taking advantage of a calling app such as Skype, FaceTime, or Google+ Hangouts.

To make cheap international calls, you can buy an international phone card in Norway; these work with a scratch-to-reveal PIN code at any phone, allow you to call home to the US for pennies a minute, and also work for domestic calls.

Another option is buying an insertable phone card in Norway. These are usable only at pay phones, are reasonable for making calls within the country, and work for international calls as well (though not as cheaply as the international phone cards). However, pay phones are becoming hard to find in Scandinavian countries. You're likely to see them only in railway stations, airports, and medical facilities. Note that insertable phone cards—and most international phone cards—work only in the country where you buy them.

Calling from your hotel-room phone is usually expensive, unless you use an international phone card. For more on phoning, see www.ricksteves.com/phoning.

Making Hotel Reservations

To ensure the best value, I recommend reserving rooms in advance, particularly during peak season. Email the hotelier with the following key pieces of information: number and type

From:	rick@ricksteves.com
Sent:	Today
To:	info@hotelcentral.com
Subject:	Reservation request for 19-22 July

Dear Hotel Central,

I would like to reserve a room for 2 people for 3 nights, arriving 19 July and departing 22 July. If possible, I would like a quiet room with a double bed and a bathroom inside the room.

Please let me know if you have a room available and the price.

Thank you!
Rick Steves

of rooms; number of nights; date of arrival; date of departure; and any special requests. (For a sample form, see the sidebar.) Use the European style for writing dates: day/month/year. Hoteliers typically ask for your credit-card number as a deposit.

Some hotels are willing to deal to attract guests—try emailing several to ask their best price. Most Scandinavian business hotels use "dynamic pricing," which means they change the room rate depending on demand—just like the airlines change their fares. This makes it extremely difficult to predict what you will pay. For many hotels, I list a range of prices. If the rate you're offered is at or near the bottom of my printed range, it's likely a good deal.

In general, hotel prices can soften if you do any of the following: offer to pay cash, stay at least three nights, or mention this book. You can also try asking for a cheaper room or discount, or offer to skip breakfast. Even though most hotels in Norway base their prices on demand, it is possible to find lower prices during the summer and on weekends. Check hotel websites for deals. The Oslo TI website also lists affordable apartments and "apartment hotels" for short-term stays; see www.visitoslo.com.

Eating

Restaurants are often expensive. Alternate between picnics (outside or in your hotel or hostel); cheap, forgettable, but filling cafeteria or fast-food fare ($20 per person); and atmospheric, carefully chosen restaurants popular with locals ($40 per person and up). Ethnic eateries—Indian, Turkish, Greek, Italian, and Asian—offer a good value and a break from Norwegian fare.

The *smörgåsbord* (known in Norway as the *store koldt bord*) is a revered Scandinavian culinary tradition. Seek it out at least once during your visit. Begin with the fish dishes, along with boiled potatoes and *knekkebrød* (crisp bread). Then move on to salads, egg dishes, and various cold cuts. Next it's meatball time! Pour on some gravy as well as a spoonful of lingonberry sauce. Still hungry? Make a point to sample the Nordic cheeses and the racks of traditional desserts, cakes, and custards.

Hotel breakfasts are a huge and filling buffet, generally included but occasionally a $15-or-so option. It usually features fruit, cereal, various milks, breads and crackers, cold cuts, pickled herring, caviar paste, and boiled eggs. The brown cheese with the texture of earwax and a slightly sweet taste is *geitost* ("goat cheese").

In Norway, alcohol is sold only at state-run liquor stores called Vinmonopolet (though weak beer is also sold at supermarkets). To avoid extremely high restaurant prices for alcohol, many Norwegians—and tourists—buy their wine, beer, or spirits at a store and then drink at a public square; this is illegal although often done. One local specialty is *akvavit*, a strong, vodka-like spirit distilled from potatoes and flavored with anise, caraway, or other herbs and spices—then drunk ice-cold.

Service: Good service is relaxed (slow to an American). When you want the bill, say, *"Regningen, takk."* Throughout Norway, a service charge is included in your bill, so there's no need to leave an additional tip. In fancier restaurants or any restaurant where you enjoy great service, round up the bill (about 5-10 percent of the total check).

Transportation

By Train and Bus: Trains cover many of my recommended Norwegian destinations. To see if a railpass could save you money, check www.ricksteves.com/rail. If you're buying tickets as you go, note that prices can fluctuate. To research train schedules and fares, visit the Norwegian train website: www.nsb.no. Nearly any long-distance train ride requires you to make a reservation before boarding (the day before is usually fine). If you're taking the Norway in a Nutshell route in mid-July or August, it's smart to make reservations at least a week in advance for the Oslo–Bergen train and the Myrdal-Flåm private train (Flåmsbana).

Don't overlook long-distance buses, which are usually slower than trains but have considerably cheaper and more predictable fares. On certain routes (e.g., Oslo-Stockholm), the bus is less expensive but slower than the train. Norway's biggest bus carrier is Nor-Way Bussekspress (www.nor-way.no).

By Car: It's cheaper to arrange most car rentals from the US. For tips on your insurance options, see www.ricksteves.com/cdw, and for route planning, consult www.viamichelin.com. Bring your driver's license. Local road etiquette is similar to that in the US. Ask your car-rental company for details, or check the US State Department website (www.travel.state.gov, click on "International Travel," then specify your country of choice and click "Traffic

Safety and Road Conditions"). Use your headlights da
it's required in most of Scandinavia. A car is a wort
ache in any big city—park it safely (get tips from your hotelier). To
minimize tolls in Norway, register as a visitor at www.autopass.no
and prepay a lump sum with your credit card.

By Boat: Boats are both a necessary and spectacular way to
travel through Norway's fjords or along its coast (for various routes,
see www.fjordtours.no, www.fjord1.no, and www.tide.no). Reserve
ahead if you're planning on taking overnight boats in summer or
on weekends to link Oslo and Copenhagen (www.dfdsseaways.
com). Other worthwhile ferry routes connect Norway and northern Denmark; see www.fjordline.com and www.colorline.com.

By Plane: SAS is the region's dominant airline (www.fly-
sas.com) and is affiliated with Oslo-based Widerøe Air (www.
wideroe.no). Another option is Norwegian Airlines (hubs in Oslo
and Bergen, www.norwegian.no). Well-known cheapo airlines
easyJet (www.easyjet.com) and Ryanair (www.ryanair.com) fly into
Scandinavia.

Helpful Hints

Emergency Help: To summon the **police** or an **ambulance**, call
112. For passport problems, call the **US Embassy** (in Oslo: passport services by appointment only, info tel. 21 30 85 58—available
Mon-Fri 15:00-16:30, emergency tel. 21 30 85 40, http://norway.
usembassy.gov).

If you have a minor illness, do as the locals do and go to a
pharmacist for advice. Or ask at your hotel for help—they'll know
of the nearest medical and emergency services. For other concerns,
get advice from your hotelier.

Theft or Loss: To replace a passport, you'll need to go in person to an embassy (see above). Cancel and replace your credit and
debit cards by calling these 24-hour US numbers collect: Visa—
tel. 303/967-1096, MasterCard—tel. 636/722-7111, American
Express—tel. 336/393-1111. In Norway, to make a collect call to
the US, dial 800-190-11; press zero or stay on the line for an opera-
tor. File a police report either on the spot or within a day or two;
you'll need it to submit an insurance claim for lost or stolen railpasses or travel gear, and it can help with replacing your passport
or credit and debit cards. Precautionary measures can minimize
the effects of loss—back up your photos and other files frequently.
For more information, see www.ricksteves.com/help.

Time: Europe uses the 24-hour clock. It's the same through
12:00 noon, then keep going: 13:00, 14:00, and so on. Norway, like
most of continental Europe, is six/nine hours ahead of the East/
West Coasts of the US.

Holidays and Festivals: Europe celebrates many holidays, which can close sights and attract crowds (book hotel rooms ahead). For info on holidays and festivals in Norway, check the Scandinavia Tourist Board website: www.goscandinavia.com. For a simple list showing major—though not all—events, see www.ricksteves.com/festivals.

Numbers and Stumblers: What Americans call the second floor of a building is the first floor in Europe. Europeans write dates as day/month/year, so Christmas 2016 is 25/12/16. Commas are decimal points and vice versa—a dollar and a half is 1,50, and there are 5.280 feet in a mile. Europe uses the metric system: A kilogram is 2.2 pounds; a liter is about a quart; and a kilometer is six-tenths of a mile.

Resources from Rick Steves

This Snapshot guide is excerpted from the latest edition of *Rick Steves Scandinavia,* which is one of more than 30 titles in my series of guidebooks on European travel. I also produce a public television series, *Rick Steves' Europe,* and a public radio show, *Travel with Rick Steves.* My website, www.ricksteves.com, offers free travel information, a forum for travelers' comments, guidebook updates, my travel blog, an online travel store, and information on European railpasses and our tours of Europe. If you're bringing a mobile device on your trip, you can download my Rick Steves Audio Europe app, featuring podcasts of my radio shows, free audio tours of major sights in Europe, and travel interviews about Norway. You can get Rick Steves Audio Europe via Apple's App Store, Google Play, or the Amazon Appstore. For more information, see www.ricksteves.com/audioeurope. You can also follow me on Facebook and Twitter.

Additional Resources

Tourist Information: www.goscandinavia.com
Passports and Red Tape: www.travel.state.gov
Packing List: www.ricksteves.com/packing
Travel Insurance: www.ricksteves.com/insurance
Cheap Flights: www.kayak.com
Airplane Carry-on Restrictions: www.tsa.gov
Updates for This Book: www.ricksteves.com/update

How Was Your Trip?

If you'd like to share your tips, concerns, and discoveries after using this book, please fill out the survey at www.ricksteves.com/feedback. Thanks in advance—it helps a lot.

PRACTICALITIES

INDEX

INDEX

Our website enhances this book and turns

Explore Europe

At ricksteves.com you can browse through thousands of articles, videos, photos and radio interviews, plus find a wealth of money-saving travel tips for planning your dream trip. And with our mobile-friendly website, you can easily access all this great travel information anywhere you go.

TV Shows

Preview the places you'll visit by watching entire half-hour episodes of Rick Steves' Europe (choose from all 100 shows) on-demand, for free.

ricksteves.com

your travel dreams into affordable reality

Radio Interviews

Enjoy ready access to Rick's vast library of radio interviews covering travel

tips and cultural insights that relate specifically to your Europe travel plans.

Travel Forums

Learn, ask, share! Our online community of savvy travelers is a great resource

for first-time travelers to Europe, as well as seasoned pros. You'll find forums on each country, plus travel tips and restaurant/hotel reviews. You can even ask one of our well-traveled staff to chime in with an opinion.

Travel News

Subscribe to our free Travel News e-newsletter, and get monthly updates from Rick on what's happening in Europe.

Audio Europe™

Pack Light and Right

Gear up for your next adventure at ricksteves.com

Light Luggage

Pack light and right with Rick Steves' affordable, custom-designed rolling carry-on bags, backpacks, day packs and shoulder bags.

Accessories

From packing cubes to moneybelts and beyond, Rick has personally selected the travel goodies that will help your trip go smoother.

Shop at ricksteves.com

Experience maximum Europe

Save time and energy

This guidebook is your independent-travel toolkit. But for all it delivers, it's still up to you to devote the time and energy it takes to manage the preparation and logistics that are essential for a happy trip. If that's a hassle, there's a solution.

Rick Steves Tours

A Rick Steves tour takes you to Europe's most interesting places with great

great tours, too!

with minimum stress

guides and small groups of 28 or less. We follow Rick's favorite itineraries, ride in comfy buses, stay in family-run hotels, and bring you intimately close to the Europe you've traveled so far to see. Most importantly, we take away the logistical headaches so you can focus on the fun.

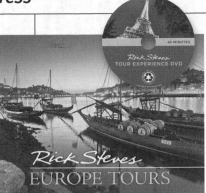

customers—along with us on 40 different itineraries, from Ireland to Italy to Istanbul. Is a Rick Steves tour the right fit for your travel dreams? Find out at ricksteves.com, where you can also get Rick's latest tour catalog and free Tour Experience DVD.

Join the fun

This year we'll take 18,000 free-spirited travelers— nearly half of them repeat

Europe is best experienced with happy travel partners. We hope you can join us.

See our itineraries at ricksteves.com

EUROPE GUIDES

Best of Europe
Eastern Europe
Europe Through the Back Door
Mediterranean Cruise Ports
Northern European Cruise Ports

COUNTRY GUIDES

Croatia & Slovenia
England
France
Germany
Great Britain
Ireland
Italy
Portugal
Scandinavia
Spain
Switzerland

CITY & REGIONAL GUIDES

Amsterdam, Bruges & Brussels
Barcelona
Budapest
Florence & Tuscany
Greece: Athens & the Peloponnese
Istanbul
London
Paris
Prague & the Czech Republic
Provence & the French Riviera
Rome
Venice
Vienna, Salzburg & Tirol

SNAPSHOT GUIDES

Basque Country: Spain & France
Berlin
Bruges & Brussels
Copenhagen & the Best of
    Denmark
Dublin
Dubrovnik
Hill Towns of Central Italy
Italy's Cinque Terre
Krakow, Warsaw & Gdansk
Lisbon
Madrid & Toledo
Milan & the Italian Lakes District
Munich, Bavaria & Salzburg
Naples & the Amalfi Coast
Northern Ireland
Norway
Scotland
Sevilla, Granada & Southern Spain
Stockholm

POCKET GUIDES

Amsterdam
Athens
Barcelona
Florence
London
Paris
Rome
Venice

Rick Steves guidebooks are published by Avalon Travel,
a member of the Perseus Books Group.

NOW AVAILABLE:
eBOOKS, DVD & BLU-RAY

TRAVEL CULTURE

Europe 101
European Christmas
Postcards from Europe
Travel as a Political Act

eBOOKS

Nearly all Rick Steves guides are available as ebooks. Check with your favorite bookseller.

RICK STEVES' EUROPE DVDs

11 New Shows 2013–2014
Austria & the Alps
Eastern Europe
England & Wales
European Christmas
European Travel Skills & Specials
France
Germany, BeNeLux & More
Greece, Turkey & Portugal
Iran
Ireland & Scotland
Italy's Cities
Italy's Countryside
Scandinavia
Spain
Travel Extras

BLU-RAY

Celtic Charms
Eastern Europe Favorites
European Christmas
Italy Through the Back Door
Mediterranean Mosaic
Surprising Cities of Europe

PHRASE BOOKS & DICTIONARIES

French
French, Italian & German
German
Italian
Portuguese
Spanish

JOURNALS

Rick Steves Pocket Travel Journal
Rick Steves Travel Journal

PLANNING MAPS

Britain, Ireland & London
Europe
France & Paris
Germany, Austria & Switzerland
Ireland
Italy
Spain & Portugal

RickSteves.com 🅕🅣 @RickSteves

Rick Steves books and DVDs are available at bookstores and through online booksellers.

Photo © Patricia Feaster

Avalon Travel
a member of the Perseus Books Group
1700 Fourth Street
Berkeley, CA 94710

ISBN 978-1-63121-062-4

For the latest on Rick's lectures, guidebooks, tours, public radio show, and public
television series, contact Rick Steves' Europe, 130 Fourth Avenue North, Edmonds,
WA 98020, 425/771-8303, www.ricksteves.com, rick@ricksteves.com.

Rick Steves' Europe
Managing Editor: Risa Laib
Editorial & Production Manager: Jennifer Madison Davis
Editors: Glenn Eriksen, Tom Griffin, Cameron Hewitt, Suzanne Kotz, Cathy Lu,
    Carrie Shepherd
Editorial & Production Assistant: Jessica Shaw
Editorial Intern: Stacie Larsen
Researchers: Glenn Eriksen, Cameron Hewitt
Maps & Graphics: David C. Hoerlein, Sandra Hundacker, Lauren Mills, Mary Rostad

Avalon Travel
Senior Editor & Series Manager: Madhu Prasher
Editor: Jamie Andrade
Associate Editor: Maggie Ryan
Copy Editor: Patrick Collins
Proofreader: Jennifer Malnick
Indexer: Beatrice Wikander
Production & Typesetting: Tabitha Lahr, Rue Flaherty
Cover Design: Kimberly Glyder Design
Maps & Graphics: Kat Bennett, Mike Morgenfeld

Photo Credits
Front Cover: Solvorn on the Lustrafjord © Cameron Hewitt
Additional Photography: Dominic Arizona Bonuccelli, Tom Griffin, Sonja Groset,
    Cameron Hewitt, David C. Hoerlein, Lauren Mills, Moesgaard Museum, Rick
    Steves, Ian Watson, Chris Werner (photos are used by permission and are the
    property of the original copyright owners).

ABOUT THE AUTHOR

RICK STEVES

 Since 1973, Rick Steves has spent 100 days every year exploring Europe. Along with writing and researching a bestselling series of guidebooks, Rick produces a public television series *(Rick Steves' Europe)*, a public radio show *(Travel with Rick Steves)*, and an app and podcast *(Rick Steves Audio Europe)*; writes a nationally syndicated newspaper column; organizes guided tours that take over 20,000 travelers to Europe annually; and offers an information-packed website (www.ricksteves.com). With the help of his hardworking staff of 100 at Europe Through the Back Door—in Edmonds, Washington, just north of Seattle—Rick's mission is to make European travel fun, affordable, and culturally enlightening for Americans.

Connect with Rick:

facebook.com/RickSteves   twitter: @RickSteves

More for your trip!
Maximize the experience with Rick Steves as your guide

Guidebooks
Dozens of European city and country guidebooks

Planning Maps
Use the map that's in sync with your guidebook

Rick's TV Shows
Preview where
you're going
with 6 shows
on Scandinavia

Free! Rick's Audio Europe™ App
Hear Scandinavia travel tips from Rick's radio shows

Small Group Tours
Take a lively Rick Steves tour through Scandinavia

For all the details, visit ricksteves.com